The Reading Connection

READING SKILLS AND COLLEGE SUCCESS

The Reading Connection

READING SKILLS AND COLLEGE SUCCESS

Linda D. Meagher
Middlesex Community College
Bedford, Massachusetts

Thomas G. Devine
University of Massachusetts Lowell
Lowell, Massachusetts

IRWIN
MIRROR PRESS

Chicago • Bogotá • Boston • Buenos Aires • Caracas
London • Madrid • Mexico City • Sydney • Toronto

© Richard D. Irwin, A Times Mirror Higher Education Group, Inc., company, 1997

All rights reserved. No part of this publication may be
reproduced, stored in a retrieval system, or transmitted,
in any form or by any means, electronic, mechanical,
photocopying, recording, or otherwise, without the prior
written permission of the publisher.

Mirror Press: *David R. Helmstadter*
Managing editor: *Elizabeth R. Deck*

Marketing manager: *Carl Helwing*
Project supervisor: *Karen M. Smith*
Senior production supervisor: *Laurie Sander*
Designer: *Crispin Prebys*
Prepress Buyer: *Jon Christopher*
Compositor: *Precision Graphic Services, Inc.*
Typeface: *11/13 Times Roman*
Printer: *Times Mirror Higher Education Group, Inc., Print Group*

**Times Mirror
Higher Education Group**

Library of Congress Cataloging-in-Pulication Data

Meagher, Linda D.
　The reading connection : reading skills and college success /
Linda D. Meagher, Thomas G. Devine.
　　p.　cm.
　Includes index.
　ISBN 0-256-22036-0
　1. Reading (Higher education)　2. Study skills.　3. College
students--Books and reading.　4. Academic achievement.　I. Devine,
Thomas G., 1928-　　．II. Title.
　LB2395.3.M43　1997
428.4′071′1—dc20　　　　　　　　　　　　　　96–9298

Printed in the United States of America
1 2 3 4 5 6 7 8 9 0 WCB 3 2 1 0 9 8 7 6

To our teachers

PREFACE

This is a book about connections—connections between students' lives and the books they read, connections between their reading and their college achievements, and, more specifically, connections between how well they read their books and their course grades.

Goals of the Text

As the authors of this text, our goals are clear and well defined:

- We show students how to connect what they already know about life with the content of the textbooks they must read in college courses.
- We explain how to use these connections systematically to relate the know to the new in order to better comprehend unfamiliar material.
- We teach specific strategies to help students improve grades and achieve success in college.

Features of the Text

In order to make these connections clear to students, this book uses several approaches, some now widely used in other similar books and some unique to this book. For example:

1. Overviewing Looking ahead is emphasized. Considerable research now documents that when students make overviews or surveys, they tend to get more out of reading assignments. From Francis Robinson's SQ3R in the 1940s to PORPE and other techniques today, the surveying technique has demonstrated its effectiveness. When students know what lies ahead, they better grasp their study goals and read more purposefully. Chapter One explains "looking ahead" and other chapters reinforce the importance of overviewing, predicting, and self-questioning.

2. Self-Testing Each chapter includes a simple self-test to give students an idea of their present proficiency in that area and to activate relevant prior knowledge they may possess. Knowing where one stands at any given moment of academic development may clarify expectations; realizing what one already knows about a topic helps make connections between the new and the known.

3. Clear Explanations Each chapter topic is clearly explained. Explanations are readily understandable and may be used by students independently, or as preclass reading before an instructor more formally introduces the material. Throughout, explanations are presented in a structured, unambiguous way with regular references to student experiences.

4. Vignettes Each chapter includes Vignettes, which are brief narratives collected from college students in which they relate their own experiences. The vignettes help clarify the topic of the chapter and relate it to the lives of the students who use this text. For example, rather than presenting critical reading solely in "academic" terms, two students tell of actual experiences in their lives when they benefited from their knowledge of key critical reading skills.

5. Idea Boxes Interspersed through the chapters are highlighted Idea Boxes. These are 2- or 3- paragraph suggestions on using a particular strategy in college reading assignments. Some are previously discussed in the book, but most are effective ideas recommended by actual college students.

6. Classroom-Tested Exercises Exercises are sequenced so that students are led carefully from relatively easy passages to increasingly difficult textbook assignments. All the exercises are taken from college textbooks in history, management, chemistry, and other areas. Thus, college students are given opportunities to use a specific strategy on topics they may encounter in other classes.

7. Authentic Texts Throughout this book, there are exercises, examples, and selections from actual college textbooks. Materials are not "made up" or created for the chapters. Students learn to master the new skills and strategies using the exact language of textbook authors. They learn, for example, approaches to unfamiliar vocabulary, SQ3R, and organizational patterns using popular college textbooks, some of which may be found in their own courses.

8. Textbook Excerpts Every chapter includes an extensive excerpt from an actual college textbook. These, again, are selected from a wide range of college courses to present opportunities to put new skills to immediate use. Using the excerpts (some are an entire chapter in length), students are carefully guided through an assignment and shown how to transfer new skills to other course's reading assignments.

9. Writing Activities Throughout the chapters, students respond regularly in writing. Often, because a specific strategy in reading is better understood when viewed from a writer's point of view, reading exercises are coupled with writing activities. Many times, written activities are designed to elicit personal responses from students to help them better see the connections between their own experiences and new skills.

10. Reflective Journals Every chapter ends with an opportunity for students to think about what they have learned. These end-of-chapter writing activities allow students to examine new ideas from a personal perspective, to organize new skills, and to reflect upon connections between the content of the chapters and their own experiences. The entries also give instructors insight into students' personal and academic development, as well as additional opportunities to establish firmer connections between reading and college achievement.

11. Multicultural Selections Readings explore problems associated with bilingualism or misunderstandings and misinterpretations of various cultural characteristics. Frequently, the text examines the advantages fostered by differing points of view and varied traditions. Appropriate selections are included in all chapters.

12. Study Alerts Each chapter ends with a Study Alert! In these brief descriptions of related study skills and strategies, students are shown how to use effective study techniques as they complete their reading assignments. For example, one chapter includes a Study Alert demonstrating the use of concept mapping; another shows how to use an index efficiently. By using the Study Alerts, students will complete the book with an array of highly effective study skills that are appropriate for all their college courses.

Everything in this text comes from college classrooms. The explanations have been tried with countless students and then checked and rechecked for effectiveness. The exercises and activities have been tested and refined. The Vignettes are from actual students telling of their own experiences in their own words. The suggestions in the "Idea" boxes come from students who have benefited from them and are eager to share their ideas. The selections and chapter excerpts come directly from real textbooks currently in use. All the connections underlying the book are rooted in the realities of lively college classes. The reading connection itself—which became the title of this book—has been well-demonstrated to its authors through their own teaching: Reading success is truly connected to success in college and life.

Although this book grew from the teaching of its authors, it was further shaped by the experiences of other college teachers. The authors are especially grateful to Joyce K. Henna of Honolulu Community College, Natalie J. Miller of Joliet (Illinois) Junior College, Bob Rogers of San Antonio College, and Jim Roth of Spokane Community College.

Linda D. Meagher
Thomas G. Devine

CONTENTS

CHAPTER 1
Previewing 1

Previewing Skills Survey 1 / Plan of the Chapter 2 / The Importance of Looking Ahead 2 / Checking Out Your Textbooks 3 / Defining the Assignment 7 / Keeping Track of Assignments 9 / Skimming 10 / Reading Rate 13 / Textbook Chapter Excerpt 1.1 15 / Study Alert! Related Study Skills #1: Using the Index 16 / Making the Connection: Reflection Entry #1 21

CHAPTER 2
Reading with Purpose 23

Reading with Purpose Survey 23 / Plan of the Chapter 24 / Previewing 24 / Setting a Purpose 30 / Textbook Chapter Excerpt 2.1 32 / Textbook Chapter Excerpt 2.2 53 / Study Alert! Related Study Skills #2: KWL 72 / Making the Connection: Reflection Entry #2 74

CHAPTER 3
Keys to Learning and Remembering New Vocabulary 75

Vocabulary Skills Survey 75 / What Do College Students Say about Vocabulary? 76 / Defining Words through Context Clues 77 / Word Parts 86 / Prefixes 86 / Suffixes 88 / Roots 89 / SSCD Approach to New Vocabulary 97 / Remembering New Vocabulary 100 / How to Learn Technical Vocabulary 100 / Textbook Chapter Excerpt 3.1 105 / Study Alert! Related Study Skills #3: Grouping Words 106 / Making the Connection: Reflection Entry #3 108

CHAPTER 4
Understanding Main Ideas 109

Main Idea Survey 109 / Plan of the Chapter 110 / What Do Other Students Say about the Problem? 110 / Topics 111 / Topics versus Main Ideas 113 / Textbook Chapter Excerpt 4.1 114 / Locations of Main Ideas in Paragraphs 115 / Textbook Chapter Excerpt 4.2 125 / Study Alert! Related Study Skills #4: Concept Mapping 127 / Textbook Chapter Excerpt 4.3 127 / Making the Connection: Reflection Entry #4 129

CHAPTER 5

Identifying Major and Minor Details 131

Major and Minor Details Survey 132 / Plan of the Chapter 132 / Major Details 132 / Careful Reading 148 / Principles of Motivation 150 / Textbook Excerpt 5.1 / Study Alert! Related Study Skills #5: Note Taking 154 / Making the Connection: Reflection Entry #5 157

CHAPTER 6

Patterns of Organization 159

Patterns of Organization Survey 159 / Plan of the Chapter 160 / Five Patterns of Organization 163 / Two Important Points about Patterns of Organization 164 / Something to Think About 185 / Chapter Excerpt 6.1 186 / Study Alert! Related Study Skills #6: Visuals 188 / Making the Connection: Reflection Entry #6 192

CHAPTER 7

Fact and Opinion 193

Plan of the Chapter 194 / Distinguishing Fact from Opinion 195 / Critical Reading 208 / Chapter Excerpt 7.1 211 / Study Alert! Related Study Skills #7: Reviewing 213 / Making the Connection: Reflection Entry #7 214

CHAPTER 8

Inferences 217

Inference Survey 217 / Plan of the Chapter 218 / Inferences in Daily Life 218 / Understanding Inferences 221 / Inferences in Reading 228 / Textbook Chapter Excerpt 8.1: Final Review 239 / Study Alert! Related Study Skills #8: Memory Tricks 241 / Making the Connection : Reflection Entry #8 243

CHAPTER 9

Understanding Arguments 245

Argument Survey 245 / Plan of the Chapter 246 / Understanding Arguments 247 / False Argumentation or Unsound Arguments 258 / Tricking Readers: Appeals in Arguments 262 / Textbook Excerpt 9.1 265 / Study Alert! Related Skills #9: Library Research Skills 267 / Making the Connection: Reflection Entry #9 270

CHAPTER 10
Summarizing 271

Summarizing Survey 271 / Plan of the Chapter 272 / Summarizing 272 / A Word about Paraphrasing 275 / Summarizing Longer Excerpts 278 / Informal Types of Summarizing 279 / Textbook Excerpt 10.1 287 / Study Alert! Related Study Skills #10: Graphic Materials 289 / Making the Connection: Reflection Entry #10 292

Ten Practice Tests 293

1: The Chemical Senses 293 / 2: Extrasensory Perception 293 / 3: Stages of Sleep 299 / 4: Parenting Styles 302 / 5: Do Animals Have Language? 306 / 6: Culture and the Expansion of Emotion 309 / 7: What Is Language? 312 / 8: Gender Similarities and Differences 315 / 9: Smoking 319 / 10: Attraction 323

Sources and Acknowledgments 327

Index 329

The Reading Connection

READING SKILLS AND COLLEGE SUCCESS

CHAPTER ONE

Previewing

One of the keys to success in reading college textbooks is to look ahead, to check things out in advance. Successful college readers try to know the territory before they move in. They survey the new area. Specifically, they try to get an idea of the book, the chapter, and the assignment before they spend valuable time reading.

There is a good deal of actual research on looking ahead. In an effort to discover what distinguishes good from poor readers, researchers have found that poor readers tend to read one word at a time, moving at the same pace from line to line, page to page. Successful readers, on the other hand, check out the chapter and book in advance. They especially check out the assignment before they begin by noting the author's purpose, headnotes, illustrations, typographical aids, and summaries; they look at picture captions, built-in questions, maps, charts, graphs, and the organization of the material.

This chapter will show you some basic approaches to textbook reading assignments. Some of these have been used by successful students for years and can help you, almost at once, to get more from the time you spend reading assignments.

Before you begin this chapter, take the previewing survey that follows. This survey will help you determine your strengths and weaknesses in previewing.

Previewing Skills Survey

	Never	Sometimes	Always
1. I read the title of the chapter before I read the chapter.		✓	
2. I read the headings and subheadings before I read the chapter.		✓	
3. I define new vocabulary words before I read the chapter.	✓		
4. I read all of the illustrative material before I read the chapter.	✓		
※5. I read the introduction and summary before I read the chapter.		✓	
6. I read the end of the chapter questions before I read the chapter.	✓		
7. I figure out the chapter plan before I read it.	✓		
8. I check out each of my textbooks before I read them.	✓		

9. I use a specific textbook reading strategy.
10. I define a purpose for reading.

Plan of the Chapter

Chapter One is arranged in three main sections:

- The first shows you how to check out a college textbook at the beginning of the course so that you will better understand its organization and the purpose and plan of its authors.
- The second helps you with the very important job of specifically defining what you are supposed to do in an assignment.
- The third explains skimming and suggests ways to skim more efficiently.

This chapter gives you several effective approaches to successful reading, ideas that you can also use when reading newspapers, magazine articles, handbooks, and other work-related materials. With the explanations and suggestions, you will find several sequentially arranged exercises to help you master the recommended strategies. Chapter One, like the other chapters in this book, also includes Vignettes (in which college students relate their experiences), an Idea Box with tips for success, self-tests, and an opportunity to reflect in writing upon your new learnings. Like the other chapters, too, Chapter One ends with a Study Alert, a brief activity focusing upon a related study skill.

The Importance of Looking Ahead

Looking ahead is important in textbook reading—and in life in general. Think about these comments from a former—and very successful—student.

Years ago I worked as a musician in traveling bands. We drove hundreds of miles each week to areas outside the city, usually going in one or two cars. One of the regular drivers, Frank, the bass player, prided himself on his driving skills. He was good. No question. He'd driven thousands of miles, safely, always getting us to our destinations with time to spare.

Frank taught me something about driving that is enormously important, something that has been of great value to me through the years since, something not only important about driving but about successful study in college, even about successful living.

"Look ahead" was his constant advice. "Don't just look at the other guy's rear bumper: look over and around his car, through his rear window even. The trick is always to see way ahead of the next car, and the car in front of it, and the car in front of that one. The farther you can see in front, the better for you."

I've followed Frank's advice on the road. There's no question he was right: if you look only at the car in front of you, you are in potential trouble. The bad things are almost always up ahead. You need to see as far ahead on the road as you can. The farther the better. If you can see what's way up on the road, you can brake, slow down, turn off the road, reverse. You have options.

But this is also true, it seems to me, in life. Some people only look ahead to the next day or week (or even the next hour). They don't have a clue about what might happen in their lives and they have no options. They are unprepared. They could avert trouble but they don't see it coming. Like a poor driver, they can't change directions, stop, pace themselves sensibly. They get bogged down—or worse—because they don't look ahead.

These comments tell us much about driving success and maybe something about successful living. They also tell us a great deal about college learning and, especially, about textbook reading.

This leads to an important piece of advice about college reading (as well as driving and leading a successful life): WHEN YOU KNOW WHAT'S COMING UP, YOU HAVE A BETTER CHANCE OF DEALING WITH IT.

College students who understand how their textbooks are organized have an advantage over those who don't. Students who understand the specific assignment have an edge. Students who have a definite purpose in reading an assignment are ahead of the game before they begin. Students who preview an assignment are already on their way to the goal.

Checking Out Your Textbooks

Most people check out movies they plan to see, restaurants they intend to visit, colleges they think they might attend. Most people check a map before taking a long trip. Most check over a book, tape, video, or CD before buying it. People seem to realize, almost instinctively, that it's wise to look at reviews, maps, travel guides, or other guides; most sense the wisdom of talking to other people first, before they spend their time and money on a film, CD, trip, or college.

Textbooks are different. You don't simply go to a bookstore and buy the book you like; you are told the title of the textbook used in the course. However, you still need to do considerable previewing—even when the choice of textbook is not yours. The book will be a major part of your life for the course, so you need to know as much about it as possible.

Checking out your textbook is time well spent. You'll get a view of the course in advance, see what material is covered (and what is not), find out in advance the kind of study helps built into the book, and, best of all, you can get the confidence that comes with knowing where you are going and how you'll get there.

Here are eight suggestions for you as you examine your textbook. Think about each and then complete Exercise 1 that appears after the suggestions.

1. Examine the title page, back and front. Sometimes students have no idea of the title of their book and don't even know its author! They refer to a book they live with (intimately!) for several weeks of their lives as "the one with the green cover" or "you know, the blue one." Your textbook, whether you like it or not, is crucial to your success in the course. Read the title page to discover the exact title, the author's name. Find out who published it. Discover where and, especially, when it was published. (You may have to go to the reverse side for the date.) Here are some questions to think about as you study the title page, back and front:

- What are the author's credentials? Is he or she well known in the field? Associated with a well-known college or university?
- Is the publisher known to you? Could the place of publication be important? Why?
- Does the date matter? Is the information in the book dated or up-to-date? Why are such matters important?
- Is there a catalog number for the Library of Congress? Why might this be important?

2. Check the table of contents. You can get an idea of the range of topics covered, not only by the book but usually by the teacher of the course. Find out what is covered and what is not. You can also get an approximate idea of time frame for the course when you note what comes early and what later on. Such information is valuable when you prepare for mid-term quizzes and final examinations. Just as a skillful driver knows what's up ahead, a skillful student tries to have a notion of what lies in store.

3. Look at the index. A good book usually has a good index. You can get a preview of topics to be treated and, at the same time, be aware of areas you already know about. Familiarity with the index may also prove invaluable when you are studying for exams.

4. Read introductory pages. Many students don't bother to read the introduction or preface, yet these pages often provide clues about the author's intentions and plan of organization. You need to see, before you start to study the book, what its major purpose is and what the author has to tell you *before you read*.

5. Actually read the first and last chapters. Not only do you begin the course with a better perspective but you get a feeling of confidence. Often, you come away with a strong notion of what the course is all about even before the first class!

6. Look for vocabulary aids. Vocabulary is the key to success in many courses: when you have a handle on the words, your understanding is clearer. Check your book to see if there is a glossary, vocabulary aids (such as underscoring or inserted definitions of new words), or previews of technical terms.

7. Skim the book. This means going over all the pages. If you have read the first and last chapters and studied the table of contents, you have a pretty good idea of the book; now, skim quickly each page to get an even better idea of how the book is put together. The time you spend skimming will add to your confidence and learning.

8. Look ahead for study aids. Often textbooks include valuable helps along the way: illustrations, graphs, charts, maps, inserted questions, reviews, summaries, references, and so on. Before the course starts, you need to have a handle on all available assistance.

Now let's put this information to practical use!

> **idea**
>
> Even when you have a clear idea of the reading assignment, you sometimes have trouble reading it because your concentration is poor. What can you do about concentration? Here are five tips.
>
> **1.** Study alone. Despite the natural urge to work with others, there are times when you need solitude and quiet. You'll be better able to rethink the assignment, clarify the task, and concentrate, by yourself. Group work may be more effective when preparing for a test.
>
> **2.** Position your body for alertness. You can (and probably do) read flat out in a bed or cot, but your brain probably functions better when you are upright, sitting on a chair and before a table or desk. (Remember, the more you relax your body, the more likely you are to fall asleep.)
>
> **3.** Choose the right area. Libraries are good but your room is fine if you have a good chair, table, desk, light, and NO radios, TVs, and other distractions.
>
> **4.** Be in good physical condition. This means that you need to be (reasonably) well fed, not thirsty, and so on. It just doesn't pay to doze off from fatigue when you need to read a key chapter in the book.
>
> **5.** Keep materials nearby. Make sure you have pencils, dictionaries, colored markers, scissors, paper clips, and so on. One advantage to working in your room is that you can establish a little stockpile.

Defining the Assignment

What Am I Supposed to Do (Exactly)?

One of the major problems in college reading is that many students don't really know what they are supposed to do on particular assignments. Many students begin a reading assignment without understanding exactly what they are expected to do. They jump in cold. They read for hours and still have problems on tests and quizzes.

One secret of success in college reading is knowing what the assignment really is. In a series of studies done at the University of Texas a few years ago, it was discovered that defining the study task was the single most important factor in success. This is not far-fetched when you stop to think about it. In life most of our failures seem to lie in our ignorance of what is expected. People on the job frequently botch a task simply because they didn't quite understand what they needed to do. In our personal lives, too, we often fail to achieve our goals because we didn't define them. We aim in a general direction but don't specify.

To improve your own reading, then, the first step is to have a plan that clearly defines and specifies goals. Instructors make assignments, but students don't copy them down, or don't listen. Exercise 3 is designed to make you more aware of this problem.

EXERCISE 1.3

Here are several assignments copied from student notebooks. Read each and decide whether it is clear enough to proceed or so fuzzy that you will probably have trouble with it.

8   Chapter 1 Previewing

1. Read Chapter 7 and list the nine causes of labor trouble given by the author. Comments: _____
   _____
   _____

2. Read Chapter 7. Comments: _____
   _____
   _____

3. Read the section in Chapter 9 discussing the developmental tasks of adolescence according to Havighurst. Make note of these and be prepared to rank them by the order they seem to develop in most American teenagers. Comments: _____
   _____
   _____

4. Read Chapter 11 and be prepared to discuss its main points. Comments: _____
   _____
   _____

5. Read Chapter 11 and list what appear to be the main points. Comments: _____
   _____
   _____

6. Read the textbook section on civil rights law. Comments: _____
   _____
   _____

7. Read the chapter on the stock market crash for the mid-term. Comments: _____
   _____
   _____

8. Read the chapter on migrations westward and prepare an outline that notes each in chronological order. Comments: _____
   _____
   _____

Your own records of reading assignments can make or break you. If you keep inexact records, you are never quite sure of what the task is. If you keep no records at all, you are in serious trouble from the start, because, of course, the human memory is much too treacherous. You think you know what to read but you haven't remembered it quite as you should.

The next Exercise can help you with this problem.

EXERCISE 1.4

Either buy a small assignment notebook or set aside pages in a loose-leaf course notebook (with lecture and reading notes) for assignments. For this exercise, keep careful track of all your course assignments for one week. Copy them down as exactly as you can. At the end of the week, copy the assignments here and then *evaluate each*. It's the second part of this exercise that will help you become more aware of the importance of clarifying and defining assignments.

Follow a plan like this:

Course: _____

Date given: _____

Date due: _____

Assignment as given: _____

My opinion of its clarity: _____

You may have discovered as you completed Exercise 4 that some of your assignments were inexact and hard to follow. You can turn fuzzy assignments into clear ones by rewriting them. For example, "Read Chapter 3 on infant development" is unclear. It is too vague. You can read that chapter three or four times and still not get much out of it. What you can do is specify yourself by saying, "Read the chapter and list chronologically the stages given in the book." or "Read and make a time-line of the stages." How can fuzzy assignments be made more clear? You can make lists, charts, comparisons and contrasts, or a list of questions you can answer through reading. Don't just read about the causes of the American Revolution; instead read to make a list of the causes or to compare the causes of the American Revolution with those that triggered, say, the Russian revolution.

EXERCISE 1.5

Directions: Go back to Exercise 1.4 and identify the assignments you believed needed clarification and rewrite them so that they better define the reading task. Get rid of those that say "Read Chapter 3" and substitute ones that specify. If you had no fuzzy assignments in your personal collection, look at Exercise 3: there were a few here.

Keeping Track of Assignments

Most successful students do keep track of reading assignments. They know that planning is important and that exact knowledge of assignments is needed for effective planning. When asked, "What are the first three things you do when given an assignment?" three people responded as follows.

VIGNETTE 1

The first thing I do is make sure that I understand the assignment completely. If I do not understand it, or only partly understand it, I go directly to the teacher and ask him or her to explain it to me better. If I still don't get it, I ask the teacher to go over it with me slowly one more time. If I'm absent the day the assignment was made, I check the syllabus and either go and see the teacher or call a friend for details.

Chuck

VIGNETTE 2

The first thing I do when I receive an assignment is write it down. Without this information I will either forget to do it or forget what it's about or when it's due. When I am planning on reading, I make sure I can be alone in my room with my door shut. The reason for this is I need to be able to read aloud. My mind tends to wander while I read so if I read aloud, I have to concentrate on it completely. Finally, when I'm comfortable I begin to read. Sometimes I'll take a break in the middle and other times I'll read it a second time if I couldn't understand it fully.

Wilma D.

VIGNETTE 3

When an instructor gives you an assignment to read there are always three things you should do. First, write the assignment down in a planner so you don't forget what pages to read. Next, do the assignment in order to get credit, and also if the instructor wants to talk about the reading in the next class period you will be able to participate in the class discussion. Finally, the third thing you should do is turn in the assignment to the teacher so it is on the record that you did complete the assignment.

Andrew W.

As you continue to read this chapter, keep these student responses in mind. Have these successful students mentioned all important points? Would you add anything? Why is it useful to know what other students do as they handle study assignments in their classes?

Skimming

Sometimes college students are confused about the concept "reading rate." They pick up heavy textbooks, flip the pages, and see hundreds and hundreds of pages. "How can I ever read this much material in a semester?" they ask. "This is *too* much. I can't go to classes, work a job, have a social life, study, sleep, and read all these pages!" Many decide to check out "speed reading" programs, enroll in special courses, or purchase expensive self-help books.

Actually, the situation isn't as dreadful as many believe. In the first place, your reading rate will improve. As you read more and more through the semester, you'll find your rate getting better and better. Also, as you become more comfortable with textbook reading, you'll discover that frequently you can *skim*. Much textbook material must be read rather slowly: the material is new and difficult, and you should—without the least embarrassment—move at a careful pace. However,

3. Why is it difficult to educate many Hispanics about AIDS?

Textbook Chapter Excerpt 1.1

Each chapter in this book ends with an activity based on an excerpt taken from an actual college textbook. These activities give you opportunities to demonstrate some of the skills you have learned so far in the book.

Textbook Chapter Excerpt 1.1 is from a college textbook on marketing called *Marketing: Creating Value for Customers*, by Gilbert A. Churchill, Jr., and J. Paul Peter (Burr Ridge, Ill.: Richard D. Irwin, 1995). Here are the directions for Excerpt 1.1:

1. **Look ahead.** Read the excerpt quickly to get an idea of its content. Ask yourself such questions as:

   Is this about Ben and Jerry? About ice cream? About how it is marketed? About how decisions are made at the company?

2. **Define the assignment.** In this case, there is no instructor to spell out the assignment. You must define it. Ask yourself:

   Do I read to find out about Ben and Jerry? Do I focus on ice cream as a product? Should I read to remember how the company grew? Do I read for examples of decision making?

3. **Read to complete the assignment.** Once you have surveyed the excerpt and spelled out exactly what your purpose is in reading, read carefully to "complete the assignment." If your purpose was to find out more about Ben and Jerry, that defines your purpose for reading. If your "look ahead" tells you to read to find out how decisions are made, that becomes your reading assignment.

4. **Record.** At the end of the excerpt you will find a place to record your responses: "I am reading to _____" (that's the assignment) and "I found _____."

BEN AND JERRY'S HOMEMADE

Chunky Monkey, Rainforest Crunch, Cherry Garcia, Chocolate Chip Cookie Dough. Everyone knows what these names stand for—flavors of that sweet, rich, incredibly delicious, all-natural ice cream made by two "counterculture" businessmen who settled in Vermont and decided that ice cream might be cheaper to produce than bagels. (By the time they learned that ice cream was actually more expensive, they were well into manufacturing it and were headed for success.) Ben Cohen and Jerry Greenfield have become household names, their ice cream is household ice cream, and their way of doing business has become a household example to many larger companies.

Ben & Jerry's started as a small company with a small-company atmosphere. In 1988, the organization still operated out of one major business site, with 150 employees and $32 million in sales. Today the firm operates four major business sites, employs 500 people, and draws in sales of $130 million. As the company grew, distribution had to expand, and its owners chose a team organization to accomplish this while maintaining their firm's focus on the importance of its people.

When it became evident that the ice-cream producer needed a new distribution center, Ben & Jerry's selected a cross-functional team to carry out the tasks of planning and designing it (instead of hiring an outside agency). The eight-member team, consisting of employees from marketing, sales, finance, and other departments, scouted other plants around the country, then reported what they concluded Ben & Jerry's needed. Management gave them the go-ahead. In 1992, the $3.5 million distribution center opened in Bellows Falls, Vermont. At the same time, Ben & Jerry's adopted the use of just-in-time manufacturing, receiving deliveries as needed rather than bearing the cost of holding an inventory of materials.

With the success of the first team, Ben & Jerry's established another team to design a manufacturing plant. Explains company president Chuck Lacy, "The passion you get by doing things in-house overcomes the expertise you can buy on the outside."

Employee empowerment through the use of cross-functional teams is helping Ben & Jerry's grow, not only in its distribution and production capabilities but in other areas as well. Now the company has what it calls "Big Nine" process teams—nine groups of employees that meet on a regular basis to find solutions to everything from training problems to flavor selection. At one point, distributors complained that they couldn't get enough of the right flavors for their customers. Employees, rather than upper management, solved the problem. Decision making at all levels is paramount. "The name of the game is creating more ownership at all levels in the mission of the company, which consists of a profit-making component and a social responsibility component," explains Elizabeth Bankowski, who holds the title of Director, Social Mission Development.

Source: Reprinted by permission of *Hemisphere,* the In-flight Magazine of United Airlines, Pace Communications, Inc., Greensboro, N.C.

My Responses to the Excerpt

1. My survey, or look ahead, told me that

_____

_____

2. I, therefore, defined my reading assignment as "Read to

_____

_____"

3. I learned

_____

_____

Related Study Skills #1: Using the Index

In each chapter of this book you'll find a STUDY ALERT! These brief sections are designed to sharpen the study skills you need to read textbooks successfully.

This chapter's STUDY ALERT! focuses upon an important but much neglected study skill—*using the index.* Many college students look at the Table of Contents of their textbook and, sometimes, skim the book itself before reading it, but few take advantage of the index at the back of the book.

The index of a textbook tries to include references to all the important items in the book—names, places, events, topics, subjects, and so on. These are listed alphabetically with the page numbers you need to go back and read.

Why is using the index an important study skill?

- You can use it to preview the book. A few minutes checking the index gives you a general picture of what the book is about. You see the major and minor topics covered, and you get an idea of what the book does not cover.
- You can use it for research. When preparing a paper for a class, the index can indicate where exactly you can locate specific information. When you need some supplementary data for a class discussion, you can speedily put your finger on the material needed.
- You can use the index for study and review. One excellent way to prepare for a test is to go through your lecture and reading notes and list all important items (names, events, places, and so on) and then check the index to make sure you have copied correct information in your notes. To prepare for an end-of-semester test, go through the index item by item to make sure you remember the material covered by the book.

Here are two exercises to sharpen your ability to make maximum use of the index.

EXERCISE 1.7

On page 19 is the first page of an index from a textbook used by students preparing for careers as Certified Travel Agents (from *Travel Career Development*, by Patricia J. Gagnon and Karen Silva, Burr Ridge, Ill.: Irwin/Mirror Press, 1990, p. 303). Look it over and then answer these questions.

1. On what page will you find information on traveling by train from London to Liverpool?

2. Where can you find out about inexpensive places to stay in a South American city?

3. Where can you discover the size and weight acceptable for a carry-on piece of luggage?

4. Where might you learn if flights to Mexico City serve Kosher food?

5. Where do you find out about backroom systems?

6. On what page might you find how rainy it is in Dublin, Ireland, in the summer months.

7. Where might you find information on writing up a ticket for an unmarried couple (with two names) traveling together?

_____

8. If a customer had to cancel a flight because of illness, where might you get information?

_____

9. On what page would you look to discover if a customer would need a birth certificate to get an automobile driving license in Montreal, Canada?

_____

10. Where would you find the difference between a regional and a commuter airline?

_____

EXERCISE 1.8

One of the best ways to use your knowledge of the index as a study skill is to actually make an index. Stop and think about it. When you reread a textbook passage in order to prepare your own index, you are forced to identify important items. You have to think carefully. By writing the items in your notebook, you are helping get them into memory. By thinking about what is and what isn't important, you are stimulating your brain to operate at a high level.

In this exercise, you must read the passage carefully and then list all items that stand out on the page. You would not list ordinary words, such as *separate, publisher,* or *today.* They appear in the passage but are not really important. On the other hand, *Hispanic, Anglos,* and *Nicaraguan* are important. Of course, you don't need to worry about page numbers, because this is a learning exercise.

Try making an index. You'll find that when you do this to prepare for an examination, you'll learn and remember much more.

MIAMI—LANGUAGE AND A CHANGING CITY

In the years since Castro seized power in Cuba, the city of Miami has been transformed from a quiet southern city to a Latin American mecca. Few thing better capture Miami today than its ethnic divisions, especially its long-simmering fight over language: English versus Spanish. The 1990 census found that half of the city's 358,548 residents have trouble speaking English—possibly the highest proportion in any large American city. Ten years ago, at 30 percent, the figure was high. Today's 50 percent who have difficulty communicating in English reflects the recent influx of Hispanic and Creole-speaking Haitian immigrants.

As this chapter stresses, language is a primary means by which people learn—and communicate—their social world. Consequently, language differences in Miami reflect a community not just of huge cultural diversity but of people who live in separate worlds. Sandra Laurin, a community college student, put it this way: "Everyone is in their own little group: the Haitians in their group, the Spanish in theirs, the Anglos in theirs." As classmate Nicole Allen added, "Language is a big barrier. It's so hard to communicate with everybody, you just don't bother.

Although the ethnic stew makes Miami culturally one of the richest cities in the United States, the lan-

Index

A

Access	238
Accommodations	
Airport hotels	152
All-suites	152
History of	147
Hotel affiliations	148–149
Hotel guides	161
Making a reservation	158–160
Market segmentation	149–153
Organization of	147
Overbooking	163
Spas	153
Accounting	259
Advertising	231–233
Africa	50
Agency income	260
Air Travel Card	266
Airfares, International	87–88
Airfares, Promotional	66
Airline club lounges	78
Airline codes	73
Airline default	80
Airline meals	74
Airline ticket	59–60, 62
Airlines	
Charters	58
Commuter	57
Rate desks	88
Regional	57
Service	57
Trunk carriers	57
Airplanes	69–70
Airport codes	73
Airports	74–78
Airline club lounges	78
Check-in procedures	76–77
Security	77–78
All-suites	152
AHMA	163
Amtrak	104–106
ARC	59
ARC Industry Agents' Handbook	269
Area-bank settlement plan	267–268
ARINC	237
Asia and the Pacific	46–50
Assets	262–263
ASTA	179
ATC	55
Automation, History of	236–237

B

Back-room systems	241
Baggage	62
Balance sheet	262–263
Ballooning	59
Bankruptcies	80, 208
Bias	238
Bilateral pacts	86
Boarding passes	77
Booking information	248
Bookkeeping	259
BritRail	109, 111
Bumping	65
Business travelers	200–201

C

Canada	35–38
Cancellation charges	268–269
Car rentals	111–118
Age	111
Automobile partnerships	113
Benefits	112
Computerized innovations	117
Credit qualifications	112
Driver's license	111–112
Insurance	115–116
International car purchase	118
International driver's permit	112
Qualifying clients	113–116
Career Planning	275–284
Cover letter	278, 281
Interviews	282–283
Job search	276–277
Resume	277–280
Caribbean	39–40
Cash flow	264
Central America	40–41
Changes in plans	208–210
Charters	204–205
Checks	266, 268
Circle trip	72
City codes	73
CLIA	123
Climate	27
Club Med	152, 227
Communications	
Fax	253
Interoffice	254
Letter writer's guidelines	252
Letters	249–252
Mail services	252–253
Telephone	254–255
Vouchers	249
Complaints	216–217
Computers	
Back-room systems	241
Components of	235–236
Computer Reservations Systems	239
Future	242
Hardware	235–236

guage gap sometimes creates anger and misunderstanding. The aggravation of Anglos—tinged with hostility—is seen in the bumper stickers reading "Will the Last American Out Please Bring the Flag?"

But Hispanics, now a majority in Miami, are equally frustrated. Many feel Anglos should be able to speak at least some Spanish. Nicaraguan immigrant Pedro Falco, for example, is studying English and wonders why more people won't try to learn his language. "Miami is the capital of Latin America," he says. "The population speaks Spanish."

In the past ten years, Miami's population grew only 3.4 percent, but its Spanish-speaking population grew 15 percent, making the city 62 percent Hispanic. Throughout the United States, 83 percent of residents speak English at home, but only 25 percent of Miami residents do so.

What's happening in Miami, says University of Chicago sociologist Douglas Massey, is what happened in cities such as Chicago at the beginning of the century. Then, as now, the rate of immigration exceeded the speed with which new residents learned English, creating a pile-up effect in the proportion of non-English speakers. Becoming comfortable with English is a slow process, he points out, whereas immigration is fast.

Language and cultural flare-ups sometimes make headlines in the city. The Hispanic-American community was outraged in 1991 when an employee at the Coral Gables Board of Realtors lost her job for speaking Spanish at the office. And in 1989, protesters swarmed a Publix supermarket after a cashier was fired for chatting with a friend in Spanish.

David Lawrence, Jr., publisher of the *Miami Herald*, the area's dominant newspaper, sees the language gap as "a challenge and opportunity." Lawrence now publishes *El Nuevo Herald*, a Spanish-language edition with a circulation of 100,000, which has become a favorite of the Cuban elite. "The key to making any community work is obviously communication," notes Lawrence. "While lots of people, including myself, work hard to learn Spanish, part of being successful is being able to communicate in English."

Massey expects the city's proportion of non-English speakers to rise with continuing immigration. But he says that this "doesn't mean in the long run that Miami is going to end up being a Spanish-speaking city." Instead, Massey believes, bilingualism will prevail. "Miami is the first truly bilingual city," he says. "The people who get ahead are not monolingual English speakers or monolingual Spanish speakers. They're people who speak both languages."

Source: Copyright 1992, *USA Today.* Reprinted by permission.

Index items selected for "Miami—Language and a Changing City"

_____   _____

_____   _____

_____   _____

_____   _____

CHAPTER TWO

Reading with Purpose

Successful college readers read with a purpose. They read to discover the answers to specific question, to verify information, to get a general view of a topic, to discover an author's point of view, to check predictions they have made, or often simply to enjoy the reading experience. Unlike less successful readers who tend to read simply to satisfy a course assignment, effective readers have a clear goal in mind. They know that a well-defined purpose not only helps them direct their energies but focuses their attention.

Chapter One recommended that in addition to knowing your textbook well, you thoroughly know each assignment. Often a good assignment carries with it a purpose, but more often you need to establish a purpose for reading. Fortunately, there are a variety of tricks and techniques available to you. This chapter suggests several.

Before you begin the chapter, take the survey below. This survey will help you determine your strengths and weaknesses when reading with a purpose.

Reading with Purpose Survey

		Never	Sometimes	Always
1.	I establish a purpose for reading textbook assignments.		✓	
2.	I make predictions about what the author is going to say.	✓		
3.	I check my predictions for accuracy.	✓		
4.	I use study guides to help set my purpose.	✓		
5.	I use a specific study method like SQ3R to help set my purpose.	✓		
6.	I read to discover answers to specific questions.		✓	
7.	I read to verify information.		✓	
8.	I read to discover an author's point of view.	✓		

9. I use assignments to help establish a purpose.
10. I just sit down and read when I have a reading assignment.

Plan of the Chapter

Chapter Two has two main sections. The first explains previewing. It explains the value of looking at an assignment carefully for clues you might use in establishing a purpose for reading. It also explains one of the most effective tools available, the SQ3R approach. SQ3R has been used by college students for more than 50 years, and countless thousands of students testify to its effectiveness in getting the most information from a reading assignment—and in remembering it!

The second section of the chapter describes several other strategies for setting a purpose, particularly predicting. Readers who make predictions in advance of reading and then read to test out their own predictions learn and remember more. Both sections are supported by exercises, tips, and stories of college students who have experimented with techniques for establishing purposes for their reading.

Previewing

Once you know the exact assignment, you need to look at it carefully, to check it out in advance. Here are five suggestions to help you.

1. Read—and think about—the title. Many students start to read the assigned pages immediately, but experience shows that reading the title—and considering its meaning—pays big dividends. The title of the chapter or chapter section may hint at the main idea. It certainly specifies the topic or area to be examined. Often it helps you activate from your long-term memory information you already possess and can use as you try to make sense of the new material. A minute or two of thoughtful consideration may make the difference between getting meaning and perplexity.

2. Look for breakdowns within the assigned section or chapter. These are usually signaled by bold type or some other clue, such as color, underlining, italics, or white space. Once you can see the breakdowns, you can get a better grasp of the way the assignment is organized and what it covers. The knowledge of the individual parts in the assigned reading can help you plan your time and also lead, as we shall see, to use of self-questioning techniques.

3. Look for any study guides and study helps. Often, authors give built-in questions to guide readers; sometimes they define tricky words or concepts; sometimes they stop and summarize as they go along. Check, then, for a glossary, questions, highlighted points, marginal explanations, and, certainly, illustrations, maps, charts, graphs, and similar aids.

4. It doesn't hurt to count the pages and make a time estimate. We know that little children count the pages of books their teachers tell them to read, but that isn't such a bad idea. When you start the reading assignment, you should know whether it is 10

or 50 pages, so that you can better judge the time needed to handle the job efficiently. Also, look at the density of print. Some books load each paragraph with material, packed in closely and hard on the eyes. Of course, a densely packed page will take longer to read and you need, therefore, to allow extra time in your study planning.

5. <u>The most famous previewing technique of all is also a highly effective study tool called SQ3R.</u> It was developed for college students years ago and has proven its effectiveness for thousands of students through the years. Here's how it works.

- First, you preview the assignment by noting all the points discussed in the preceding paragraphs, but you pay particular attention to titles, subtitles, and all headings. You should get a good overall view of the assignment in advance.
- The second step is crucial: you make up personal questions based on your reading of the titles and headings. For example, if the section on the economic depression of the 1930s is divided by subheadings such as Probable Causes, Immediate Consequences, Steps to Remedy, and Worldwide Consequences, then you create four questions: What were the probable causes? What were the immediate consequences? What steps were taken to remedy the problem? What were the worldwide consequences? You should actually write these questions into your notebook.
- Next you Read. (That's the first "R.") You read as you normally would read an assignment, but now you have specific questions you need answered: you read to answer your questions. You should write the answers into your notebook as you find them.
- The second "R" is Recite. After you have finished the reading, go back and recite the answers to your questions to make sure you know them.
- The last step (and final "R") is Review. Before a test or class quiz, you can go over the questions and review all your answers.

Why does SQ3R work so well? Experiments have been done for years with SQ3R and it seems that it focuses your reading. It makes you attentive and thoughtful. Your mind is less apt to wander because you are looking for answers to specific question, and, of course, you are more likely to remember the new material.

Now let's try putting some of these ideas to work.

EXERCISE 2.1

The following passages have been taken from a college textbook. Before you start to read, check the suggestions made above and then use the SQ3R technique. Space has been set aside for your questions on the page after the actual reading assignment.

UNDERSTANDING HUMAN MEMORY

Memory plays a crucial role in learning. All new information and ideas that we may later need must be stored in memory, but human memory is fragile and not always to be trusted. Some of the material we want to remember seems not to be stored while other material pops up when we least expect it. What have psychologists learned in recent years about our ability to remember?

Kinds of Memory Psychologists who study human memory have discovered several kinds of memory.

When we first encounter new material, we seem to hold onto it for fractions of a second in *sensory-storage memory*. Here the mind makes decisions, not understood by psychologists, about the value of the data. If the mind decides the new material may be important, then it is stored for a very brief time in *short-term memory*. Here we hold the new information and ideas for seconds, minutes, maybe hours, but rarely more than a few days. During the time we hold data in short-term memory, we evidently consider it carefully or use it. We consider it (or our minds do without our really thinking much about the matter) in relation to what we need to know to survive and succeed in life. If the mind decides it is valuable, the new material seems to go into *long-term memory*. Often, however, the material in short-term memory is useful only for a moment (an example might be a telephone number we look up).

Long-term memory When we put new data into long-term memory this material seems to go into networks of associated data, all related. For example, when you learn a new (and important) fact about health, it is stored in a network of related information pertaining to health. Sports information is stored in the same way: into your network systems pertaining to sports (broken down, of course, by individual sports, players, times, personal associations, and so on). One interesting aspect of long-term memory that intrigues psychologists is that once an item gets into long-term memory, it seems to stay forever. We may not always be able to remember the item, but it can come back to us at unexpected times. One reason elderly people seem to be able to recall data from childhood, often 60 or 70 years before, is that they have less interference in their minds from daily business and current distractions. The general finding is that once an item gets into long-term memory we have it forever.

How Does Material Get into Long-Term Memory? Psychologists are still not sure how we get certain items into long-term memory while other material disappears after minutes or days from short-term memory. One way is certainly *repetition*. When we repeat a new fact over and over again, the drill seems to work; we often can remember it when we want even though years have elapsed. School teachers have always known the efficacy of drill and repetition: recall your own experiences learning the multiplication tables in elementary school. Another sure-fire way to get a fact into long-term memory is through *association*. We remember by associating the new item with information we already have stored in long-term memory. For example, a friend tells you a telephone number and you realize you do not need to write it down because the last four digits are the year you graduated from high school. Because the date of your high school graduation is already firmly in your long-term memory, it is easy to establish a connection for the new information. Another way we seem to get new material into long-term memory is if the new material is *odd* or *unusual*. When the new item fails to fit into expected patterns, we seem to remember it more readily. Thus, we cannot remember all the chairs we have sat in but we will remember one that collapsed under us or one we may have been sitting in when we heard especially good (or bad) news. *Personal connections* also lead to long-term storage. You may sit through a long lecture and remember very little except the fact that a politician had the same name as one of your sisters or that a particular law might have directly influenced your life. There are other suggestions that try to explain why certain items get into long-term memory and others do not, but the four cited here seem to account for most instances.

Semantic and Episodic Memory There is one further distinction that psychologists have found useful. When we put an item into long-term memory, it may be entirely personal or entirely general. The personal items are called *episodic*; they are ours and ours alone. The word "mother," for example, helps us recall our own mother; we can visualize her face, dress, or manner, her speaking voice or style. Over time, as we emerged from childhood, we began to realize that other people also had mothers and, although they had different voices and appearances, they shared common characteristics. We discovered—probably in early childhood—that the word "mother" had a general significance. In our memories, therefore, we still have both episodic and *semantic*, or generalized, memories. If you try to recall a variety of items from long-term memory (teacher, school, car, job, and so on), you will find a wealth of both episodic and semantic memories.

Mnemonic Devices One way to control what goes into long-term memory (and what comes out!) is through *mnemonic devices*. These are formal schemes designed deliberately to improve memory. They range from tying strings to fingers to simple rhymes such as "Thirty days hath September . . ." Students learn to distinguish a Bactrian camel from a dromedary camel by turning the initial letters on their sides to note that Bactrian has two humps and the dromedary one. Some students remember the reciprocal of pi (0.318310) by remembering the phrase "Can I remember the reciprocal?" in which the numbers of letters in each word indicate the numbers. Why do mnemonic devices work? They are retrieval systems built into the initial learning; when you learn the new data, you associate it with material already networked in your long-term memory and can get it out efficiently.

Worksheet for Exercise 2.1

After you have *surveyed* the textbook selection for Exercise 2.1, write your *questions* here. You should have at least five. Once you have surveyed and written your questions, go back and *read* the selection and answer the questions. When your answers are on paper here, you are ready to *recite* and *review*.

List here your personal questions prepared after your survey:

1. How many different kinds of memory are there.
2. What is Long-term memory?
3. How does material get into Long-term Memory?
4. What is Semantic Memory?
5. What are Mnemonic Devices?

Write your answers to your questions here:

1. There are 4 different kinds of memory.

---

idea.

SQ3R has proved so effective through the years that many instructors and students have created several similar techniques. You may want to try one or two to see if another better fits your personal learning/reading style.

- PQRST — Preview, Question, Read, State, Test
- OK5R — Overview, Key Idea, Read, Record, Recite, Review, Reflect
- PQ4R — Preview, Question, Read, Reflect, Recite, Review
- LAQ/PV — Look Ahead, Question/Predict, Verify
- SPIN — Survey, Predict, Infer, Note

And then there's the simplest of all, the famous *triple S technique*. Using it, you simply Scan, Search, and Summarize.

The value in using any of these techniques is that it reminds you to look ahead, preview, survey, or take an overview. You are reminded, too, to make up questions or predictions to guide you through the reading and help hold your attention. These techniques have the additional value of having you follow up your reading by testing, reviewing, verifying, noting, or summarizing.

Remember, whether you choose to use one of these techniques or not, that you must look ahead or preview, set a purpose through questions or predictions, and follow up by reviewing or summarizing. However labeled, these are the three signposts on the road to reading success.

2. _When you learn a new (and important) fact about health, it is stored in a network of related information pertaining to health._
3. _One way is certainly repetition._
4. _Generalized memories_
5. _They are retrieval systems built into the initial learning; when you learn the new data, you associate it with material already networked in your long-term memory and can get it out efficiently._

VIGNETTE 1

One of the best things I learned in the reading course was Questioning. We were told to make up questions before we read, and I thought at first that was dumb. I tried by using the headings as we were told, and that didn't work. I tried making questions from first sentences and that didn't work for me. I settled on another approach. I skimmed the whole assignment and then asked myself, "If the author were sitting here with me, what would I ask him or her?" Let me explain. I tried a section on the end of World War II. I knew what the pages were about because it had large headings that even a kid could understand and it was loaded with great pictures. I thought that, say, I was blind. I couldn't read. What would I do? I have the author here and I can ask him direct. I made up a list of ten questions, like "Did they have to drop the bomb? Who decided? How many might have been killed if they didn't drop it? Who says?" and so on. Then, I read—as if the blindness went away!—and tried to answer my own questions. The approach worked and I've used it ever since. It's a great way to tackle an assignment.

Constantine C.

VIGNETTE 2

This recommendation about setting up a purpose for reading means a lot to me. I've thought about it in connection with all my nonreading activities and decided that, of course, it's true. We do things in life because we have some purpose. The jobs that aren't based on a purpose are meaningless and nasty to do. I think of tasks in my work. Some I jump into and do right away. I can see a meaning for them and have a purpose. Other things the boss tells me to do have no meaning. I can't see why she wants me to do them and I hate every minute doing them. To me, the same applies to college assignments. When an instructor says, "Write a paper on such-and-such," and I can't see the point, I hate the assignment and do it poorly. When she says to do something that makes sense and that I really want to do, I do it and get it right.

Emily D.

EXERCISE 2.2

This exercise is more difficult than the last. The textbook selection here has no subtitles or subheadings. You must survey it, paying attention to the first lines in each paragraph, and making up your personal questions on the basis of information not provided in subheadings and subtitles. Again, space is provided at the end of the exercise for your questions and answers.

If your preferred learning style is auditory, you might also want to keep a cassette recorder in your study area to play back lectures or listen to tapes. Recite key words, formulas, and summaries of chapters into the recorder and play them back. Read out loud.

If you are primarily a kinesthetic learner, you may want to have a display table or bulletin board with models, graphs, samples, and pictures of your subjects. You may find that you want a computer chair, a stool, or even a drafting table that lets you stand while you work. You may want a learning space that allows you to walk around while you read.

If you are a visual learner, you will want to make your study area as visually appealing as possible. You might want to install a bulletin board so that you can display a calendar, course syllabi, schedules, and a daily to-do list. You also might want to use a project board to list all the projects due this semester.

You'll find that if you keep all your tools in one area, you'll reduce interruptions. Nothing is more frustrating than sitting down to work and being unable to find your favorite pen or your dictionary. So try to study at that space and make it your own private place, where no one else can work.

To further organize your materials, make a folder for each class. This folder can hold all class handouts, your schedules, phone numbers of classmates, and returned papers and tests. It can also hold works in process—a draft of a paper, or notes for a speech, for example. You should also have a folder for registration materials, grades, school planning, and a school catalog. To avoid mixing up projects, keep only one on the top of your desk at a time. To reduce distraction from the project at hand, put everything else in a file drawer or on a shelf. After each semester, keep a success file of your best papers, speeches, and tests.

If you have a typewriter, set it on a small table next to your desk. A computer and all its hardware take up lots of space, though, so if you have a computer, you might want to invest in a specialized computer desk or table that has enough space for the keyboard, monitor, printer, disks, and so on. If you enjoy using a computer, you may want to create your semester calendar, redo your course outlines, and write out projects.

When you don't want to study at home or can't find a private space, study in the school or a public library. Most libraries, even public libraries, have carrels that provide some privacy and protection from distractions. Try to pick the same spot each time you go to the library and carry all your essential tools with you. You can invest in an inexpensive backpack or canvas briefcase that has pockets of all sizes for holding pens and pencils, rulers, and different sizes of notebooks. You can carry a pocket dictionary or choose a carrel that's positioned near the reference area of the library, where you can use a larger dictionary. The key again is to keep only one project on the desk at a time, to use the same space if possible, and to pick a quiet place so that you're not distracted or interrupted. It might take some scouting around to find the best place. Some campus libraries have study areas that are quieter than others; check with other students for information, or do your own research. Sometimes the magazine stacks are a quiet area.

Source: Sharon K. Ferrett, *Peak Performance*. All rights reserved. Copyright ©1994 by Richard D. Irwin, Burr Ridge, Ill. Reprinted with permission.

Worksheet for Exercise 2.2

List here your personal questions prepared after your survey:

1. _____

2. _____

3. _____

4. _____

5. _____

Write your answers to your questions here:

1. _____

2. _____

3. _____

4. _____

5. _____

Setting a Purpose

SQ3R helps you set a purpose for reading an assignment: you read to find the answers to your questions. There are other effective ways to set a purpose for reading. You can read to answer questions given in the book itself. Sometimes authors start a chapter with specific questions designed to guide readers, and sometimes there are questions at the end of the chapter that you can read *first* to give you purpose. Often you read to discover some specific information for a class discussion or to write a paper. Sometimes, too, you read in order to pass a test, in which case you take copious notes and hope for the best. One of the best ways is the one we will explain here: it is *reading to check your predictions*.

How does predicting help reading comprehension? Here's how it works. The reader—you—previews the assignment and makes predictions about what the author is going to say. Then the reader reads to discover if the predictions are accurate. Let's use the example given earlier about a textbook chapter on the economic depression of the 1930s. There were four headings, if you remember, about the probable causes, the immediate consequences, the steps to remedy, and the worldwide consequences. Using SQ3R, you can make up questions such as: What were the causes of the depression? Using the prediction

idea:

SQ3R suggests that you get questions from headings, illustrations, or first sentences. There is another way that many students prefer. You can get questions to set a purpose for reading from the "5Ws plus H." This is supposed to be an old newspaper reporters' technique of finding the answers to the basic questions: Who? What? Where? When? Why? and How? Reporters sent to get information on a news story used these six question-headers to guide them. They'd ask, "Who did it? When did it happen?" and so on. You can use the same technique in setting up your own personal questions for reading an assignment. Look at the title, illustrations, headings, and so on, to get a rough idea of what the reading assignment is all about, and then make up six basic questions. You read to find the answers to these questions, and that's your purpose. Better than "just reading!" The questions focus your reading and help you pay attention to the assignment.

approach, you would write in your notebook your predictions of what the author is going to say! You'd write that the depression was caused by taxes, debts, the enormous amounts of money spent on the war that preceded it, and the stock market crash. These are your predictions, your personal predictions. Once you have written them in your notebook, you read the passages to discover the answers given by the author. You are testing your predictions. Some may be right and others incorrect.

Why does this technique work so well? For one thing, it helps focus your attention on the material; your mind is less apt to wander. You have a vested interest in the prediction and really want to find out if you are right or wrong. Another value to predicting is that it keeps your mind alert to all other possibilities: you read more carefully the thoughtfully. The major value, of course, is that predicting gives your reading purpose. You aren't just letting your eyes move over the pages; you are attentive and thinking critically. Chances are, too, that you will remember the material much better than if you read passively.

Let's try setting a purpose through predicting.

EXERCISE 2.3

In the following textbook reading assignment there are good opportunities for prediction. First, read the assignment quickly; preview it. Note subheadings and subtitles and the first lines of paragraphs. Then, on the lines that follow the chapter excerpt, write out your predictions. Next, read the assignment and go back to comment on the predictions you made: were they on target, inaccurate, almost right? Tell, too, what you think of this technique.

Textbook Chapter Excerpt 2.1

CHAPTER 10

CREATIVITY AND HUMAN RELATIONS

CHAPTER OUTLINE

The Creativity Connection
What Is Creativity?
Perception and Creativity
Creative Intelligence
 STRATEGY 10–1 Increase Your Creativity
Creativity in the Workplace
Creative Methods for Groups

LEARNING OBJECTIVES

This chapter will help you learn:

- The relationship between creativity and effective decision making.
- The relationship between the positive reinforcement by others and the originality and frequency of creative ideas.
- How to remove the barriers that keep you from being as creative as possible.
- How to create a climate for creativity in the workplace.

The community college business club held its first annual flea market. Despite hard work and planning, the results were disappointing. It was an indoor event, and customers wanted to be outdoors on what turned out to be a beautiful day. Also, a similar event was being held nearby.

Around lunch, the club met to decide how to salvage the day. One member suggested giving the participants back their table-space rental money and taking only the 10 percent of sales, rather than both, as contracted. Someone else suggested the opposite: just keep their rental money, but don't ask for a percentage. Then, members took sides and argued. After 20 minutes, the members with the loudest voices and the greater persuasive ability won. The participants in the event were told they wouldn't be asked to pay a percentage of the money they took in.

When the club advisor, a management instructor, heard about the decision two hours later, she was irate. "What happened to creative problem solving? You've made the mistake of choosing one of two alternatives and ignoring all other possibilities." Earlier, the advisor had informally polled the participants. Only 12 out of 40 were really unhappy with the sales situation. "With a little creativity, you could have come up with a solution to make everyone happy and still realize a nice profit. I hope you've all learned a lesson from this." The club later estimated that they had lost over $700 just from one bad decision.

Textbook Chapter Excerpt 2.1 (continued)

Creativity clearly has workplace implications. The boom in high technology portable office equipment, including portable phones and FAX machines, is a product of creative thinking and a factor in increased productivity. (Tom McCarthy/PhotoEdit.)

THE CREATIVITY CONNECTION

Creativity

You may be wondering what a chapter on **creativity** is doing in a human relations textbook. At first the connection might indeed seem vague. However, you will see in this chapter how much our ability to come up with new ideas—to create—has to do with our self-esteem, and in turn with our relationships with other people. Business factors like the number of good ideas and products created, and their quality, are affected both by self-esteem and by human relations in general.

The importance of creativity cannot be overstated. In the 1990s very few people deny how crucial an issue it is. International competition is forcing the United States to take a look at our own creative levels compared to other nations. Americans are frustrated that the Japanese (whom many of us had always believed were less creative than we) are "out-creating" us on a regular basis.

American companies are putting a new emphasis on creativity, to an extent that hasn't been seen since the "Sputnik" era of the late 1950s. When the Russians launched the first satellite in 1957, Americans feared

Textbook Chapter Excerpt 2.1 (continued)

that the Russians were going to win the race for space. Nationwide campaigns for better scholarship and creativity were begun. Now, once again we are trying to increase creativity, though for a new reason: international business competition. Hewlett-Packard has built a "factory of the future" in Puerto Rico, where computer-systems people are hired on their creative ability.[1] Like Hewlett-Packard, many other companies both large and small have started taking the creativity issue seriously.

Creativity is something that we don't completely understand. As British comedian John Cleese says, "It's like Mozart's music or Van Gogh's paintings or Saddam Hussein's public relations."[2] We can usually tell the difference between what is creative and what isn't. But can we really put our finger on what causes creativity? If we didn't have at least some notion, this chapter would have no point. To understand creativity, we need to understand ourselves better.

WHAT IS CREATIVITY?

Let's start by looking at what creativity definitely *is not*. Research has shown that creativity has little to do with personality patterns, with the media used, with the products produced, or with the particular environment. People can be creative whether they are outgoing or shy, naive or sophisticated, impulsive or steady as a rock, hermits or good mixers. They can also be creative whether they are involved in painting, writing, architecture, mathematics, teaching, or child rearing; and they can be creative in the city or the country, in poverty or in plenty.[3] Willa Cather was able to produce great American literature while living in a small Nebraska town.

Because we often use the word *genius* when we talk about extremely creative people, many have made the mistake of linking creativity to traditional intelligence. Most of us know stories about creative people who did badly in school. Thomas Edison and Albert Einstein are both examples. Actually, **intuition** (direct perception or insight) has been shown to be much more important to creativity than scholastic ability. "You don't have to have a high IQ to be intuitive," says Frank Barron, a psychologist at the University of California at Santa Cruz. Barron has been studying creativity for the last 40 years. "Intuition depends less on reasoning and verbal comprehension [the main device used to measure IQ] than it does on feelings and metaphor," he concludes.[4]

Intuition

PERCEPTION AND CREATIVITY

Most of the researchers who have studied creativity agree that creative people are somehow able to get away from the ordinary, everyday way of

Textbook Chapter Excerpt 2.1 (continued)

seeing things. In his book *The Act of Creation,* Arthur Koestler describes all of the major scientific inventions of the past, and shows the creative process that produced them. Koestler says that *habit* is the stumbling block to creativity. How many people who could have done so, never even tried to invent an airplane, for example, because they simply accepted the common belief that man was not meant to fly?[5] Galileo, the great pioneer astronomer, fell into the trap of habits. He saw comets through his telescope, but refused to accept them as they really are, because he believed firmly that all heavenly bodies must move in a circle, and that those that don't must just be optical illusions.

Likewise, groups of people (such as companies, committees, and even universities) are often unable to move beyond habits of thinking.[6] Groups often have their own beliefs about what should be done and how. These have become **collective habits of thought.** Both as individuals and as groups, we need to get past the old, established ways of seeing things if we are going to be creative.

Collective habits of thought

Perception

Perception is the way we view the world. When you are sitting in a classroom with 25 other students listening to your instructor, there are, in a sense, 26 different instructors teaching the class. Each person in the room *perceives* the instructor in a slightly different way. Everything we see is similarly filtered through our own perceptions.

Looking at the world from different angles makes a great difference in how creatively we deal with that world, and how we solve problems. When Albert Einstein was 14 years old, he asked an interesting question that had a lot to do with his perceptions of the world. "What would the world look like," he asked, "if I rode on a beam of light?" As an adult, he finally answered the question, and that answer became the principle of relativity.[7] Einstein was not unlike many others we label as "creative geniuses." He started out with a perception that was not the ordinary one, and built an answer. It's easy to see why Einstein once said, "Imagination is more important than knowledge."[8]

Let's look again at Einstein's question: "What would the world look like if I rode on a beam of light?" Research has shown that creative people aren't afraid to ask what might seem to be silly or childish questions. They might ask questions such as "Why do rivers rarely run north?" or "Why don't spiders get tangled up in their webs?" The curiosity we all have as children is an essential part of the creative process. Whatever we can do to retain or regain some of that childlike curiosity will help us produce more creative ideas.

Abraham Maslow, the psychologist who is best known for his needs hierarchy, has said about highly creative people: "They tend to be called childish by their more compulsive colleagues, irresponsible, wild,

Chapter 2 Reading with Purpose 35

Textbook Chapter Excerpt 2.1 (continued)

crazy, . . . emotional, and so on." He is not saying that such a judgment is false, though. ". . . It should be stressed, I suppose," he goes on, "that in the early stages of creativeness, you've got to be a bum or a Bohemian or an eccentric."9 By this remark, Maslow means that by remaining in conventional society, our thinking is likely to become conventional and noncreative. The lesson for people in business is to learn to look beyond the conventional business world.

No matter how you scored in the accompanying perception test, be aware that your perceptions are just that: your perceptions. They are open to be challenged, re-examined, and evaluated. Other people's perceptions also have their own life and reality.

CREATIVE INTELLIGENCE

Earlier, we discussed the lack of relationship between creativity and traditional views of intelligence. For many years, people assumed that **intelligence** was a one-dimensional concept. For example, a person could either make it through college or fail. Those who made it were smart; those who failed weren't. Lately we have come to understand that intelligence comes in many forms. Researchers have discovered **the seven intelligences**— seven separate areas that creative people put their perceptiveness to work (see Figure 10–1 on p. 215).10

[margin notes: Intelligence; The seven intelligences]

1. Language. People who are gifted writers, poets, songwriters, and speakers fall into this category. If you love language and are fascinated by its meanings, expressions, and rhythms, your intelligence falls into this category.

2. Math and logic. Scientists and mathematicians find pleasure in using the logical, reasoning parts of the brain. Most of the standardized intelligence tests measure ability levels in this area.

3. Music. Most people whose intelligence falls into this category have a fond relationship with sound. As children, they likely tried to produce new combinations of sound on their own.

4. Spatial reasoning. A person who excels in this area has a knack for seeing how elements fit together in space. This type of intelligence can be expressed by building things, or by perfecting the art of flying a hand glider. The talent is physical and mechanical, rather than tied to ideas and concepts.

5. Movement. Traditionally, we haven't thought of physical movement as a part of intelligence. But the ability to use your body or parts of your body

Textbook Chapter Excerpt 2.1 (continued)

TESTING THE 'ORDINARINESS' OF YOUR PERCEPTIONS

Maybe you don't know whether your perception of reality is ordinary or unusual. Here are a few statements about our perceptions. Read each statement, and decide whether it is true or false.

___ 1. A fact is a fact. There can be no difference of views on something that is a fact.
___ 2. If two people view the same event differently, it is only logical to conclude that one of them is right and the other one wrong.
___ 3. Our perceptions of people and events are almost always colored by our attitudes, values, and beliefs.
___ 4. Intelligent people do not ascribe meanings to things and events. They take them as they are.
___ 5. People usually see what they want to see.
___ 6. In our perception of people, events, and objects, we have a natural tendency to leave out certain aspects that don't square with our views.
___ 7. Besides a person's qualities and mannerisms, there are other factors that can influence the way we see that person.
___ 8. If we are careful, we can always trust our eyes and ears to give us a true picture of the world around us.
___ 9. We view the world around us through our own colored glasses.
___ 10. Differences in views about people, objects, and events usually result from different levels of intelligence.

How did you do? If you got more than two wrong, you need to take a closer look at perception.

Answers: 1. F,   2. F,   3. T,   4. F,   5. T,   6. T,   7. T,   8. F,   9. T,   10. F

Based on Sugato Lahiry, "A Blueprint for Perception Training," reprinted from *Training and Development* (August 1991), pp. 21–25. Copyright August 1991, the American Society for Training and Development. Reprinted with permission. All rights reserved.

Textbook Chapter Excerpt 2.1 (continued)

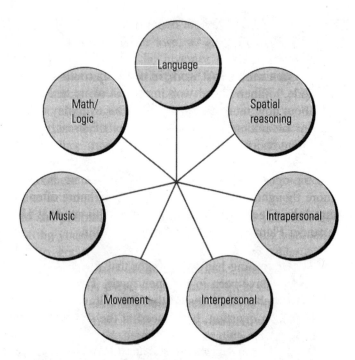

FIGURE 10–1

The Seven Dimensions of Creative Intelligence

to solve problems is a type of intelligence. Athletes and ballet dancers are examples of people who excel in this area.

6. Interpersonal intelligence. This area of intelligence deals with one's ability to understand and deal with the world of people. It is an essential skill in all aspects of life, and particularly important in business.

7. Intrapersonal intelligence. *Intra*personal intelligence means knowledge of oneself. A person with a large amount of this type of intelligence knows his or her own strengths and weaknesses, desires and fears, and can act on that knowledge realistically.

Examine your talents and abilities, to see which of these intelligence categories best describes you. If you are a manager, watch for the type of intelligence each of your workers exhibits and learn to use the abilities of each worker to the fullest capacity possible. Such knowledge can help to raise the level of an organization's creative output greatly.

STRATEGY 10–1
INCREASE YOUR CREATIVITY

The question "How can I become more creative?" has no easy answer. However, we can learn some basic steps. Only you know what specific

Textbook Chapter Excerpt 2.1 (continued)

barriers keep you from reaching your own creative potential; you can apply these steps to your own progress.

1. Get into the "open mode." At work, in our daily routine, most of us are in a "closed mode." When we're working, most of us feel pressured, we keep thinking about how much we have to do. Our everyday mode contains a certain amount of anxiety, little humor, a lot of stress, and a definite element of fear. But it doesn't contain creativity.

Open mode

The **open mode** on the other hand, is relaxed, expansive, and less purposeful. In the open mode, we tend to let things come as they may; we tend to be more thoughtful; and we smile and laugh more often. "Playful" is a word that John Cleese uses when discussing this mode.[11] He tells the story of Alexander Fleming, who discovered penicillin:

> When Alexander Fleming had the thought that led to the discovery of penicillin, he must have been in the open mode. The previous day, he had arranged a number of dishes so that the cultures would grow in them. On the day in question, he glanced at the dishes and discovered that on one of them no culture had appeared. Now, if he'd been in the closed mode, he would have been so focused upon his need for dishes with cultures grown in them, that when he saw that one dish was of no use for that purpose, he would have quite simply thrown it away. It was useless to him. Like some magazine articles. But, thank goodness, he was in an open mode. He became curious about why the culture had not grown on this particular dish. And that curiosity led him to penicillin. In the closed mode, an uncultured dish is an irrelevance; in the open mode, it's a clue.[12]

Operating in the open mode often involves giving yourself sufficient time. Although you are likely to meet many people who claim they do their most creative work under time pressure, the truth is that most of us produce better when we've given ourselves enough time to do the job justice.

We are not at all suggesting that you should stay in the open mode permanently. Important parts of our lives require that we stay in the closed mode, just so we can concentrate on a noncreative task, for example. As mentioned, asking childlike questions is important. Answering those questions, though, may involve the closed mode, and may even require it.

2. Think of yourself as a creative person. One of the biggest stumbling blocks to creativity is the belief that you can't do it—that you somehow aren't good enough to create anything worthwhile. Many people carry around a self-image that includes statements like, "Oh, I couldn't come up with a new idea if somebody paid me." This kind of self-image with its

Textbook Chapter Excerpt 2.1 (continued)

accompanying low self-esteem causes a person to put creative people on a pedestal and look at them with awe, as if they were a different kind of person. But Nolan Bushnell, the inventor of the video game, is a good example of just how easy creativity can be. He says that he noticed that people like to watch television and that they also enjoy playing games. He just put the two ideas together.[13]

The key to this step, then, is **self-perception.** Research has shown that people who produce more creative output are different in one major way from those who create less: the more creative people *believe that they are creative.* The others have serious doubts. Believe in yourself creatively, and you will have accomplished an important step.[14]

_{Self-perception}

3. Learn to see problems as opportunities. Once you have gotten to this point by putting yourself into an open mode and seeing yourself as creative, you'll need to get a mind set that doesn't see problems as events or situations to get depressed about. An athletic coach at the University of Oregon noticed that his players were having great difficulty with sore feet and blisters. After examining the shoes his players were wearing, he decided that he could make a better shoe, one that would work with nature, rather than against it. Using the most lightweight and tough materials he could find, he made a shoe that improved both cushion and traction. His name was Bill Browerman, and he went on to form what is now the billion-dollar Nike company.[15] Browerman saw the problem as a challenge, and he met that challenge in a remarkable way.

4. Look for more than one or two solutions to a problem. A major stumbling block with our methods of learning is that we are taught to look for *the one right answer.* When we should be casting about for the many right answers and numerous ways to view a problem, we tend to go after that one surefire answer that will please the teacher or the boss and make us feel that we have succeeded. If you think there is only one right answer, you behave accordingly, and stop looking once you have found an answer that works.[16]

We settle for the one right answer out of a tendency to grab the first idea that comes. We make this error especially when we feel pressured, frustrated, or afraid we aren't going to succeed in solving the problem.[17] That first idea might be good, but how do you know it's the best? Again, taking some extra time might be the only way to proceed. Here is a story from the creative life of John Cleese:

> I was always intrigued that one of my Monty Python colleagues, who seemed more talented than I was, did not produce scripts as original as mine. I watched for some time and then began to see why. If he was faced with a problem and fairly soon saw the solution, he was inclined

Textbook Chapter Excerpt 2.1 (continued)

to take it, even though the solution was not very original. Whereas if I was in the same situation, although I was sorely tempted to take the easy way out, and finish by 5 PM, I just couldn't! I'd sit there with the problem for another hour and a quarter and, by sticking at it, would almost always come up with something more original. It was that simple. My work was almost always more creative than his because I was prepared to stick with the problem longer.[18]

Either/or fallacy

Another common mistake we make in decision making is called the **either/or fallacy.** This approach sees only one of two extremes as possible for a solution, without really looking at the great number of compromises and other creative choices that might exist between the two extremes. When we are in the closed mode, we are much more likely to fall for this blunder in thinking. The business club members in our opening story fell into either/or thinking, and that mistake cost them dearly.

The second right answer

To get beyond this trap, learn to look for **the second right answer**—and the third, the fourth, and so on. Think of an idea as a letter in the alphabet. Everything ever written in English was written with the same 26 letters. Yet the relationship of those letters to other letters form words and ideas in a limitless number of possibilities. Don't stop until you've found at least three right answers. Chances are, once you discover three, you won't need to stop there.

Many people feel a need to seem decisive, to be able to make decisions rapidly. After all, such a reputation is certainly better than one of being "wishy-washy." If you *are* truly decisive, great. It you're not, don't fake it. Even very decisive people aren't decisive all the time. Examine the alternatives. This author tries to get *at least five* different possible solutions before going on to finish solving a problem. Don't be too proud to use combinations of ideas other people have thought of, bringing them together for your own creative result. The French philosopher Emile Chartier said, "Nothing is more dangerous than an idea when it is the only one you have."[19] Of course, even in the world of business, one will sometimes encounter a problem that truly has only one right answer. In such a case, methods of discovery still need to be varied, rather than limited.

5. Learn to "play the violin." Management expert Peter Drucker was once asked how one can become a better manager. "Learn to play the violin," was Drucker's reply. Of course, he didn't mean literally that violin playing would directly help. He was trying to say that anything that really gets people outside of their regular context will force them out of their comfort zone. You are more likely to be creative when you are outside of your comfort zone.[20] As an added bonus, you may get to be really good at the violin, or at golf, or at wind surfing—and your self-esteem will grow. That is a bonus that improves your performance in all areas of your life.

Textbook Chapter Excerpt 2.1 (continued)

> About 15 years ago, a young mother went toy shopping for her two-year-old daughter. She discovered to her dismay that all she could find were poorly made plastic toys. She had thought she could find some of the durable, long-lasting toys like those her daughter played with at her day-care center. Although she had no business experience, this woman borrowed $5,000 from her grandmother to start her own small company. Today, Lane Nemeth owns Discovery Toys, a company that makes over $70 million in gross sales every year. Ms. Nemeth saw a need that probably thousands of parents had already seen. Her important contribution to the creative process was *putting the solution of that need into action.* Thomas Edison once said, "Creativity is 1 percent inspiration and 99 percent perspiration." He was right. Without this sixth step, any creativity is meaningless.
>
> Source: Victor M. Parachin, "Seven Ways to Fire Up Your Creativity," *Supervision* (January 1992), p. 4.

6. Turn your ideas into action. How many ideas have you thought of, then dismissed, only to find later that someone else who thought of the same idea had put it into action? But that was *your* idea! Painful, isn't it? The author had a friend who had totally thought out the idea for what is now called multilevel marketing. Three years later, the founders of Amway, Inc., put the same idea (which they certainly didn't get from him) into action. Amway is now a billion-dollar corporation. Creativity doesn't do anyone much good if its products aren't followed through into action. What if all of Renoir's paintings, Robert Frost's poems, or Paul McCartney's songs had simply remained unexecuted ideas?

7. Don't be afraid to break the rules. Another related issue is our attitude toward rules. Whatever we do, we feel compelled to follow the rules. For 13 years, from kindergarten through high school, we are taught the rules. After we graduate, society has more rules for adulthood, and breaking them can get us into a lot of trouble. Many of those rules aren't rules at all, only customs—customs that everyone has been afraid to change.

Sometimes rules outlive their usefulness, but we continue to follow them anyway, as in the following story told by Roger von Oech, creativity guru of California's Silicon Valley:[21]

> ... I like to run, and I have three or four runs that I'll take depending on how far I want to go. One of these is a route which goes through my neighborhood for about four miles. As a rule, the run ends about two blocks from our house, because two years ago, when I started this route, there was a big, friendly golden retriever living at the house where I stopped. His name was Aslan. After my run, I would take some time to

Textbook Chapter Excerpt 2.1 (continued)

"... But Officer, isn't it great that I'm learning to overcome my fear of breaking the rules?"

pet him and cool down. So stopping at Aslan's house became the rule for having a nice ending to a fun run.

But things have changed. His owner moved away a year ago, and took Aslan with her. Nevertheless, whenever I take this route, I still stop at the same place—even though Aslan no longer lives there. There are probably more pleasurable places to end my run, but because I am following an obsolete rule, I haven't looked for them.

(Reprinted by permission of Warner Books/New York. From *A Whack on the Side of the Head.* Copyright © by Roger von Oech.)

The Aslan phenomenon

For obvious reasons, von Oech calls this problem with rules **the Aslan phenomenon:**

- We make rules based on reasons that make a lot of sense.
- We follow these rules.
- Time passes, and situations change. The original reasons for the generation of these rules may no longer exist, but the rules are still in place and we continue to follow them.

8. Don't be afraid to make mistakes. Most people have two selves: the safekeeping self, which keeps us fed, clothed, and out of trouble, and the spontaneous self, which allows us the freedom and fun of doing things without structure and detailed planning. Our childhood training warns us not to be too spontaneous, not to be messy, and most importantly, not to make fools of ourselves. Actually, making mistakes is one of the most

Textbook Chapter Excerpt 2.1 (continued)

effective ways of learning, and being a bit foolish is part of being human. The president of a successful, fast-growing computer company tells his employees, "We're innovators. We're doing things nobody has ever done before. Therefore, we are going to be making mistakes. My advice to you: make your mistakes, but make them in a hurry."[22]

CREATIVITY IN THE WORKPLACE

Unfortunately, positive reinforcement is often missing in the workplace. Creativity is often discouraged as a result. Managers themselves are often notorious creativity killers. Many managers have a vocabulary of "killer phrases" which are designed to stop creative thoughts before they start. "It's not in the budget." "Top management won't go for it." "We could never sell it to the stockholders." "We tried it last year." Managers need to realize that workers' ideas are often better than the ideas that come out of boardrooms. Also, discouraging creative ideas damages morale in the workplace. Looking back to Chapter 9, we see that these phrases are the same ones that destroy change efforts in companies.

An effective manager encourages creativity among workers by creating a climate of deferred judgment. All ideas will not be useful, but all will be listened to. He or she uses a formal method for receiving suggestions, with all employees knowing the procedure. Many companies use reward systems to encourage employees to make creative suggestions that save money for the company.

For a creative spirit to emerge from a company or a department, the environment must encourage enthusiasm and commitment from the whole person. Many workers bring only a part of themselves to work. The author once asked a truck driver for his opinion on company policy. "I'm not paid to think," was the only answer he could get. "I leave my brains at home," the driver explained. "I've found it's safer that way." Managers should not make creativity a dangerous route for employees.

Work must be made rewarding, challenging, and fulfilling for a creative atmosphere to exist. As discussed earlier, job enrichment is one key to employee motivation. It is also a key to increased creativity. If the company shows that the worker's mind is respected and valued, it will logically follow that the worker's creative solutions to problems will be valued as well. Figure 10–2 illustrates the interrelatedness of these conditions with creativity.

Although there are stories about lone mad scientists and poets such as Emily Dickinson who wrote in isolation with few readers, for most of us creativity has a social aspect. One could ask how many songs Paul

Textbook Chapter Excerpt 2.1 (continued)

FIGURE 10–2

Nurturing a Creative Workplace Climate

McCartney would have written if he had not been discovered along with the rest of the Beatles. How many inventions would Thomas Edison have completed if absolutely everything he did had been rejected? To what extent does the quality and quantity of our creative output depend on the opinions of others?

To be truly creative, says Howard Gardner of Harvard University, an idea must be able to be taken seriously by others. "I mean, I could talk while standing on my head, and that would be unusual," Gardner says. "But unless I and other people found it was somehow adaptive, I couldn't be called creative for it."[23] The way any creative effort is received does make a difference. The received group or audience ultimately determines the value of the creative work and whether it is to have a large impact.

Experiments in classrooms have shown that positive reinforcement improves both the quality of creative work and the number of projects attempted. If college students are complimented on a project, even with a brief, "That's really good; keep it up," the difference in creative output is remarkable, even when the students for the experiment are chosen totally at random. The opposite is also true. Creativity is often discouraged when it is *not* positively reinforced. When our creative output is rejected, we tend to take the rejection personally. The negatives affect our self-esteem, and the lowered self-esteem results in less effort and lower quality of work.

CREATIVE METHODS FOR GROUPS

More and more in today's workplace, creative problem solving is being done in group settings. Whatever an individual can produce creatively, a

Textbook Chapter Excerpt 2.1 (continued)

FIGURE 10–3

The Brainstorming Process

First Session
1. Participants speak in phrases.
2. Hitchhiking on others' ideas is encouraged.
3. Criticism is forbidden.
4. Silliness is encouraged.
5. Climate is relaxed.
6. All ideas are recorded and quantity of ideas encouraged.

Second Session
1. Return to rational mode.
2. All ideas are analyzed and prioritized.
3. Idea duplications are eliminated.
4. Ideas are ranked in order of importance.
5. Everyone gives evaluative input, just as all gave creative input in Session One.

group can usually produce more effectively. Groups can produce more ideas in shorter time periods if the creative process is structured carefully. Approach any process of group creativity carefully; it must contain just enough structure to be effective and sufficient freedom to remain creative.

Brainstorming

In 1934, a sales manager named Alex Osborne devised a method of getting creativity to happen in a group situation. He called his idea **brainstorming.** The process starts with a small group of people. Groups of five to eight work best. With a leader in front to record their ideas, they begin with session one by addressing a problem. In this first session, nothing is allowed except free-flowing ideas. Everyone is encouraged to speak in phrases, rather than in sentences, to "hitchhike" on the ideas of others, and to be as wild and crazy as they can be within the social context. No one is allowed to put down anyone else's ideas. Statements such as "Get serious!" or "That's stupid!" are forbidden.

When the first session is over, the second session begins. In this part of the brainstorming process, the adult part of everybody's personality takes over. The group examines the ideas that have come up, noticing if any of them duplicate each other. The group can then prioritize the ideas, agreeing together which is the most important, second, and so on. (These rules are expanded upon in Figure 10–3.) When a group brainstorms correctly following these rules, it can produce an amazing number of high-quality ideas in a fairly short period of time. Note that brainstorming works best for the solving of simple, well-defined problems, although it can be used in nearly any context. Although a lot of shallow, even useless ideas are suggested, there are usually gems among the dust.[24]

Brainstorming

Textbook Chapter Excerpt 2.1 (continued)

This method of group creativity is designed to provide a structure that encourages individual creativity within a group framework. The reason we call it *nominal* is because the members are actually a group in name only. The group is basically a tool for voting. Usually, nominal grouping involves six steps:

1. Each employee puts his or her ideas down in writing.
2. The leader lists all of the ideas up on a board or chart where everyone can see them.
3. The leader leads a discussion to clarify the ideas and to add new ones.
4. Each group member rates the ideas and votes; the voting eliminates other ideas at this point.
5. After the vote, there is a brief discussion of the voting results. The purpose is to clarify points, not to persuade anyone.
6. The group casts a final vote to select the proposal or proposals that will be used.

As time goes on, group creativity is likely to become increasingly important. Creative problem solving is one of the hot topics of the 1990s. New ideas for group creativity will continue to be invented. Of course, they will all have one thing in common: all will be attempts to get the greatest number of new high-quality ideas from a group of people.

SUMMARY

Creativity is important in the workplace for sound decision making, for maintaining high morale, and for keeping our companies competitive. Creativity requires getting away from the normal ways of seeing the world. How we perceive the world makes a great difference in terms of how creatively we deal with that world and with problems that need solutions.

In the past, we have defined intelligence narrowly. Today, we recognize at least seven types or areas of intelligence, all of which can be expressions of the creative process. Self-esteem affects both our perceptions and our level of creativity. The child ego state is important for creativity. The ability to play, to experiment, and to be curious are all related to the child within us.

We can take many steps to improve our creativity. Encouraging creativity in groups and organizations requires the manager to develop a climate for independent expression and deferred judgment. The manager should strive to make jobs more meaningful and fulfilling. Brainstorming and the nominal group method are two group creativity approaches used widely in business.

Textbook Chapter Excerpt 2.1 (concluded)

KEY TERMS

Creativity
Intuition
Collective habits of thought
Perception

Intelligence
The seven intelligences
Open mode
Self-perception

Either/or fallacy
The second right answer
The Aslan phenomenon
Brainstorming

QUESTIONS TO CONSIDER

1. Why is creativity in the workplace an important issue?
2. Briefly explain the role of perception in the creative process.
3. Why does the workplace so often lack creativity?
4. What steps can managers take to increase the quality and quantity of their workers' creative output?
5. Explain the difference between brainstorming and the nominal group method? How can both help produce more creative group results?
6. What does it mean to be in the open mode? How can the open mode allow for greater creativity?
7. Explain the seven areas of intelligence, showing their relationship to creativity.
8. How do the opinions of others affect the creative output of most people?
9. What is meant by "the second right answer?" Explain.
10. List at least six steps you can take to improve your own creativity.

Source: Lowell Lamberton and Leslie Minor, *Human Relations: Strategies for Success* (Burr Ridge, Ill.: Richard D. Irwin, 1995), pp. 209–225 Copyright 1995 by Richard D. Irwin. All rights reserved. Reprinted by permission.

Your Predictions

1. _____
_____

2. _____
_____

3. _____
_____

4. _____
_____

5. _____
_____

6. _____
_____

7. _____
_____

8. _____
_____

9. _____
_____

10. _____
_____

11. _____
_____

12. _____
_____
13. _____
_____
14. _____
_____
15. _____
_____
16. _____
_____
17. _____
_____
18. _____
_____
19. _____
_____
20. _____
_____
21. _____
_____
22. _____
_____

Accuracy of Your Predictions

1. _____

2. _____

3. _____

4. _____

5. _____

6. _____

7. _____

8. _____

9. _____

10. _____

11. _____

12. _____
_____

13. _____
_____

14. _____
_____

15. _____
_____

16. _____
_____

17. _____
_____

18. _____
_____

19. _____
_____

20. _____
_____

21. _____
_____

22. _____
_____

What Did You Think of This Technique?

Textbook Chapter Excerpt 2.2

Directions: Use the SQ3R method of study on the following excerpt taken from a college textbook.

Textbook Chapter Excerpt 2.2 (continued)

CHAPTER 16

Population Ecology

Chapter Outline

Population Characteristics
Reproductive Capacity
The Population Growth Curve
Population-Size Limitations
Limiting Factors
  Extrinsic and Intrinsic Limiting Factors
  Density-Dependent and Density-Independent Limiting Factors
Human Population Growth
Box 16.1 Thomas Malthus and His Essay on Population

Purpose

Populations of organisms exhibit many kinds of characteristics that can vary significantly from one population to another. Recognizing that populations differ from one another is necessary to understanding differences in population growth rates. While not specifically about growth of the human population, much of the material in this chapter relates to the problems associated with the human population explosion.

For Your Information

China is the most populous country in the world, with over one billion people—approximately one-fourth of the world's population. The government has tried to limit the size of families by encouraging later marriages, providing conception-control information, making small family size a patriotic duty, and giving financial incentives to couples who have no children or limit themselves to one child. Most families desire a male child. Consequently, many baby girls are left to die so the parents can have another opportunity to have a male child. The government must now deal with the problems of infanticide and an aging work force.

Learning Objectives

- Recognize that populations vary in gene frequency, age distribution, sex ratio, size, and density.
- Describe the characteristics of a typical population growth curve.
- Understand why populations grow.
- Recognize the pressures that ultimately limit population size.
- Understand that human populations obey the same rules of growth as populations of other kinds of organisms.

Textbook Chapter Excerpt 2.2 (continued)

Population Characteristics

A **population** is a group of organisms of the same species located in the same place at the same time. Examples are the number of dandelions in your front yard, the rat population in the sewers of your city, or the number of people in your biology class. On a larger scale, all the people of the world constitute the human population. The terms *species* and *population* are interrelated because a species is a population—the largest possible population of a particular kind of organism. Population, however, is often used to refer to portions of a species by specifying a space and time. For example, the size of the human population in a city changes from hour to hour during the day and varies according to where you set the boundaries of the city.

Since most populations are small portions of a species, we should expect different populations of the same species to show differences. One of the ways in which they can differ is in gene frequency. Chapter 11 on population genetics introduced you to the concept of **gene frequency,** which is a measure of how often a specific gene shows up in the gametes of a population. Two populations of the same species often have quite different gene frequencies. For example, many populations of mosquitoes have high frequencies of insecticide-resistant genes, whereas others do not. The frequency of the genes for tallness in humans is greater in certain African tribes than in any other human population. Figure 16.1 shows that the frequency of the allele for type B blood differs significantly from one human population to another.

Since members of a population are of the same species, sexual reproduction can occur, and genes can flow from one generation to the next. Genes can also flow from one place to another as organisms migrate or are carried from one geographic location to another. **Gene flow** is used to refer to both the movement of genes within a population due to migration and the movement from one generation to the next as a result of gene replication and sexual reproduction.

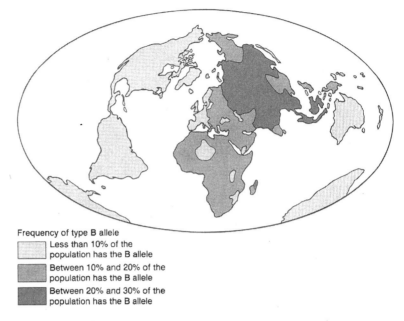

Figure 16.1 **Distribution of the Allele for Type B Blood.** The allele for type B blood is not evenly distributed in the world. This map shows that the type B allele is most common in parts of Asia and has been dispersed to the Middle East and parts of Europe and Africa. There has been very little flow of the allele to the Americas.

Another feature of a population is its **age distribution,** which is the number of organisms of each age in the population. Organisms are often grouped into the following categories: (1) prereproductive juveniles—insect larvae, plant seedlings, or babies; (2) reproductive adults—mature insects, plants producing seeds, or humans in early adulthood; or (3) postreproductive adults no longer capable of reproduction—annual plants that have shed their seeds, salmon that have spawned, and many elderly humans. A population is not necessarily divided into equal thirds (figure 16.2). In some situations, a population may be made up of a majority of one age group. If the majority of the population is prereproductive, then a "baby boom" should be anticipated in the future. If a majority of the population is reproductive, the population should be growing rapidly. If the majority of the population is postreproductive, a population decline should be anticipated.

Populations can also differ in their sex ratios. The **sex ratio** is the number of males in a population compared to the number of females. In bird and mammal species where strong pair-bonding occurs, the sex ratio may be nearly one to one (1:1). Among mammals and birds that do not have strong pair-bonding, sex ratios may show a larger number of females than males. This is particularly true among game species, where more males are shot than females. Since one male can fertilize several females, the population can remain large. However, if the population of these managed game species becomes large enough to cause a problem, it becomes necessary to harvest some of the females as well, since their number determines how much reproduction can take place. In addition to these examples, many species of animals like bison, horses, and elk have mating systems in which one male maintains a harem of females. The sex ratio in these small groups is quite different from a 1:1 ratio (figure 16.3). There are very few

Textbook Chapter Excerpt 2.2 (continued)

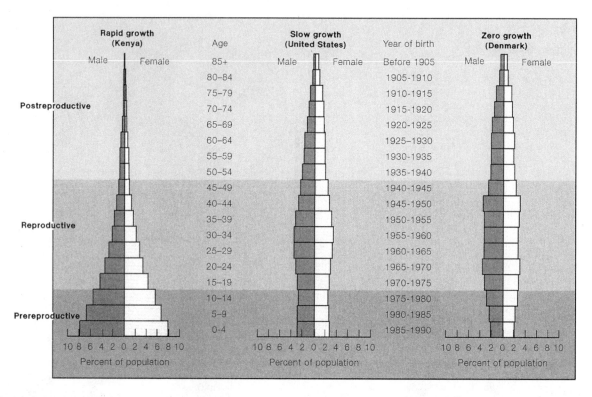

Figure 16.2 **Age Distribution in Human Populations.** The relative number of individuals in each of the three categories (prereproductive, reproductive, and postreproductive) can give a good clue to the future of the population. Kenya has a large number of young individuals who will become reproducing adults. Therefore, this population will grow rapidly and will double in about nineteen years. The United States has a declining proportion of prereproductive individuals, but a relatively large reproductive population. Therefore, it will continue to grow for a time, but will probably stabilize in the future. Denmark's population has a large proportion of postreproductive individuals and a small proportion of prereproductive individuals. Its population is stable.

Source: U.S. Bureau of the Census and the United Nations, as reported in Joseph A. McFalls, Jr., "Population: A Lively Introduction," *Population Bulletin*, Vol. 46, No. 2 (Washington, D.C.: Population Reference Bureau, Inc., October 1991).

Figure 16.3 **Sex Ratio in Elk.** Some male animals defend a harem of females; therefore, the sex ratio in these groups is several females per male.

Textbook Chapter Excerpt 2.2 (continued)

situations in which the number of males exceeds the number of females. In some human and other populations, there may be sex ratios in which the males dominate if female mortality is unusually high or if some special mechanism separates most of one sex from the other.

Regardless of the specific sex ratio in a population, most species can generate large numbers of offspring, producing a concentration of organisms in an area. **Population density** is the number of organisms of a species per unit area. Some populations are extremely concentrated into a limited space, while others are well dispersed. As the population density increases, competition among members of the population for the necessities of life increases. This increases the likelihood that some individuals will explore new habitats and migrate to new areas. Increases in the intensity of competition that cause changes in the environment and lead to dispersal are often referred to as **population pressure.** The dispersal of individuals to new areas can relieve the pressure on the home area and lead to the establishment of new populations. Among animals, it is often the juveniles who participate in this dispersal process. If dispersal cannot relieve population pressure, there is usually an increase in the rate at which individuals die due to predation, parasitism, starvation, and accidents. In plant populations, dispersal is not very useful for relieving population density; instead, the death of weaker individuals usually results in reduced population density.

Reproductive Capacity

Sex ratios and age distributions within a population have a direct bearing on the rate of reproduction. Each species has an inherent **reproductive capacity** or **biotic potential,** which is the theoretical maximum rate of reproduction. Generally this biotic potential is many times larger than the number of offspring needed simply to maintain the population. For example, a female carp may produce one to three million eggs in her lifetime. This is her reproductive capacity. However, only two or three of these offspring would ever develop into sexually mature adults. Therefore, her reproductive rate is much smaller than her reproductive potential.

A high reproductive capacity is valuable to a species because it provides many opportunities for survival. It also provides many slightly different individuals for the environment to select among. With most plants and animals, many of the potential gametes are never fertilized. An oyster may produce a million eggs a year, but not all of them are fertilized, and most that are fertilized die. An apple tree may have thousands of flowers but only produce a few apples because the pollen that contains the sperm cells may not be transferred to the female part of the flower in the process of pollination. Even after the new individuals are formed, mortality is usually high among the young. Most seeds that fall to the earth do not grow, and most young animals die as well. But usually enough survive to ensure continuance of the species. Organisms that reproduce in this way spend large amounts of energy on the production of potential young, with the probability that a small number of them will reach reproductive age.

A second way of approaching reproduction is to produce relatively fewer individuals but provide care and protection that ensure a higher probability that the young will become reproductive adults. Humans generally produce a single offspring per pregnancy, but nearly all of them live. In effect, the energy has been channeled into the care and protection of the young produced rather than into the production of incredibly large numbers of potential young. Even though fewer young are produced by animals like birds and mammals, their reproductive capacity still greatly exceeds the number required to replace the parents when they die.

The Population Growth Curve

Because most species of organisms have a high reproductive capacity, there is a tendency for populations to grow if environmental conditions permit. For example, if the usual litter size for a pair of mice is four, the four would produce eight, which in turn would produce sixteen and so forth. Figure 16.4 shows a graph of change in population size over time known as a **population growth curve.** This kind of curve is typical for situations where a species is introduced into a previously unutilized area.

The change in the size of a population depends on the rate at which new organisms enter the population compared to the rate at which they leave. The number of new individuals added to the population by reproduction per thousand individuals is called **natality.** The number of individuals leaving the population by death per thousand individuals is called **mortality.** When a small number of organisms (two mice) first invades an area, there is a period of time before reproduction takes place when the population remains small and relatively constant. This part of the population growth curve is known as the **lag phase.** Mortality and natality are similar during this period of time. In organisms that take a long time to mature and produce young, such as elephants, deer, and many kinds of plants, the lag phase may be measured in years. With the mice in our example, it will be measured in weeks. The first litter of young will reproduce in a matter of weeks. Furthermore, the original parents will probably produce an additional litter or two during this time period. Now we have several pairs of mice reproducing more than just once. With several pairs of mice reproducing, natality increases and mortality remains low; therefore, the population begins to grow at an ever-increasing (accelerating) rate. This portion of the population growth curve is known as the **exponential growth phase.** The number of mice (or any other organism) cannot continue to increase at a faster and faster rate because, eventually, something in the environment will cause an increase in the number of deaths. Eventually, the number of individuals entering the population will equal the number of individuals leaving it by death or migration, and the population size becomes stable. Often there is both a decrease in natality and an increase in mortality at this point. This portion of the population growth

Textbook Chapter Excerpt 2.2 (continued)

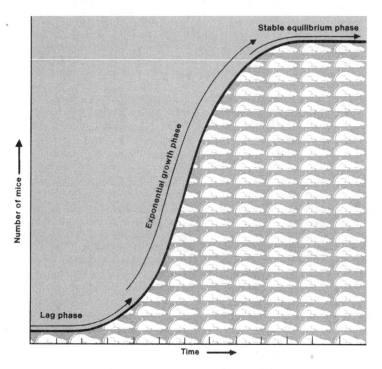

Figure 16.4 **A Typical Population Growth Curve.** In this mouse population, the period of time in which there is little growth is known as the lag phase. This is followed by a rapid increase in population as the offspring of the originating population begin to reproduce themselves; this is known as the exponential growth phase. Eventually the population reaches a stable equilibrium phase, during which the birth rate equals the death rate.

curve is known as the **stable equilibrium phase.** Reproduction continues and the birthrate is still high, but the death rate increases and larger numbers of individuals migrate from the area.

Population-Size Limitations

Populations cannot continue to increase indefinitely; eventually, some factor or set of factors acts to limit the size of a population leading to the development of a stable equilibrium phase or even to a reduction in population size. The specific identifiable factors that prevent unlimited population growth are know as **limiting factors.** All of the different limiting factors that act on a population are collectively known as **environmental resistance.** In general, those organisms that are small and have short life spans tend to have fluctuating populations, while large organisms that live a long time tend to reach an optimum population size that can be sustained over an extended period known as the **carrying capacity** (figure 16.5). For example, a forest ecosystem contains populations of many insect species that fluctuate widely, but the number of specific tree species or large animals such as owls or deer is relatively constant.

Carrying capacity, however, is not an inflexible rule. Often such environmental changes as successional changes, climate changes, disease epidemics, forest fires, or floods can change the capacity of an area to support life. In addition, a change that negatively affects the carrying capacity for one species may increase the carrying capacity for another. For example, the cutting down of mature forests followed by the growth of young trees increases the carrying capacity for deer and rabbits, which use the new growth for food, but decreases the carrying capacity for squirrels, which need matured, fruit-producing trees as a source of food and hollow trees for shelter.

The size of the organisms in a population also affects the carrying capacity. For example, an aquarium of a certain size can support only a limited number of fish, but the size of the fish makes a difference. If all the fish are tiny, a large number can be supported, and the carrying capacity is high; however, the same aquarium may be able to support only one large fish. In other words, the biomass of the population makes a difference (figure 16.6). Similarly, when an area is planted with small trees, the population size is high. But as the trees get larger, competition for nutrients and sunlight becomes more intense, and the number of trees present declines, while the biomass increases.

Limiting Factors

Limiting factors can be placed in four broad categories: (1) availability of raw materials, (2) availability of energy, (3) production and disposal of waste products, and (4) interaction with other organisms.

The first category of limiting factors is the availability of raw materials. For plants, magnesium is necessary for the manufacture of chlorophyll, nitrogen is necessary for protein production, and water is necessary for the transport of materials and as a raw material for photosynthesis. If these are not present in the soil, the growth and reproduction of plants is inhibited. However, if fertilizer supplies these nutrients, or irrigation is used to supply water, the effects of these limiting factors can be removed, and some other factor becomes limiting. For animals, the amount of

Textbook Chapter Excerpt 2.2 (continued)

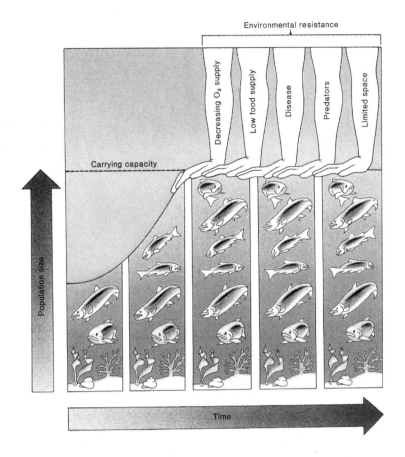

Figure 16.5 **Carrying Capacity.** A number of factors in the environment, such as food, oxygen supply, diseases, predators, and space, determine the number of organisms that can survive in a given area—the carrying capacity of that area. The environmental factors that limit populations are collectively known as environmental resistance.

Figure 16.6 **The Effect of Biomass on Carrying Capacity.** Each aquarium can support a biomass of 2 kilograms of fish. The size of the population is influenced by the body size of the fish in the population.

Textbook Chapter Excerpt 2.2 (continued)

water, minerals, materials for nesting, suitable burrow sites, or food may be limiting factors. Food for animals really fits into both this category and the next because it supplies both raw materials and energy.

The second major type of limiting factor is the availability of energy. The amount of light available is often a limiting factor for plants, which require light as an energy source for photosynthesis. Since all animals use other living things as sources of energy and raw materials, a major limiting factor for any animal is its food source.

The accumulation of waste products is the third general category of limiting factors. It does not usually limit plant populations because they produce relatively few wastes. However, the buildup of high levels of self-generated waste products is a problem for bacterial populations and populations of tiny aquatic organisms. As wastes build up, they become more and more toxic, and eventually reproduction stops, or the population may even die out. When a few bacteria are introduced into a solution containing a source of food, they go through the kind of population growth curve typical of all organisms. As expected, the number of bacteria begins to increase following a lag phase, increases rapidly during the exponential growth phase, and eventually reaches stability in the stable equilibrium phase. But as waste products accumulate, the bacteria literally drown in their own wastes. When space for disposal is limited, and no other organisms are present that can convert the harmful wastes to less harmful products, a population decline known as the **death phase** follows (figure 16.7).

Wine makers deal with this same situation. When yeasts ferment the sugar in grape juice, they produce ethyl alcohol. When the alcohol concentration reaches a certain level, the yeast population stops growing and eventually declines. Therefore, wine can naturally reach an alcohol concentration of only 12% to 15%. To make any drink stronger than that (of a higher alcohol content), water must be removed (to distill) or alcohol must be added (to fortify). In small aquatic pools like aquariums, it is often

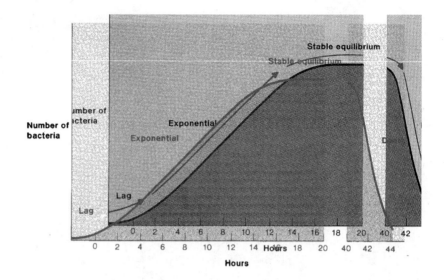

Figure 16.7 **Bacterial Population Growth Curve.** The rate of increase in the population of these bacteria is typical of population growth in a favorable environment. As the environmental conditions change as a result of an increase in the amount of waste products, the population first levels off, then begins to decrease. This period of decreasing population size is known as the death phase.

difficult to keep populations of organisms healthy because of the buildup of ammonia in the water from the waste products of the animals. This is the primary reason that activated charcoal filters are commonly used in aquariums. The charcoal removes many kinds of toxic compounds and prevents the buildup of waste products.

The fourth set of limiting factors is organism interaction. As we learned in chapter 15 on community interaction, organisms influence each other in many different ways. Some organisms are harmed and others are benefited. The population size of any organism would be negatively affected by parasitism, predation, or competition. Parasitism and predation usually involve interactions between two different species. Cannibalism is rare, but competition among members of the same population is often very intense. Many kinds of organisms perform services for others that have beneficial effects on the population. For example, decomposer organisms destroy toxic waste products, thus benefiting populations of animals. They also recycle materials needed for the growth and development of all organisms. Mutualistic relationships benefit both of the populations involved.

Often, the population sizes of two kinds of organisms will be interdependent because each is a primary limiting factor of the other. This is most often seen in parasite–host relationships and predator–prey relationships. A good example is the relationship of the *lynx* (a predator) and the *varying hare* (the prey) as it was studied in Canada. The varying hare has a high reproductive capacity that the lynx helps to control by using the varying hare as food. The lynx can capture and kill the weak, the old, the diseased, and the unwary varying hares, leaving stronger, healthier ones to reproduce. Because the lynx is removing unfit individuals, it benefits the varying hare population by reducing the spread of disease and reducing the amount of competition among varying hares. At the same time, the varying hare gene pool benefits because individuals that are less fit have their genes removed from the gene pool. While the lynx is helping to

Textbook Chapter Excerpt 2.2 (continued)

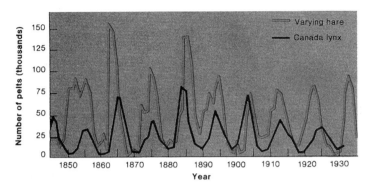

Figure 16.8 **Organism Interaction.** The interaction between predator and prey species is complex and often difficult to interpret. These data were collected from the records of the number of pelts purchased by the Hudson Bay Company. It shows that the two populations fluctuate, with changes in the lynx population usually following changes in varying hare population.

Source: Data from D. A. MacLulich, *Fluctuations in the Numbers of the Varying Hare (Lepus americanus).* University of Toronto Press, 1937, reprinted 1974.

limit the varying hare population, the size of the varying hare population determines how many lynx can live in the area, since varying hares are their primary food source. If such events as disease epidemics or unusual weather conditions cause a decline in the varying hare population, the population of the lynx also falls (figure 16.8).

Extrinsic and Intrinsic Limiting Factors

Some of the factors that help control populations come from outside the population and are known as **extrinsic factors.** Predators, loss of a food source, lack of sunlight, or accidents of nature are all extrinsic factors. However, many kinds of organisms self-regulate their population size. The mechanisms that allow them to do this are called **intrinsic factors.** For example, a study of rats under crowded living conditions showed that as conditions became more crowded, abnormal social behavior became common. There was a decrease in litter size, fewer litters per year were produced, mothers were more likely to ignore their young, and many young were killed by adults. Thus, changes in the behavior of the members of the rat population itself resulted in lower birth rates and higher death rates, leading to a reduction in the population growth rate. As another example, trees that are stressed by physical injury or disease often produce extremely large numbers of seeds (offspring) the following year. The trees themselves alter their reproductive rate. The opposite situation is found among populations of white-tailed deer. It is well known that reproductive success is reduced when the deer experience a series of severe winters. When times are bad, the female deer are more likely to have single offspring rather than twins.

Density-Dependent and Density-Independent Limiting Factors

Many populations are controlled by limiting factors that become more effective as the size of the population increases. Such factors are referred to as **density-dependent factors.** Many of the factors we have already discussed are density-dependent. For example, the larger a population becomes, the more likely it is that predators will have a chance to catch some of the individuals. Furthermore, a prolonged period of increasing population allows the size of the predator population to increase as well. Large populations with high population density are more likely to be affected by epidemics of parasites than are small populations of widely dispersed individuals, since dense populations allow for the easy spread of parasites from one individual to another. The rat example discussed previously is another good example of a density-dependent factor operating, since the amount of abnormal behavior increased as the size of the population increased. In general, whenever there is competition among members of a population, its intensity increases as the population increases. Large organisms that tend to live a long time and have relatively few young are most likely to be controlled by density-dependent factors.

A second category, made up of population-controlling influences that are not related to the size of the population, is known as **density-independent factors.** Density-independent factors are usually accidental or occasional extrinsic factors in nature that happen regardless of the size or density of a population. A sudden rainstorm may drown many small plant seedlings and soil organisms. Many plants and animals are killed by frosts that come late in spring or early in the fall. A small pond may dry up, resulting in the death of many organisms. The organisms most likely to be controlled by density-independent factors are small, short-lived organisms that can reproduce very rapidly.

So far we have looked at populations primarily from a nonhuman point of view. Now it is time to focus on the human species and the current problem of the world population.

Human Population Growth

It is important to realize that human populations follow the same patterns of growth and are acted upon by the same kinds of limiting factors as populations of other organisms. When we look at the curve of population growth over the past several thousand years, estimates are that the human population remained low and constant for thousands of years but has

Textbook Chapter Excerpt 2.2 (continued)

increased rapidly in the last few hundred years (figure 16.9). For example, it has been estimated that when Columbus discovered America, the Native American population was about one million. Today, the population of North America is over 280 million people. Does this mean that humans are different from other animal species? Can the human population continue to grow forever?

The human species is no different from other animals. It has a carrying capacity but has been able to continuously shift the carrying capacity upward through technology and the displacement of other species. Much of the exponential growth phase of the human population can be attributed to the removal of diseases, improvement in agricultural methods, and destruction of natural ecosystems in favor of artificial agricultural ecosystems. But even this has its limits. There must be some limiting factors that will eventually cause a leveling off of our population growth curve. We cannot increase beyond our ability to get raw materials and energy, nor can we ignore the waste products we produce or the other organisms with which we interact.

To many of us, raw materials consist simply of the amount of food available, but we should not forget that in a technological society, iron ore, lumber, irrigation water, and silicon chips are also raw materials. However, most people of the world have only more basic needs. For the past several decades, large portions of the world's population have not had enough food. Although it is biologically accurate to say that the world can currently produce enough food to feed all the people of the world, there are many reasons why people can't get food or won't eat it. Many cultures have food taboos or traditions that prevent the use of some available food sources. For example, pork is forbidden in some cultures. Certain groups of people find it almost impossible to digest milk. Some African cultures use a mixture of cow's milk and cow's blood as food, which people of other cultures might be unable to eat.

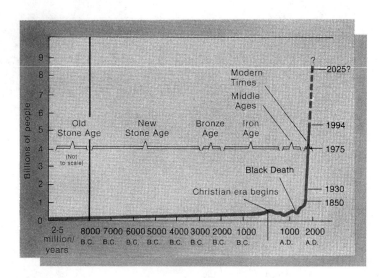

Figure 16.9 **Human Population Growth.** The number of humans doubled from A.D. 1850 to 1930 (from one billion to two billion), then doubled again by 1975 (four billion), and could double again (eight billion) by the year 2025. How long can the human population continue to double before the earth's ultimate carrying capacity is reached?

In addition, complex political, economic, and social problems are related to the production and distribution of food. In some cultures, farming is a low-status job, which means that people would rather buy their food from someone else than grow it themselves. This can result in underutilization of agricultural resources. Food is sometimes used as a political weapon when governments want to control certain groups of people. But probably most important is the fact that transportation of food from centers of excess to centers of need is often very difficult and expensive.

A more fundamental question is whether the world can continue to produce enough food. In 1992 the world population was growing at a rate of 1.7% per year. This amounts to nearly three new people being added to the world population every second, which will result in a doubling of the world population in forty years. With a continuing increase in the number of mouths to feed, it is unlikely that food production will be able to keep pace with the growth in human population (see box 16.1). A primary indicator of the status of the world food situation is the amount of grain produced for each person in the world (per capita gain production). World per capita grain production peaked in 1984. The less-developed nations of the world have a disproportionately large increase in population and a decline in grain production because they are less able to afford costly fertilizer, machinery, and the energy necessary to run the machines and irrigate the land to produce their own grain.

The availability of energy is the second broad limiting factor that affects human populations as well as other kinds of organisms. All species on earth ultimately depend on sunlight for energy—including the human species. Whether one produces electrical power from a hydroelectric dam, burns fossil fuels, or uses a solar cell, the energy is derived from the sun. Energy is needed for transportation, building and maintaining homes, and food production. It is very difficult to develop unbiased, reasonably accurate estimates of global energy "reserves" in the

Textbook Chapter Excerpt 2.2 (continued)

BOX 16.1 Thomas Malthus and His Essay on Population

I(1, 2, 3, 4, 5, 6, etc.). The ultimate outcome of these different rates would be that population would outgrow the ability of the land to produce food. He concluded that wars, famines, plagues, and natural disasters would be the means of controlling the size of the human population. His predictions were hotly debated by the intellectual community of his day. His assumptions and conclusions were attacked as being erroneous and against the best interest of society. At the time he wrote the essay, the popular opinion was that would take less procreative forms and human population would be limited. Only within the last fifty years, however, have really effective conception-control mechanisms become widely accepted and used, and they are used primarily in developed countries.

Malthus did not foresee the use of contraception, major changes in agricultural production techniques, or the exporting of excess people to colonies in the Americas. These factors, as well as high death rates, correct—and that we are seeing his predictions come true today.

Another important impact of Malthus's essay was the effect it had on the young Charles Darwin. When Darwin read it, he saw that what was true for the human population could be applied to the whole of the plant and animal kingdoms. As overreproduction took place, there would be increased competition for food, resulting in the death of the less fit organisms. This theory he called *natural selection*.

---

form of petroleum, natural gas, and coal. Therefore, it is difficult to predict how long these "reserves" might last. We do know, however, that the quantities are limited and that the rate of use has been increasing, particularly in the developed and developing countries.

If the less developed countries were to attain a standard of living equal to that of the developed nations, the global energy "reserves" would disappear overnight. Since the United States constitutes 4.72% of the world's population and consumes approximately 25% of the world's energy resources, raising the standard of living of the entire world population to that of the United States would result in a 500% increase in the rate of consumption of energy and reduce theoretical reserves by an equivalent 500%. Humans should realize there is a limit to our energy resources; we are living on solar energy that was stored over millions of years, and we are using it at a rate that could deplete it in hundreds of years. Will energy availability be the limiting factor that determines the ultimate carrying capacity for humans, or will problems of waste disposal predominate?

One of the most talked-about aspects of human activity is the problem of waste disposal. Not only do we have normal biological wastes, which can be dealt with by decomposer organisms, but we generate a variety of technological wastes and by-products that cannot be efficiently degraded by decomposers. Most of what we call pollution results from the waste products of technology. The biological wastes can usually be dealt with fairly efficiently by the building of waste-water treatment plants and other sewage facilities. Certainly these facilities take energy to run, but they rely on decomposers to degrade unwanted organic matter to carbon dioxide and water. Earlier in this chapter we discussed the problem that bacteria and yeasts face when their metabolic waste products accumulate. In this situation, the organisms so "befoul their nest" that their wastes poison them. Are humans in a similar situation on a much larger scale? Are we dumping so much technological waste, much of which is toxic, into the environment that we are being poisoned? Some people believe that disregard for the quality of our environment will be a major factor in decreasing our population growth rate. In any case, it makes good sense to do everything possible to stop pollution and work toward cleaning our nest.

The fourth category of limiting factors that determine carrying capacity is interaction among organisms. Humans interact with other organisms in as many ways as other animals do. We have parasites and occasionally predators. We are predators in relation to a variety of animals, both domesticated and wild. We have mutualistic relationships with many

Textbook Chapter Excerpt 2.2 (continued)

of our domesticated plants and animals, since they could not survive without our agricultural practices and we would not survive without the food they provide. Competition is also very important. Insects and rodents compete for the food we raise, and we compete directly with many kinds of animals for the use of ecosystems.

As humans convert more and more land to agricultural and other purposes, many other organisms are displaced. Many of these displaced organisms are not able to compete successfully and must leave the area, have their populations reduced, or become extinct. The American bison (buffalo), African and Asian elephants, the panda, and the grizzly bear are a few species that are much reduced in number because they were not able to compete successfully with the human species. The passenger pigeon, Carolina parakeet, and great auk are a few that have become extinct. Our parks and natural areas have become tiny refuges for plants and animals that once occupied vast expanses of the world. If these refuges are lost, many organisms will become extinct. What today might seem to be an insignificant organism that we can easily do without may tomorrow be seen as a link to our very survival. We humans have been extremely successful in our efforts to convert ecosystems to our own uses at the expense of other species.

Competition with one another (intraspecific competition), however, is a different matter. Since competition is negative to both organisms, humans must be harmed. We are not displacing another species, we are displacing some of our own kind. Certainly when resources are in short supply, there is competition. Unfortunately, it is usually the young that are least able to compete, and high infant mortality is the result.

Humans are different from most other organisms in a fundamental way: we are able to predict the outcome of a specific course of action. Current technology and medical knowledge are available to control human population and improve the health and well-being of the people of the world. Why then does the human population continue to grow, resulting in human suffering and stressing the environment in which we live? Since we are social animals that have freedom of choice, we frequently do not do what is considered "best" from an unemotional, unselfish point of view. People make decisions based on historical, social, cultural, ethical, and personal considerations. What is best for the population as a whole may be bad for you as an individual. The biggest problems associated with control of the human population are not biological problems, but require the efforts of philosophers, theologians, politicians, sociologists, and others. As population increases, so will political, social, and biological problems; there will be less individual freedom, and herd politics will prevail. The knowledge and technology necessary to control the human population are available, but the will is not. What will eventually limit the size of our population? Will it be lack of resources, lack of energy, accumulated waste products, competition among ourselves, or rational planning of family size?

• Summary •

A population is a group of organisms of the same species in a particular place at a particular time. Populations differ from one another in gene frequency, age distribution, sex ratio, and population density. Organisms typically have a reproductive capacity that exceeds what is necessary to replace the parent organisms when they die. This inherent capacity to overreproduce causes a rapid increase in population size when a new area is colonized. A typical population growth curve consists of a lag phase in which population rises very slowly, followed by an exponential growth phase in which the population increases at an accelerating rate, followed by a leveling-off of the population in a stable equilibrium phase. In some populations, a fourth phase may occur, known as the death phase. This is typical of bacterial and yeast populations.

The carrying capacity is the number of organisms that can be sustained in an area over a long period of time. It is set by a variety of limiting factors. Availability of energy, availability of raw materials, accumulation of wastes, and interactions with other organisms are all categories of limiting factors. Because organisms are interrelated, population changes in one species sometimes affect the size of other populations. This is particularly true when one organism uses another as a source of food. Some limiting factors operate from outside the population and are known as extrinsic factors; other are properties of the species itself and are called intrinsic factors. Some limiting factors become more intense as the size of the population increases; these are known as density-dependent factors. Other limiting factors that are more accidental and not related to population size are called density-independent factors.

Humans as a species have the same limits and influences that other organisms do. Our current problems of food production, energy needs, pollution, and habitat destruction are outcomes of uncontrolled population growth. However, humans can reason and predict, thus providing the possibility of population control through conscious population limitation.

Textbook Chapter Excerpt 2.2 (continued)

If you return to figure 16.9, you will note that it has very little in common with the population growth curve shown in figure 16.4. What factors have allowed the human population to grow so rapidly? What natural limiting factors will eventually bring this population under control?

• **Thinking Critically** •

What is the ultimate carrying capacity of the world? What alternatives to the natural processes of population limitation could bring human population under control?

Consider the following in your answer: reproduction, death, diseases, food supply, energy, farming practices, food distribution, cultural biases, and anything else you consider to be appropriate.

• **Experience This** •

Place a male and a female fruit fly in a bottle with half a banana. (You may use prepared fruit fly medium if you have it available.) The fruit flies can be wild or from cultures. Males have solid black tail ends, while females have striped tail ends. Count the fruit flies each day for four weeks and plot them on a graph.

Number of flies

Date ⟶

• **Questions** •

1. Draw the population growth curve of a yeast culture during the wine-making process. Label the lag, exponential growth, stable equilibrium, and death phases.
2. List four ways in which two populations of the same species could be different.
3. Why do populations grow?
4. List four kinds of limiting factors that help to set the carrying capacity for a species.
5. How do the concepts of biomass and population size differ?
6. Differentiate between density-dependent and density-independent limiting factors. Give an example of each.
7. Differentiate between intrinsic and extrinsic limiting factors. Give an example of each.
8. As the human population continues to grow, what should we expect to happen to other species?
9. How does the population growth curve of humans compare with that of other kinds of animals?
10. All organisms overreproduce. What advantage does this give to the species? What disadvantages?

Textbook Chapter Excerpt 2.2 (concluded)

• Chapter Glossary •

age distribution (āj dis″tri-biu′shun) The number of organisms of each age in the population.

biotic potential (bi-ah′tik po-ten′shul) See **reproductive capacity.**

carrying capacity (ka′re-ing kuh-pas′i-te) The optimum population size an area can support over an extended period of time.

death phase (deth fāz) The portion of some population growth curves in which the size of the population declines.

density-dependent factors (den′si-te de-pen′dent fak′tōrz) Population-limiting factors that become more effective as the size of the population increases.

density-independent factors (den′si-te in″de-pen′dent fak′tōrz) Population-controlling factors that are not related to the size of the population.

environmental resistance (en-vi-ron-men′tal re-zis′tants) The collective set of factors that limit population growth.

exponential growth phase (eks-po-nen′shul grōth fāz) A period of time during population growth when the population increases at an accelerating rate.

extrinsic factors (eks-trin′sik fak′tōrz) Population-controlling factors that arise outside the population.

gene flow (jēn flo) The movement of genes within a population due to migration or the movement of genes from one generation to the next by gene replication and reproduction.

gene frequency (jēn fre′kwen-se) A measure of how often a specific gene shows up in the gametes of a population.

intrinsic factors (in-trin′sik fak′tōrz) Population-controlling factors that arise from within the population.

lag phase (lag fāz) A period of time following colonization when the population remains small or increases slowly.

limiting factors (lim′i-ting fak′tōrz) Environmental influences that limit population growth.

mortality (mor-tal′i-te) The number of individuals leaving the population by death per thousand individuals in the population.

natality (na-tal′i-te) The number of individuals entering the population by reproduction per thousand individuals in the population.

population (pop″u-la′shun) A group of organisms of the same species located in the same place at the same time.

population density (pop″u-la′shun den′si-te) The number of organisms of a species per unit area.

population growth curve (pop″u-la′shun grōth kurv) A graph of the change in population size over time.

population pressure (pop″u-la′shun presh-yur) Intense competition that leads to changes in the environment and dispersal of organisms.

reproductive capacity (re-pro-duk′tiv kuh-pas′i-te) The theoretical maximum rate of reproduction; also called **biotic potential.**

sex ratio (seks ra′sho) The number of males in a population compared to the number of females.

stable equilibrium phase (sta′bul e-kwi-lib′re-um fāz) A period of time during population growth when the number of individuals entering the population and the number leaving the population are equal, resulting in a stable population.

Source: Eldon D. Enger et al., *Concepts in Biology,* 7th ed. (Dubuque, Ia.: Wm C. Brown, 1994), pp. 240–52. Copyright 1994 by Wm C. Brown. All rights reserved. Reprinted by permission.

Survey

Describe what you did when you surveyed this chapter. In addition, tell what you learned after surveying this chapter.

Question

Write your questions based on headings, subheadings, and boldface words on the lines below.

_____

_____

_____

_____

_____

_____

_____

_____

_____

_____

_____

_____

_____

_____

_____

_____

Read

As you read the chapter, note the answers to your questions on the lines below.

_____
_____
_____
_____
_____
_____
_____
_____
_____
_____
_____
_____
_____
_____
_____
_____
_____
_____

Recite

Discuss what you were reciting and how reciting helped you.

Let's try KWL. First, read the title of the following section from a sociology textbook and then skim the passage. Into your first column, you may write the names of westerns you've seen on television or in the movies. Maybe you'll write the names of actors or events and characters. You may note that westerns are popular or that you like or dislike them. This is what you know already.

In the next column, write out questions you have, such as: Do Native Americans like westerns? or whatever. Then read to find the answers to your questions. You'll discover that you'll read with greater understanding and that you'll be more apt to remember.

WHY DO NATIVE AMERICANS LIKE WESTERNS?

American audiences (and even German, French, and Japanese) have devoured westerns. In the United States, it is easy to see why Anglos might like this genre, for it is they who seemingly defy odds and emerge victorious. It is they who are portrayed as heroically taming a savage wilderness, who fend themselves from cruel, barbaric Indians intent on their destruction. But why would Indians like westerns?

Sociologist JoEllen Shively, a Chippewa who grew up on Indian reservations in Montana and North Dakota, found that westerns are so popular that Native Americans bring bags of paperbacks into taverns to trade with one another. They even call one another "cowboy."

Intrigued, Shively decided to investigate the matter by showing a western movie to adult Native Americans and Anglos in a reservation town. To select the movie, Shively (1991) previewed over seventy westerns and then chose a John Wayne movie, *The Searchers*, because it focuses not only on conflict between Indians and cowboys but also shows the cowboys defeating the Indians. The viewers were matched on education, age, income, and percentage of unemployment. After the movie, she had the viewers fill out questionnaires and interviewed them.

Shively found something surprising: all Native Americans and Anglos identified with the cowboys; none identified with the Indians.

The ways in which Anglos and Native Americans identified with the cowboys, however, were quite different, for each projected a different fantasy onto the story. While Anglos saw the movie as an accurate portrayal of the Old West and a justification of their own status in the social system, Native Americans saw it as embodying a free, natural way of life. In fact, Native Americans said that they were the "real cowboys." By this, they referred to their idealization of freedom and being "one's own man."

Shively concludes:

In westerns, Indians express the ways in which they are different from the dominant society through one of the core myths of the dominant society. . . . To express their real identity—a combination of marginality on the one hand, with a set of values which are about the land, autonomy, and being free—they (use) a cultural vehicle (that is) written for Anglos about Anglos, but it is one in which Indians invest a distinctive set of meanings that speak to their own experience, which they can read in a manner that affirms a way of life they value, or a fantasy they hold to.

In other words, values, not ethnicity, are the central issue. If a Native American film industry were to portray Native Americans with the same values as the Anglo movie industry projects onto cowboys, then Native Americans would identify with their own group. Thus, says Shively, Native American viewers make cowboys "honorary Indians," for the cowboys express their values of bravery, autonomy, and toughness.

Source: James M. Henslin, *Sociology: A Down-to-Earth approach* (New York: Allyn and Beacon, 1993). Copyright © 1993 by Allyn and Beacon. Reprinted by permission.

Making the Connection

Reflection Entry #2

Directions: After taking a few moments to reflect on the information in this chapter, write an essay summarizing what you have learned about reading with a purpose and how you will apply that knowledge to your textbook reading assignments.

CHAPTER THREE

Keys to Learning and Remembering New Vocabulary

New vocabulary can be an obstacle to fully comprehending textbook reading assignments. These words can range from general vocabulary words to specialized and technical vocabulary used by authors and experts in a specific discipline. The simple fact is that the inability to unlock the meanings of these words means that you will most likely not understand what you are reading.

This chapter will help you unlock the meanings of unfamiliar vocabulary. It will discuss several methods for learning and defining new vocabulary such as: becoming familiar with structural clues, acquiring meaning through context clues, and using the SSCD approach. The chapter also includes ideas for remembering your new vocabulary words once you have unlocked their meanings.

Before you begin this chapter, take the vocabulary skills survey. This survey will help you determine the strengths and weaknesses in your vocabulary.

Vocabulary Skills Survey

	Never	Sometimes	Always
1. I look up new words.	___	___	___
2. I keep track of new vocabulary in a notebook.	___	___	___
3. I try to use new vocabulary words in class discussions.	___	___	___
4. I try to use new vocabulary words in written assignments.	___	___	___
5. I try to improve my vocabulary by learning five new words each day.	___	___	___
6. I use context clues to help unlock the meaning of an unfamiliar word.	___	___	___

7. I use structural clues to help unlock the meaning of an unfamiliar word. _____ _____ _____

8. I use a dictionary or glossary to help define unfamiliar words. _____ _____ _____

9. I use mnemonic devices to help me remember new words. _____ _____ _____

10 I review new vocabulary words often. _____ _____ _____

Plan of the Chapter

This leads us to the goals of this chapter:

1. Show you how to figure out meanings from the way words are used in context.
2. Show you how to use word parts (like prefixes, roots, and suffixes) to get at meanings.
3. Show you a famous shortcut, the renowned SSCD approach to vocabulary problems.
4. Give you suggestions for dealing with the technical vocabulary found in textbooks.
5. Give you some tips for remembering new words.

This may seem like a lot for one chapter, but it isn't. These ideas have been used for years by students in colleges all over America. They are tried and true. They work.

And to make sure they work for you, you will find the chapter loaded with practical exercises and activities. Again, these are also tried and true. They, too, have been used by thousands of college students and they work.

Take time to read the chapter carefully and do all the exercises and activities. You are on your way to a positively magnificent vocabulary (not to mention, better grades).

What do College Students Say about Vocabulary?

What do typical college students say about vocabulary study? Do they find problems with new and unfamiliar words? Do they have trouble remembering word meanings? What tricks do they use to unlock the meanings of strange words? Here are three responses from students.

VIGNETTE 1

When reading a textbook assignment, I have problems with the vocabulary. One problem I have is that I am not familiar with many of the words used in the textbook readings. As a result, I have to read and reread the paragraphs I do not understand and hope that they will somehow explain the meanings of the words. Another problem with not having good vocabulary skills is that I have to stop reading and look up words in the dictionary. Even after doing this, I still did not always know what the words meant. This makes the textbook reading assignments much longer than they really are. Also, textbooks use words that occasionally have more than one meaning, and not knowing which meaning fits makes the reading assignment confusing and frustrating.

Shawna T.

VIGNETTE 2

It seems to me that even though I know how to get the meaning of a word through its context, I still have some trouble understanding unfamiliar words. For instance, if there is a word I do not know in a paragraph and I do not know its antonym or synonym, then I cannot figure out what the word means. Moreover, if I have to figure out the word from the general sense of the sentence, and I am not really familiar with the topic, it is hard for me to figure out the definition of the word.

I think that it is extremely important to have a good vocabulary to function in today's society. Words and language are all part of our life and if you do not understand the half of it, how can you communicate or even function within society? A strong vocabulary allows you to express your thoughts and opinions clearly.

Dan F.

VIGNETTE 3

I learn words by writing the words and their definitions on index cards. I use these cards like flash cards to help me memorize them. I then have someone quiz me using these index cards. I also try to write sentences using the new words. I believe that if I can do this, it means that I really understand the word and its definition.

Paul D.

As you can see, many people have similar problems. They note:

Unfamiliar words.

Trying to figure out meanings from context.

Stopping to look words up in the dictionary.

Multiple meanings.

Remembering meanings.

Confusion and frustration.

Confusion and frustration, yes. But we also get a sense from these people that *vocabulary* is *important*. They all seem to imply that having skills to attack new words and possessing a good vocabulary is important to success in college.

Defining Words through Context Clues

The context of an unfamiliar word refers to the words, sentences, and paragraphs that surround that unfamiliar word. Context clues are features within the sentence or paragraph that can help you to define the unfamiliar word. For example, you may or may not know the meaning of the word *aptitude* by itself. However, when this word appears in context, you can guess the meaning: Picasso revealed his *aptitude* for painting at an early age. You're correct if you guessed talent.

You can become skillful at using context clues if you practice. Here is a brief description of some of the most common types of context clues.

Types of Context Clues

1. Definition. Some authors will tell readers what a word means.

    Example 1   *Social stratification* is a system in which people are divided into layers according to their relative power, property, and prestige.

    Example 2   *Self-disclosure* refers to the process of letting yourself be known to others.

2. Examples. Writers will often provide examples within the sentences.

    Example 1   *Street crime* often involves such things as rape, mugging, and robbery.

    Example 2   *Suffixes,* such as -ly and -ate, change the part of speech of words.

3. Synonyms. Authors may introduce a new word by using a familiar word with the same meaning.

    Example 1   The *sternum,* or breastbone, is a flat, narrow bone located in the center of the anterior thoracic wall

    Example 2   The *dividends,* or payments received from the company, were reinvested so I could get bigger returns.

4. Antonyms. They can also introduce a new word by using a familiar word that means the opposite.

    Example 1   Some people are *introverts,* while others are very outgoing.

    Example 2   My colleagues prefer an *urban* setting. I, on the other hand, enjoy the country.

5. Description. Sometimes writers will use enough description so that the meaning can be determined through the details.

    Example 1   Many companies find that protecting the environment helps sell their products. This has spurred the rise of *green marketing*. Even companies that at one time cared little about the environment are producing environmentally sound products.

    Example 2   The *griffin* was a mythological creature with an eagle's wings, head, and beak, but with the body, legs, and tail of a lion.

6. Summary. Authors at times will give a series of items and summarize them into a single word.

    Example 1   The soup was cold. The salad greens were wilted. The meat was practically raw. The vegetables were mushy. The dessert was burned. In short, the whole meal was *inedible.*

    Example 2   Mike refused to take work home. He lacked respect for his co-workers. He disregarded company policies. He was often late for meetings. *Disciplinary* action was taken.

Grammatical Clues

In addition to the six types of context clues just mentioned, there are four types of grammatical clues that you can use to determine the meaning of an unfamiliar word. They are:

1. The verb *to be*.
2. Clause markers.
3. Appositives.
4. Punctuation.

Verb *to be*. Authors will often follow the verb *to be* (is, are, was, were, will be, etc.) with a definition.

Example   To enhance your writing skills *is* to improve upon them.

Clause markers. These are words that give the meanings or clues to the meanings of nouns. Some examples of clause markers are: who, which, that, where, and whom.

Example   Most textbooks have an index *that* lists the page numbers of specific topics covered in the book.

Appositives. This type of clue consists of phrases of explanation that follow the unfamiliar word.

Example   The centaur, *a creature that is half man and half horse,* is often found in Greek mythology.

Punctuation. At times, the meaning of an unfamiliar word follows commas, dashes, parentheses, or other quotation marks.

Example   One country that epitomizes, *or closely represents*, the ideal government is Canada.

Example   Being raised with the same family values, it seems ironic—*contrary to what some would expect*—that my brother and I share none of the same values in life.

Example   My view of life in general is totally nonconforming (*lacking in agreement*) with the view of life among my colleagues.

Example   "*Components*" is another word for parts.

Using context clues can clearly save you time, improve your reading rate, and, more importantly, increase your overall understanding of textbook reading assignments. Apply what you have learned about context clues to the exercises that follow.

EXERCISE 3.1

Directions: Define the words in italics and identify the type of context clue in the following sentences.

1. *Kinetics* is the study of communication through body movement, posture, gestures, and facial expressions.

80 Chapter 3 Keys to Learning and Remembering New Vocabulary

Definition: _____
_____
_____

Type of context clue: _____

2. *Surrogate* mothers replaced the real mothers for nine months.

Definition: _____
_____
_____

Type of context clue: _____

3. There are four basic *components* to a personal computer system: the keyboard, the monitor, and the disk drives.

Definition: _____
_____
_____

Type of context clue: _____

4. During business negotiations the vice president was *feckless*, while the president was efficient and competent.

Definition: _____
_____
_____

Type of context clue: _____

5. More colleges should have *computer literacy* as part of their core requirements, thus giving students the basic skills needed to survive in a computer age.

Definition: _____
_____
_____

Type of context clue: _____

6. The *trachea,* or windpipe, is a passageway for air that is located anterior to the esophagus.

Definition: _____
_____
_____

Type of context clue: _____

7. The amendment includes many *facets*, or aspects, that may require much discussion.

Definition: _____

_____

Type of context clue: _____

8. A flexible work-schedule plan in which employees set their own arrival and departure times is called *flextime*.

Definition: _____

_____

Type of context clue: _____

9. The *scapulae*, or shoulder blades, are large, triangular, flat bone situated in the posterior part of the thorax between the second and seventh ribs.

Definition: _____

_____

Type of context clue: _____

10. Some workers are rather lazy, but others are *diligent*.

Definition: _____

_____

Type of context clue: _____

EXERCISE 3.2

Directions: Using your knowledge of context clues, fill in the blanks with the terms below so that they fit grammatically and logically.

| craft | industrial union | labor union |
| industrial | craft union | working conditions |

A. For more than 200 years, individual workers have sought methods of improving their living standards, working conditions, and job security. Over time, as workers began to unite, they realized that their collective strength was often sufficient to elicit responses to their demands. And so labor unions were born. A _____ _____ is a group of workers who have banded together to achieve common goals in the key areas of wages, hours, and _____ _____. Two types of labor unions exist in the United States: _____ and _____. A _____ _____ consists of skilled workers in a specific craft or trade, such as carpenters, painters, printers, and heavy-equipment operators. An _____ _____ is made up of all workers in a given industry, regardless of their occupation or skill level. Industrial unions include the United Steelworkers, the United Auto Workers, the Amalgamated Clothing Workers, and the United Transportation Union.

Directions: Using your knowledge of context clues, fill in the blanks with the terms below so that they fit grammatically and logically. *Some words may be used more than once.*

> violations   imprisonment   littering   felonies   penitentiary
> misdemeanors   embezzlement   disorderly conduct

B. Crimes are usually divided into categories related to their seriousness. _____, the most serious type of crime, are punishable by more than one year in a state or federal _____. Common _____ include treason, murder, arson, burglary, _____, grand larceny, aggravated assault, rape, and manslaughter. _____ are less serious offenses, punishable by a fine or _____. Common _____ include petty larceny, simple assault, reckless endangerment, and _____ _____. The least serious types of criminal conduct are classified as _____. These crimes are not usually punishable by imprisonment (although they can be) but are punishable by _____. Common _____ include the breaking of traffic rules, failing to inspect one's automobile, spitting on the sidewalk, and _____.

EXERCISE 3.3

Directions: One way to understand the use of context clues is to write your own sentences that include them. Write a sentence for each of the words below and include at least one context for each.

1. **admonish** (to warn) - verb

_____

_____

_____

2. **sporadic** (happening from time to time) - adjective

_____

_____

_____

3. **ubiquitous** (present everywhere at the same time) - adjective

_____

_____

_____

4. **elapse** (slip by) - verb

5. **velocity** (swiftness) - noun

6. **stringent** (strict) - adjective

7. **taciturn** (uncommunicative) - adjective

8. **meticulous** (precise) - adjective

9. **dissipate** (scatter; disperse) - verb

10. **enigmatic** (mysterious) - adjective

84 Chapter 3 Keys to Learning and Remembering New Vocabulary

EXERCISE 3.4

Directions: Read through your textbooks to find sentences that clearly use each of the types of context clues. On the lines below, copy the sentence and identify the type of context clue used.

1. Textbook sentence: _____
_____
_____

Type of context clue: _____

2. Textbook sentence: _____
_____
_____

Type of context clue: _____

3. Textbook sentence: _____
_____
_____

Type of context clue: _____

4. Textbook sentence: _____
_____
_____

Type of context clue: _____

5. Textbook sentence: _____
_____
_____

Type of context clue: _____

6. Textbook sentence: _____
_____
_____

Type of context clue: _____

7. Textbook sentence: _____
_____
_____

Type of context clue: _____

8. Textbook sentence: _____

_____

_____

Type of context clue: _____

9. Textbook sentence: _____

_____

_____

Type of context clue: _____

10. Textbook sentence: _____

_____

_____

Type of context clue: _____

EXERCISE 3.5

Directions: Use your knowledge of context clues to fill in the blanks with the correct word.

| chagrin | impede | attrition | complacent | cajole |
| facetious | aversion | emulate | poignant | integrity |

1. After receiving his grade, the student had a _____ look on his face.
2. This is a _____ novel about the relationship between an unmarried, only son and his aging mother.
3. Much to my _____, I learned that the proposal for my pattern was rejected.
4. Someone in the audience made a _____ remark about the speaker.
5. Some people have an _____ to going to the dentist, while I like to go.
6. The football coach had to _____ his losing team to get them to go back onto the field at the end of halftime.
7. When faced with a moral dilemma, you must maintain your _____, the honesty to stand by your convictions.
8. The _____ (dropout) rate at most European schools is quite low.
9. Most students do not realize that poor vocabulary skills will _____ their academic progress.
10. Children often will _____ their parents' words and actions.

> **idea:** Here's an idea that has worked for many students. You do use a bookmark. Of course. What do you use? A piece of tissue? A movie ticket stub? An old postcard? An ad? The list is endless. (Watch in the library some day. People use the wildest things for bookmarks.) Here is the great idea: Take a card (like a 5 × 7-inch one) and, as you read, jot down new and unfamiliar words. Keep track, in other words. Don't look them up as you find them. Just keep track. As you complete the assignments, go back and see how many words defined themselves! In reading, you were actually using context clues without realizing it. For words you still don't know, check the dictionary and use your bookmark as a kind of word growth scorecard. You can also use it for review and self-testing. It's great for the old self-confidence.

Word Parts

The meaning of words can also be determined by using structural clues. Structural clues are the prefixes, suffixes, and roots that make up a word.

Prefixes

Prefixes are word parts that are added to the beginning of a root word or whole word. They usually change the meaning of a word. The following is a list of commonly used prefixes grouped by meaning.

Prefixes with negative meanings

Prefix	Meaning	Example
ant, anti-	against	antibiotic
contra-, contro-	against	contradict
dis-	not, apart, away	disengage
il-, im-, in-, ir-	not	immature
mal-	bad, wrong, ill	malpractice
mis-	wrong	misnomer
non-	not	nonrefundable
pseudo-	false	pseudonymous
un-	not	undisciplined

Prefixes that are numbers of quantity

Prefix	Meaning	Example
bi-	two	bilateral
di-	two	dichotomy
du-	two	dual
mono-	one	monosyllabic
multi-	many	multisyllabic
poly-	many	polygon
quad-	four	quadrangle
quint-	five	quintet
uni-	one	universal
tri-	three	triangle

Prefixes that identify placement or direction

ab, a-	away, down, from	abdicate
ad, ac, af, ag, an, ap, ar, as, at, a	to	accumulate
de-	down, remove	delouse
con, com, co, col, cor	with, together	cooperate
ex-	forth, from, out	excerpt
inter-	between	intercede
pro-	before, forward	prologue
re-	again	reevaluate
sub-	below, under	subordinate
super-	above	supernatural
tele-	far	telegraph
trans-	across	transcontinental

Prefixes that indicate time

pre-	before	predict
post-	after	postdate

Other commonly used prefixes

bene-	good	benefit
co-	together with	cooperate
equi-	equal	equidistant
hydro-	water	hydrophobia
hyper-	over, above, beyond	hyperbole
hypo-	below, beneath	hypodermic
micro-	small	microscopic
macro-	large	macroeconomics
semi-	half	semiretired
syn-	together with	synchronize

EXERCISE 3.6

Directions: Add a prefix to change the meaning of the words below.

Add a prefix that means **Word formed**

1. exist together   _____ exists

2. not coherent   _____ coherent

3. a room before   _____ room

4. small computer   _____ computer

5. a wrong understanding   _____ understanding

6. many facets   _____ facet

7. not responsible   _____ responsible

8. not enchanted   _____ enchanted

9. below normal   _____ normal

10. above the average human _____ human

Suffixes

Suffixes are word parts that are attached to the end of a root word or whole word. Their main function is to change the part of speech of a word. Suffixes can form nouns, verbs, adjectives, and even on adverb. The following is a list of commonly used suffixes.

TYPES OF SUFFIXES

Suffixes Used to Form Nouns	Examples of Nouns Formed
-tion, sion, ion	transformation
-age	voltage
-ance, ence	vigilance
-cy	vacancy
-ism	terrorism
-ment	establishment
-tude	multitude
-ure	overture
-ness	goodness
-ity	velocity
-ant, ent	migrant
-ary, ory	memory
-ery, ry	imagery

Suffixes Used to Form Adjectives	Examples of Adjectives Formed
-able, ible	adaptable
-ic	ionic
-ern	western
-esque	statuesque
-ish	impish
-al, ial	instrumental
-y, ly	steamy
-an	African
-ive	festive
-ous, ious, eous	advantageous
-less	mindless
-ful	powerful
-and, ent	recurrent

Suffixes used to Form Verbs	Example of Verbs Formed
-ify	rectify
-ize, ise	theorize
-en	enlighten
-ate	originate

Suffix Used to Form Adverbs	Example of Adverb Formed
-ly	overtly

In addition, these is also a set of suffixes that indicate a person or thing that does something.

Suffixes Used to Indicate Person or Thing	Examples Formed
-ian	librarian
-ist	archivist
-er, or, ar	teacher, professor, scholar

EXERCISE 3.7

Directions: Add a suffix to change the part of speech of the words in the first column to the part of speech indicated in the second column.

Word	New Word
1. wonder	adjective _____
2. memory	verb _____
3. marry	noun _____
4. happy	noun _____
5. vocal	verb _____
6. vacancy	adjective _____
7. observe	noun _____
8. active	adverb _____
9. skeptical	noun _____
10. exert	noun _____

Roots

Roots are word parts to which prefixes, suffixes, or both can be added. The following is a list of commonly used roots.

Root	Meaning	Example
anthro	man	anthropologist
astro	star	astrology
bio	life	biology
cept	take	accept
cess	go, move	access
demo	people	democracy
derm	skin	epidermis
dict	say, tell, speak	contradict
duc	take, lead	conduct
geo	earth	geology
graph	write	paragraph
gress	go	transgress
magni	great	magnificent
mit	send, let go	transmit
mono	one	monorail
ortho	straight	orthodontist
path	feeling	apathetic
pend	hang	impending
port	carry	transport
psych	mind	psychology
script	write	inscription
sist	stand	resistant
spec	look	introspect
tang	touch	tangible
theo	god	theology
thermo	heat	thermostat
tract	draw	attract
vers	turn	reverse
vid	see	video
voc	call	vocation
zygo	connect	zygomorphic

EXERCISE 3.8

Directions: Jot down five or six words for each of the root words below.

1. graph

a. _____   d. _____

b. _____   e. _____

c. _____   f. _____

2. psych

a. _____   c. _____

b. _____   d. _____

e. _____   f. _____

3. cess

a. _____   d. _____

b. _____   e. _____

c. _____   f. _____

4. cede

a. _____   d. _____

b. _____   e. _____

c. _____   f. _____

5. dict

a. _____   d. _____

b. _____   e. _____

c. _____   f. _____

6. script

a. _____   d. _____

b. _____   e. _____

c. _____   f. _____

7. mit

a. _____   d. _____

b. _____   e. _____

c. _____   f. _____

8. duc

a. _____   d. _____

b. _____   e. _____

c. _____   f. _____

9. port

a. _____   d. _____

b. _____   e. _____

c. _____   f. _____

10. gress

a. _____ d. _____

b. _____ e. _____

c. _____ f. _____

The following exercises use a combination of prefixes, suffixes, and roots.

EXERCISE 3.9

Directions: Using your knowledge of prefixes, suffixes, and roots, write out the meanings for the boldface words in the following sentences.

1. Why must you **contradict** everything the instructor says every time you come to class?

Meaning: _____

_____

2. Mark is studying to be a **geologist**, although he is not sure if he can get a job in this field.

Meaning: _____

_____

3. It would appear that this story is written in a **chronological** order.

Meaning: _____

_____

4. The student craft show is a **biannual** event at this college.

Meaning: _____

_____

5. There are many reasons for people to have weekly **hydrotherapy** treatments.

Meaning: _____

_____

6. **Synchronized** swimming is both a beautiful and graceful team sport.

Meaning: _____

_____

7. The students stormed the fraternity house to recover their mascot who had be **abducted** by a rival college.

Meaning: _____

8. According to the directions, the student parking lots are **adjacent** to the playing fields.

Meaning: _____

9. In order for this law to pass, we need **bipartisan** cooperation from both the house and senate.

Meaning: _____

10. The public has been forewarned about the dangers of smoking and second-hand smoke.

Meaning: _____

EXERCISE 3.10

Directions: Use your knowledge of prefixes to fill in the blanks below.

Word Formed Using Prefixes	Definition of Word
1. _____verse	situated or lying across
2. _____active	overly energetic
3. _____struct	put together or build
4. _____dict	to tell something before it happens
5. _____pathetic	not having any feelings or interest
6. _____adjusted	badly or wrongly adjusted
7. _____phobia	fear of the water
8. _____struct	to block
9. _____factor	someone who provides for someone else
10. _____chronized	happening at the same time

EXERCISE 3.11

Directions: Match the following word parts to form words. Define each of the words that you have made.

1. mit
2. cede
3. portable
4. graph
5. psych
6. script
7. vers
8. astro
9. anthro
10. gress

a. pre-
b. re-
c. trans-
d. uni-
e. im-
f. poly-
g. ex-
h. -ology
i. -tion
j. -ist

Your Word   **Definition**

1. _____   _____

2. _____   _____

3. _____   _____

4. _____   _____

5. _____   _____

6. _____   _____

7. _____   _____

8. _____   _____

9. _____   _____

10. _____   _____

EXERCISE 3.12

Directions: Using any of your current textbook reading assignments, find five words using the prefixes and five words using the roots listed in this chapter. Write them in the space below along with their definitions.

1. Textbook Word _____

Definition: _____

_____

2. Textbook Word _____

Definition: _____

_____

3. Textbook Word _____

Definition: _____

_____

4. Textbook Word _____

Definition: _____

_____

5. Textbook Word _____

Definition: _____

_____

6. Textbook Word _____

Definition: _____

_____

7. Textbook Word _____

Definition: _____

8. Textbook Word _____

Definition: _____

_____

9. Textbook Word _____

Definition: _____

_____

10. Textbook Word _____

Definition: _____

_____

EXERCISE 3.13

Directions: Answer the following questions by using the meanings of word parts to help you.

1. What does **picturesque** mean?

_____

_____

2. What is meant by **unisex** fashion?

_____

_____

3. What happens to someone who is suffering from **hypoglycemia**?

_____

_____

4. Who rules in a **theocracy**?

_____

_____

Chapter 3 Keys to Learning and Remembering New Vocabulary 97

5. What is an **intangible** object?
_____
_____
_____

6. What is **hydrotherapy**?
_____
_____
_____

7. What is meant by a **unique** situation?
_____
_____
_____
_____

8. What is a **misanthrope**?
_____
_____
_____
_____

9. What is another word for **pyrotechnic** display?
_____
_____
_____

10. Why would someone need to use a **pseudonym**?
_____
_____
_____
_____

SSCD Approach to New Vocabulary

The SSCD approach is a four-step process to figure out an unfamiliar word. Each step in the approach is described below.

1. Sound out the word. Sometimes if you sound the word out loud you may, after hearing it, recognize that this is a word that you already know. This happens because it may be a part of your listening vocabulary but not a part of your sight vocabulary. The next time that you see it, you will not have to sound it out.

2. Look for structural clues. Words are made up of word parts and although you may not recognize the whole word, you may recognize a part of it. For example, the word *indescribable* may not ring a bell. But with your knowledge of word parts, you can take away the prefix *in-*, meaning not, and the suffix *-able*, meaning able, which would leave you with *describe*, a word that you do know. Putting it back together you would then realize that the word means *not able to be described*.

3. Check for context clues. The words or sentences around an unfamiliar word often provide clues to the meaning of that word. For example, context clues in the following sentences will help you to determine the meaning of the word *redundant*. This paper is full of *redundant* statements. I don't know why the author found it necessary to consistently *repeat* himself. From the context clue you should have figured out that redundant means repetitive.

4. Use a dictionary as a last resort. When it is impossible to get the meaning of a word from structural clues or context clues, then it is time to get out the dictionary. Although this may slow you down, it is important for you to find the meaning of the word so that it does not interfere with your comprehension of the reading assignment.

EXERCISE 3.14

Directions: As you are reading your next textbook assignment, jot down ten unfamiliar words from the chapter. Then tell which method you used to figure out their meanings.

Words	Method Used
1.	
2.	
3.	
4.	
5.	
6.	

7.

8.

9.

10.

EXERCISE 3.15

Directions: In the space provided, discuss which methods worked best and why.

Remembering New Vocabulary

This is a list of suggestions for remembering the new words you learn as you read.

1. **Write down the new words.** Keep a section of your notebook for recording new and specialized vocabulary that you hear during lectures and read in your textbooks. After recording the new word, write a brief definition or synonym. By the end of the semester, you will have a set of terms for each of your courses.

2. **Use the new words in class discussions and writing assignments.** Just recording and defining a new word is not enough. You need to write and speak your new words to ensure that they stay in your memory.

3. **Use index cards for drills.** Writing each word on the front of an index card and the definition on the back allows you to drill yourself during spare moments between classes, appointments, and television commercials. The possibilities are endless. The results are rewarding.

4. **Make different forms of the words.** Practicing by writing your new words, using different forms of the word, is another way to make sure that these words stay with you. You may, for example, use suffixes to change the part of speech.

5. **Try writing sentences using your new words.** A true test of word comprehension is to use the word in a sentence that makes sense. If the word grammatically, contextually, and logically fits in the sentence, then you know that you have truly learned the meaning of the word.

6. **Use mnemonic devices.** These devices are tricks that help you remember. Some examples of mnemonic devices are: word association, visual association, and rhyming. Word association means that you associate a word that you do not know with a word that you do know. Visual association means that you associate the new word with a visual image or picture in your mind. Rhyming enables you to remember the new word by rhyming it with a word that you already know.

7. **Play a matching game with new words.** Many students put their new words on one set of index cards and their definitions on another set. They mix them up and then try to match the correct definition to each word.

How to Learn Technical Vocabulary

Each subject you study in college has its own vocabulary. Just as you need a large general vocabulary to understand and use language effectively, so do you need a large specialized vocabulary of technical terms to understand and perform successfully in each subject area. To be a chemist, for example, you need to have meanings for *element, isotope, toxicity, halogen,* and *matter.* To be a musician, you need meanings for words such as *chord, clef, transpose, theme,* and *note.* To be an economist, you need to know *barter, productivity, monopolistic, differentials,* and *capital.*

Look again at the words given in the examples above and you will see one of the fundamental problems with technical vocabulary. Some of those words are already in your general vocabulary but have special meanings in the technical vocabulary. Every child says and understands, "What's the matter?" but when a chemist uses *matter*, the meaning is quite special. It means a specific type of substance, such as *inorganic matter*. Everyone knows what a note is ("I'll drop you a note!") but note means something very specific to a musician. Schoolchildren know about capital letters, but *capital* is rather different for an economist.

Some of the words given in these examples are so specialized that most people do not include them in their general vocabularies. Three such words are *isotope, halogen,* and *clef.* Many of the new words you will encounter in textbooks are so specialized that you will not even find them in ordinary dictionaries. You will need to check a glossary or a technical dictionary.

The point to remember about technical vocabularies is that you must have meanings for the words. Just as you cannot understand spoken or written language unless you have meanings for the words speakers and writers use, so too you must have meanings for words in special fields. You cannot understand the chemistry textbook or the chemistry professor when you lack a meaning for *isotope* or *halogen* any more than you can understand a newscaster on television who discussed the *penultimate* warning when you lack a meaning for *penultimate.*

Six suggestions for learning technical vocabulary are presented here.

1. **Make up your mind to learn all technical words.** Some students learn a few new terms as they listen to lectures and read assignments—but "some" isn't enough! To really understand the material in a course, you must know the vocabulary. Words represent concepts; when you fail to learn a word, you cannot know the concept it labels. The vocabulary of the course is your basic handle on the course content. Without it, the content will slip through your mind and be gone when the examination comes.

2. **Keep lists.** As you encounter new words in courses, write them down with their meanings. This is the most effective single technique for mastering new vocabulary. Short-term memory allows us to retain new information for only a few seconds. Unless we write down new information, it will be lost to us.

We suggest that you allocate a few pages in that section of your notebook where you keep reading and lecture notes for a particular course and label it "Important Words." Make sure that every time you come across a technical word you write it here, either with the meaning you figure out for it using structure or context clues or the meaning you get from the dictionary. The list becomes your chief tool for understanding all lectures and readings in the course. Allow adequate space so that when you encounter each word a second or third time, you have room to jot down new uses or additional meanings for the word. Make sure, too, that you copy the correct spelling. You may need to use the word in an essay-type examination, so as you learn the meaning learn the proper spelling.

3. **Check for help in the textbook.** Authors and editors of textbooks know that certain words are crucial to understanding the material, and often mark these words in a special way. Sometimes they use boldface type, italics, or even color. Such signals tell you that these words are important and that a definition may be close by. The definition may be spelled out for you or it may be presented in context. Look for such built-in definitions. If you cannot locate them, check the glossary or dictionary. But be sure you have definitions for all such words.

Some textbooks present important words before the chapter text. Under a heading such as "Key Words" or "New Vocabulary," you will find those words authors and editors think may be troublesome. Copy these in your notebook, too, even though they are in the book. (The process of copying helps you get them in your memory with the proper spelling.) Then, look up the meanings and write them down with the words in your notebook.

4. Look for help during lectures. Words that are important to the course will be used repeatedly in the textbook. They will also be used in lectures and discussions. Some instructors will write new words on the board; some will slow down the pace of the presentation so that the new words stand out. Some will use the new words several times in a lecture so that you have an opportunity to learn them. Make sure you copy all such words into your notebook. When the instructor writes a word on the board, copy it on your list with the correct spelling. When it is said but not written, copy down your best approximation of the spelling, and then go to the textbook after class to locate the word in print and get the spelling. When you cannot catch the spelling of a spoken word, make a phonetic version and later ask the instructor or another student.

5. Use the glossary. Most textbooks include a glossary. This is an abbreviated dictionary listing all technical terms used in the book. It is invaluable (although it is rumored that some students have never actually looked at one!). For your purposes, it can be more useful than a dictionary, because a dictionary will give all the meanings of a word, while the glossary will give only the meaning that applies to a particular field. For example, a good general-purpose dictionary may give 13 or 14 definitions for matter, but the glossary in your chemistry book will give you only the definition that is used in chemistry.

The glossary may be one of the most unappreciated parts of the typical textbook. It can give you precise technical definitions, thus saving you the bother of picking out one from the many provided in a dictionary. It is also wonderfully available. Most students find it irksome to have to put down the textbook they are studying to get another book—a dictionary. The glossary, on the other hand, is right there. By marking the first page of the glossary for easy access, you can always locate your definitions quickly. Another important value of the glossary becomes apparent when you need to review and study for a test. Here are all the key words! At the end of a course you can go through the glossary, using it as the basis for a quick self-test. Some students place a check mark beside each glossary word as they look it up. That way, they can review for a midterm or final exam by testing themselves on only the checked words.

Does the glossary approach to new words have any drawbacks? Yes. The words in it have been selected by the book's author and editors, who have chosen words they believe are important for the book or course. Therefore, you need to know all the words they picked. Remember, however, that they do not know you. Many words in a typical textbook may not be in your personal vocabulary. An author may use terms such as *element, barter*, or *transpose,* but not include them in the glossary, assuming that everyone knows them. You may in fact not yet know them or understand how they are being used in the specific context. This realization should highlight for you the value of the personal word lists you keep in your notebooks.

6. **Make use of structure.** You have been advised to look at word parts when you want to get meanings for unfamiliar words. Often, roots and affixes provide clues to meaning. Sometimes they indicate meaning so directly that you do not need to check the glossary or a dictionary.

The use of structural clues becomes even more important when dealing with technical vocabulary. Most scientific words, for example, are relatively recent. They were created to fit specific needs, and are often made up of old parts! For example, when scientists discovered various drugs that could be used to reduce the physiological effects associated with histamine production in allergies and colds, they simply took a widely used prefix that meant *against* and coined the word *antihistamine*. Because so many scientific words have been constructed from old Latin and Greek roots plus common affixes, the study of word structure can pay you big dividends as you learn technical vocabulary.

Sample lists of specialized and technical vocabulary from college textbooks

Psychology

antisocial behavior	localization of function
bipolar disorders	micromovements
convergent thought	nonreinforcement
demonology	obsession
extrasensory perception	psychopath
functional psychosis	reciprocity
gerontologist	superordinate goal
hypoglycemia	trichromatic theory
introspection	unipolar disorder
justification	vocational interest
kinesthetic senses	work efficiency

idea

When you come across a technical word that just won't stay in your mind, try to use it as the basis of a string of words in the area. It's a challenge sometimes, but it is a good way to remember and better understand the word's meaning.

For example, you can't remember that a *spelunker* is a person who explores caves. Write the letters of the word in an up-and-down line, and then put some word associated with caves and cave exploring beside it. It stretches your mind but works wonderfully. Here's both *spelunker* and *barter*.

Stalactites	**B**argain
Person	**A**rrange
Explorer	**R**eorganize
Light	**T**rade
Under	**E**xchange
Night	**R**elease
Kneel	
Enthusiast	
Rocky	

Sociology
acculturation
bilateral
cohabitation
disengagement theory
epidemiology
fundamentalism
gerontocracy
homogamy
ideology
job deskilling
macropolitics
neocolonialism
oligopoly
polytheism
rehabilitation
socialization
totalitarianism
universal citizenship
variable

Business
autocratic leaders
compulsory arbitration
deregulation
entrepreneurship
flexible benefit plans
generic products
horizontal merger
injunction
jurisdictional strikes
liability
microcomputer
nonprogrammed decision
oligopoly
primary market
recession
sole proprietorship
telemarketing
unemployment

Biology
abiotic factors
biogenesis
coenzyme
dicot
ethology
genetics
homeotherm
interphase
kinetic energy
microorganisms
nondeciduous
polysome
recombinant DNA
subspecies
transpiration
unsaturated

Literature
antagonist
anthropomorphism
biography
coincidence
chronological order
diction
dynamic character
explicit theme
exposition
foreshadowing
genre
hyperbole
implicit theme
omniscient
primary theme
progressive plot
understatement

Philosophy
anthropomorphic
biocosmos
cosmology
dualism
epistemology
formalism
hedonism
invalid

macrocosm
naturalism
ontology
predestination

rationalize
synoptic
theology
vitalism

Textbook Chapter Excerpt 3.1

Directions: Read the following excerpt taken from a college textbook. Use your knowledge of context clues to define the vocabulary that follows the excerpt.

FUNCTIONS OF NONVERBAL MESSAGES

Albert Mehrabian, one of the first scholars to study nonverbal communication, describes three major functions of nonverbal messages: They show the attitudes and emotions of the speaker; they help *clarify* what is being said in words; and they show the reactions of the speaker to the listener, whether those reactions are negative, positive, or mixed. In other words, they reflect the relationship between speaker and listener. We will examine these in more detail.

1. Showing the speaker's attitudes and emotions. The words we speak can say a great deal about the way we feel. However, nonverbal signals in this area tend to be both more powerful and more honest. If the speaker's *nonverbal signals* disagree with the words being said, which do you believe? Which should you believe? Both questions have the same answer: the nonverbal ones.

Beware of your feelings and emotions; unless you are a practiced actor, they will show themselves when you communicate with others. Much of what we communicate, we do *unconsciously*. We communicate our feelings and opinions to others often without any awareness we are doing so. Sometimes, we are even communicating feelings and opinions that we don't know we have; they are buried somewhere beneath our consciousness.

When we communicate unconsciously, our *internal climate*—how we feel within ourselves—is bound to give us away. If we are feeling bad about ourselves, that will show. Of course, if we are feeling good toward ourselves, that will show, too. If we have other issues on our mind, our lack of complete attention will most likely get in the way of real communication. Self-esteem is the key to internal climate.

Let's say you are a manager. An employee comes into your office, hanging his head, speaking in a soft voice, and shuffling his feet. These behaviors will tell you more about the message the employee is about to give you than the message itself. Your own nonverbal reactions to such a speaker can be important.

2. Clarifying messages. Imagine watching a movie that was filmed entirely with a white sheet as a background. The frustration provided by such a movie is *analogous* to the frustration that would be caused by verbal communication with no nonverbal "background." Nonverbal communication allows us to understand and interpret meaning in terms of the *context* in which it is being said. Context is a point of reference, a place to begin.

Have you ever been forced to ask for directions in a strange city? If the person gives you just verbal signals, without quite a few nonverbals, not only might you feel slighted by the direction-giver, you are also more likely to get the directions wrong. When a direction-giver points the way, along with verbal explanations, you and that person are communicating better in many ways.

3. Showing the speaker's reactions to the listener. Watch someone walk down a hallway, greeting people along the way. You might be surprised at how many different ways one person has of saying things as simple as "hi" or "how are you." Although the words are the same, *variations* in facial expression, tone and pitch of the voice, amount of time spent in the greeting, eye contact: all are likely to show differences in emotional reaction. These differences include variations in acceptance, approval, and comfort level.

If you were to say "you're all right" to someone in a fairly neutral tone of voice, the statement could easily be taken as anything from neutral to somewhat negative. If you put your arm around the same person while saying "you're all right," the difference in *intensity* alone would be quite obvious. Thus, intensity is another dimension of this function of nonverbal communication, according to Dr. Mehrabian.

Over the years, many have commented that the English language should have perhaps a dozen different words to express various types and intensities of love. "I love chocolate" certainly means something totally different from "I love my work." Because of gaps such as this in our language, nonverbal expressions that accompany expressions of feelings toward others are often necessary to help get across the emotional reactions more completely.

Source: Lowell Lamberton and Leslie Minor, *Human Relations* (Burr Ridge, Ill.: Richard D. Irwin, 1995). Copyright 1995 by Richard D. Irwin. All rights reserved. Reprinted by permission.

1. clarify _____
_____
_____

2. nonverbal signals _____
_____
_____

3. unconsciously _____
_____
_____

4. internal climate _____
_____
_____

5. analogous _____
_____
_____

6. context _____
_____
_____

7. variations _____
_____
_____

8. intensity _____
_____
_____

Related Study Skills #3: Grouping Words

A good way to learn new words in a reading assignment is to group them. Individual words often resemble, in one way or another, other familiar words. Often words share a common root—and a common element of meaning. For example, if you know the root *bio* indicates *life* or *living* (you don't have to know that it comes from the Greek word for life!), then you can guess the meanings of many related words: *bioastronautics, biochemistry, bioclimatology, biodegradable, bioengineering, biofeedback, biography, biographer*—not to mention *biocenosis* and *biolysis*. (One popular college dictionary lists—and defines—108 words that begin with the root *bio*!)

Grouping similar-looking words leads you to examine common roots and affixes; examining these common features usually leads to insights into shared meaning elements. Once you've grouped *paragraph, telegraph, autograph,* and *biography,* you begin to realize that these words all have something to do with writing. If, by chance, you include *graphite* in your list, you begin to see further possibilities in word groupings on a larger scale.

A highly effective study technique based on word grouping is the *constellation*. You write the words that you need to know (with brief definitions) in a circle, and then enter other similar words you already know. A few seconds with a dictionary can tell you the root if you can't figure it out. Once you identify the root, place it in the middle of the circle, or constellation. You end up with a neat visual that helps you understand and remember the target word or words. An example is shown below.

```
                         Ductile
          Deduct                        Educate
          Deduce                        Education
          Deduction                     Educator


   Conduct                                        Produce
   Conductor                                      Production
                         DUCT
                    (from the Latin word
                       ducere, to lead)
       Abduct
       Abductor                                   Aquaduct


              Seduce              Introduce
              Seduction           Introduction
                         Viaduct
```

EXERCISE 3.16

Prepare two constellations of your own, based on the following two word groups:

A. geology

   geographical

   geophagus

B. anthropology

   anthropologist

   anthropocentric

Making the Connection

Reflection Entry #3

Directions: After taking a few moments to reflect on the information in this chapter, write an essay summarizing what you have learned about learning and remembering new vocabulary and how you will apply that knowledge to your textbook reading assignments.

_____

_____

_____

_____

_____

_____

_____

_____

_____

_____

_____

_____

_____

_____

_____

_____

_____

_____

_____

CHAPTER FOUR

Understanding Main Ideas

Most authors of textbooks try to present their material in an organized manner, systematically moving paragraph by paragraph, with each paragraph developing the ideas that make up the content of the chapter. Usually—but not always—they build each separate paragraph around one of the basic ideas of the chapter in such a way that each paragraph has a main idea. Sometimes textbook authors fail to organize their material so neatly and logically, and, for one reason or another, their paragraphs either fail to include well-defined, main-idea sentences or imply, rather than state, the main idea. In any case, to read college textbooks well, readers need to be aware of the main ideas that are in chapters and to look for sentences in paragraphs that express main ideas. Looking for main-idea sentences—even when they are only implied or nonexistent—stimulates active reading and learning.

Before you read this chapter, take the main idea survey. This survey will help you determine your strengths and weaknesses for understanding main ideas.

Main Idea Survey

		Never	Sometimes	Always
1.	I look for main ideas at the beginning of paragraphs.		✓	
2.	I look for main ideas in the middle of paragraphs.		✓	
3.	I look for main ideas at the end of paragraphs.		✓	
4.	I look for main ideas in introductory sentences or paragraphs.		✓	
5.	I look for main ideas in headings.		✓	
6.	I look for main ideas in titles and subtitles.	✓		
7.	I look for ideas that are often repeated in different words.	✓		
8.	I watch for phrases that are used to call my attention to main ideas.	✓		

9. I connect main ideas in paragraphs to one another.   ✓ ____ ____
10. I use main ideas to summarize the chapter.   ✓ ____ ____

Plan of the Chapter

This chapter focuses on problems associated with identifying and remembering main ideas in textbook reading assignments.

- It helps you distinguish between *topics* and *main ideas*. This is important because many readers think that when they identify the topic of a reading assignment they have its main idea. These are not the same, and confusing them may lead to trouble!

- It also shows you where main idea sentences may be placed. All authors are not considerate: some place main idea sentences at the ends or middles of paragraphs, and some fail to state the main idea clearly.

- It helps you, too, in your college writing. The main purpose of this and the other chapters of this book is to make you a better reader of college textbooks, but an indirect gain for you is that by learning to be a more skillful reader, you also become a better writer. A reader who identifies main ideas easily tends to be a writer who uses main ideas effectively on college writing assignments.

What Do Other Students Say about the Problem?

Main ideas *are* a problem. We often wish that textbook writers started each paragraph with a good, clear statement of the main idea, but they often don't. Some writers place the main idea at the end of the paragraph and some place it in the middle. Some textbook writers don't even give a definite main idea sentence; instead they *imply* (or hint at) the main idea.

When we asked a group of students what they did about main ideas, these were some of the responses we got.

VIGNETTE 1

I know that it's important to remember as much as I can about the reading assignment but no one can remember everything. So what I try to do is get the main ideas. This isn't easy. Once I copied into my notebook every single first sentence from every paragraph, but this doesn't work. What I do now is read each paragraph and then write down my version of what I think the main idea sentence might be.

Charlene W.

VIGNETTE 2

The first step that I do is to read the assignment. The next step that I do is highlight the major idea of the assignment. Then I go back and write what I highlighted into my notes. If I have trouble understanding the reading I'll go back and reread what I just read.

Bob T.

VIGNETTE 3

When I'm reading a story I try to remember the main incidents. I put these ideas on a time line, one thing after another. When it's time to review for a test, all I have to do is go over my time line and check the incidents and the main ideas of the story come right back into my mind.

Arnold Dew.

Students seem to realize that it is important to recall main ideas, both from textbook reading assignments and from stories and novels they read in English class. Most students have some tricks they use (like the time line idea) and others make efforts to keep track of main ideas. This chapter gives you some valuable suggestions and some practical exercises to help you in recalling main ideas.

Topics

Identifying the topic of a paragraph often will help you zero in on the main idea or a paragraph. To find the topic of a paragraph ask the following question: Who or what is this paragraph about? The answer to this question is the topic of the next paragraph.

Example

Effective learners engage in frequent self-instruction. In other words, they act, in a sense, as their own teachers. Typically, this takes the form of a silent dialogue, in which a person guides learning with a series of instructions or questions. For example, when you are reading, you might ask yourself at the and of each paragraph, "What is the main idea here? How does it connect with what came before? What are the implications of this idea? How does this information relate to what I already know? What details should I remember?" It is also important to ask often, "Do I really understand this information? Where are the gaps and weaknesses in my knowledge? What needs more attention? Do I need to consult other sources of information or ask for clarification?"

Who or what is this paragraph about? The answer is **self-instruction,** which is the topic of the paragraph. The topic, self-instruction, leads you to the maid ideas. **Effective learners engage in frequent self-instruction.**

112 Chapter 4 Understanding Main Ideas

EXERCISE 4.1

Directions: Write a topic for each of the following groups of words and phrases.

1. cornea
   pupil
   iris
   lens
   Topic: _Eyes_

2. sole proprietorships
   partnerships
   corporations
   limited partnerships
   Topic: _Companies_

3. solar
   hydro
   nuclear
   Topic: _Energy_

4. Maslow
   Skinner
   Freud
   Jung
   Topic: _Psychology_

5. true/false
   matching
   essay
   multiple choice
   Topic: _Tests_

6. topic sentence
   supporting details
   concluding sentence
   Topic: _Paragraphs_

7. SQ3R
   notetaking
   time management
   summarizing
   Topic: _Study Skills_

8. question mark
   exclamation point
   quotation marks
   period
   Topic: _Punctuation_

9. macro
   pre
   il
   re
   Topic: _Word Parts / Prefixes_

10. Saturn
    Jupiter
    Venus
    Mars
    Topic: _Planets_

11. Thoreau
    Emerson
    Dickinson
    Whitman
    Topic: _Writers_

12. pint
    quart
    peck
    bushel
    Topic: _Measurements_

EXERCISE 4.2

Directions: Read the following paragraphs and write a topic for each on the lines provided.

1. Current research describes two different types of self-esteem: (1) feelings, either positive or negative, about **self-worth,** and (2) feelings of confidence in our ability to deal with problems when they happen, often called **action-based self-esteem**. The first type has to do with how we feel about ourselves when we are alone. The second type has to do with actions and problem solving. Your self-esteem may be stronger in one of these areas than the other.
Topic: _Two different types of self-esteem_

2. Recent studies show that **ageism,** or negative attitudes toward older people, is still very much with us. More than most other groups, though, the elders are fighting back. Consider this startling statistic: In fiscal 1989, employers paid around $9 million in damages and compensation in cases brought under Title VII of the Civil Rights Act. In that same year, employers paid *$25 million* on lawsuits involving the Age Discrimination in Employment Act. That's a ratio of almost 3. to 1. As you can see, this is an impor-

hundred, who have battled Africans in an adjoining block, say, "It is demagoguery to ignore the achievements of the Nazis."

In France, where immigrants from North Africa make up 8 percent of the population, the National Front was dismissed as a racist fringe group just a few years ago. The party's slogan, "Let's Make France for the French," hit a national nerve. Jean-Marie Le Pen, the head of the party, says, "If integration between Islamic immigrants and the French were possible, it would have happened already. We must make these people go back to their homes." Bruno Megret, the chief strategist of the National Front, adds, "France must be made racially pure. Racial integration corrupts. There is a worldwide cosmopolitan conspiracy that seeks to abolish national identity and infect the world with the AIDS virus." In 1992, the National Front carried 14 percent of votes nationwide.

Italy is home to a million immigrants, and thousands more are arriving weekly. In the city of Florence, residents have thrown bottles and set guard dogs on North Africans. "There is a long tradition in Italy of regarding anyone from outside your own village with suspicion," explains Roberto Formigoni, a vice president of the European Parliament.

The slowing economies of Europe have made the situation even more tense. In Austria, the birthplace of Hitler, the right-wing Freedom party has scored big gains on an anti-immigration platform.

And the immigrants? They are caught between two worlds. For many, their native country has become as foreign as their adopted land. With this upsurge in racism, however, their desire for a better life—which drew them from their homelands—is now tinged with fear. As Phung Tien, a thirty-year-old factory worker from Vietnam, who is living in Germany, succinctly expresses the matter, "I don't want to go home, but I don't want to die either."

Source: Based on Horwitz and Forman 1990: Forman and Carrington 1991; Gumbel 1992; Shlaes 1992. From James M. Henslin, *Sociology: A Down-to-Earth Approach* (New York: Allyn and Bacon, 1993). Copyright © 1993 by Allyn and Bacon. Reprinted by permission.

1. Modern-day Nazis _T_
2. African and Italians don't mix. _MI_
3. Once European countries sent immigrants to the United States. _MI_
4. Booming economies and low birth rates have brought immigrants to European countries. _MI_
5. Immigration _T_
6. "Foreigners Out" _T_
7. People from European countries clash with new immigrants. _MI_
8. Immigrants are often caught between two worlds. _MI_
9. Clashing cultures _T_
10. Immigrants are unhappy and want to go home. _MI_

Locations of Main Ideas in Paragraphs

Main ideas can be located in four places in a paragraph: (1) the beginning (most common); (2) the middle; (3) the end; and (4) the beginning and the end of a paragraph.

Example of Main Idea Sentence at the Beginning of the Paragraph

> **Human beings are motivated by needs and wants.** These needs and wants build up inside, causing people to desire to buy a product—a new car or a new duplicating machine. People's **needs** result from *a lack of something desirable.* **Wants** are *needs learned by the person.* For example, people need transportation, but some want a Cadillac, while others prefer a Ford Mustang.

Example of Main Idea Sentence in the Middle of the Paragraph

> If you pride your on being one of a kind, you have good reason. There is no such thing as a "typical person" or a "typical life." Nevertheless, there are certain broad similarities in the universal **life stages** of infancy, childhood, adolescence, young adulthood, middle adulthood, and old age. **Each stage confronts a person with a new set of developmental tasks to be mastered.** These are skills that must be acquired or personal changes that must take place for optimal development. Examples are learning to read in childhood, adjusting to sexual maturity in adolescence, and establishing a vocation as an adult.

Example of Main Idea Sentence at the End of the Paragraph

> Many types of stress are *positive;* such a stress is called *eustress.* Sources of eustress might include holidays, going to a party, giving a presentation, getting married, job promotions, buying a house, vacations, and travel. Sources of eustress are associated with outcomes expected to be mostly positive, and with some sense of personal control over that outcome. On the other hand, sources of *distress* are associated with outcomes expected to be mostly **negative,** and with stress over which we feel little personal control. **Expectation and control are the two key elements that distinguish eustress and distress.**

Example of Main Idea Sentence at the Beginning and the End of a Paragraph

> **With wealth comes power.** We see this principle at work, in our homes, in our towns—whether big or small—even in our high schools. This does not mean that every wealthy person has a lot of power, of course. Some wealthy people are content to simply watch their investments grow, and celebrities in show business and sports who have made many millions may make decisions that affect few lives. **In general, however, power tends to follow money.**

EXERCISE 4.5

Directions: Read each of the paragraphs below. Then on the lines provided, write the stated main idea sentence of each paragraph.

1. "A dusty storehouse of facts." That's how many people think of **memory.** In reality, memory is an *active system* that receives, stores, organizes, alters, and recovers information (Baddeley, 1990). In some ways memory acts like a computer. Incoming information in first **encoded,** or changed into a usable form. This step is like typing data into a computer. Next, information is **stored,** or held in the system.

Chapter 4 Understanding Main Ideas 117

Finally, memory must be **retrieved,** or taken out of storage, to be useful. To remember something, encoding, storage, and retrieval all must take place.

Topic: Memory

Main Idea: To remember something, encoding, storage, and retrieval all must take place.

2. Learning to think of some foods as desirable and others as revolting obviously has much to do with eating habits. In America we would never consider eating the eyes out of the streamed head of a monkey, but in some parts of the world this dish is considered a real delicacy. By the same token, our willingness to consume large quantities of meat, to eat cows, and to cook fish would be considered barbaric in many cultures. Thus, **cultural values** greatly affect the incentive value of various foods.

Topic: Eating habits in different parts of the world. Cultural values of food.

Main Idea: Thus, cultural values greatly affect the incentive value of various foods.

3. Computer technology has transformed medicine in the United States. Computers allow medical personnel to "image" the body, to peer within the body's hidden recesses to determine how its parts are functioning, or to see if surgery is necessary. Computers also allow surgeons to operate on unborn babies and on previously inaccessible parts of the brain. Computers provide the answer to complicated tests in minutes instead of days. Physicians can feed vital information into a computer—sex, age, race, family history, symptoms, and test results—and find out what the chances are that a person has cancer or some other disease.

Topic: Computer technology with medicine

Main Idea: Computers allow medical personnel to "image" the body, to peer within the body's hidden recesses to determine... Computer technology has transformed medicine in the U.S.

4. Corporations can be classified as domestic, foreign, or alien. Your firm is considered a **domestic corporation** in the state in which it is incorporated. If you expect to do business in states other than the state of incorporation, you would register as a **foreign corporation** in those states. A firm incorporated in one nation but operating in another in known as an **alien corporation** in the operating nation.

Topic: Classification Different types of corporations

Main Idea: Corporations can be classified as domestic, foreign, or alien.

118 Chapter 4 Understanding Main Ideas

5. Creating a positive attitude is important, it alone will not result in your making the sale. To sell to someone, you also must convert a buyer's belief into a positive attitude. A **belief** is a state of mind in which trust or confidence is placed in something or someone. The buyer must believe your product will fulfill a need or solve a problem. A favorable attitude toward one product rather than another comes from a belief that one of them is better.

Topic: ~~Attitude~~ Belief

Main Idea: Creating a positive attitude is important, it alone will not result in your making the sale. A belief is a state of mind in which trust or confidence is placed in something or someone.

EXERCISE 4.6

Directions: Using one of your textbooks, find one paragraph that has been written with the main idea at the beginning of the paragraph, find a second paragraph with the main idea written somewhere in the middle, and finally, find a third paragraph with a main idea written at the end.

1. Main idea (beginning)

Textbook used: _____

Page: _____

Paragraph: _____

_____

_____

_____

_____

_____

_____

_____

_____

_____

_____

_____

2. Main idea (middle)

Textbook used: _____

Page: _____

Paragraph: _____

3. Main idea (end):

Textbook used: _____

Page: _____

Paragraph: _____

Sometimes chapters are poorly written: Authors worked too hastily and/or didn't recheck their work carefully. As a result, readers are not given main ideas clearly and, sometimes, the main ideas are not only implied but jumbled together in a way that makes reading incredibly difficult.

One trick many students have used is to simply read the assignment with the purpose of identifying what they think are the three of five (the exact number doesn't matter) main ideas of the entire piece. Here is how the trick works.

If after reading several pages it becomes obvious that the author has not placed a main idea sentence in each paragraph and has not implied one, then the reader reads along with the purpose of writing down at the completion of reading a certain number of main ideas. If I were condensing this chapter for a magazine, the reader thinks, what are the key ideas I'd need to get into the article? A second reading can confirm the choices or help revise the selections of main ideas. This trick works, not only with poorly written or especially difficult material but often as a double-check with an important assignment that you don't want to take a chance of not understanding.

EXERCISE 4.7

Directions: After selecting three of the main idea sentences below, write three paragraphs: the first with the main idea at the beginning, the second with the main idea in the middle, and the third with the main idea at the end.

Main idea sentences:

1. Some faculty members make learning interesting.
2. Minimum wages need to be raised.
3. Courses should be graded as pass or fail.
4. Smoking should be banned in restaurants.
5. Colleges need to consider lowering student fees.
6. There is too much emphasis placed on college sports.
7. Salaries for professional athletes are outrageous.
8. This country needs to address the problems of the homeless.
9. Exercise in important for several reasons.
10. Television has created a generation of nonreaders.

Your Paragraph with Main Idea at the Beginning

_____
_____
_____
_____
_____
_____

Your Paragraph with Main Idea in the Middle

Your Paragraph with Main Idea at the End

Implied or Unstated Main Ideas

Sometimes an author does not state the main idea. When this occurs, you must figure out what the main idea is by making up a general statement that is broad enough to cover all the details in the paragraph. To do this, it is often helpful to fit the details under a topic and then write the most important thing that is being said about them.

Example

The Gray Panthers illustrate the central position of conflict theorists—that competition for limited resources forms the basis of group relationships. Back in the 1960s, Margaret Kuhn (1990) decided that she was fed up with the disadvantaged position of the elderly. Taking her cue from the Black Panthers, an organization that was then striking fear into the hearts of many Americans, she founded the Gray Panthers. The purpose of organization, which encourages people of all ages to join, is to work for the welfare of both old and young. On the micro level, the goal is to develop positive self-concepts. On the macro level, the goal is to build a power base that will challenge institutions that oppress the poor, whatever their age. The Gray Panthers have actively fought ageism, regardless of the age group that is on the receiving end of discrimination. One indication of their effectiveness is that their members are frequently asked to testify before congressional committees concerning pending legislation.

Implied main idea: The Gray Panthers was formed to champion the causes of the elderly.

EXERCISE 4.8

Directions: Read each of the following implied main idea paragraphs and write your own main ideas on the lines below.

1. Values and their supporting beliefs paint their own picture of reality, as well as forming a view of what life ought to be like. Because Americans value individualism so highly, for example, they tend to see people as free to pursue whatever legitimate goals they desire. This value blinds them to the many social circumstances that impede people's efforts. The dire consequences of family poverty, parents' lack of education, and dead-end jobs tend to drop from sight. Instead, Americans cling to the notion that anyone can make it—with the right amount of effort. And to prove it, dangled before their eyes are success stories of individuals who have succeeded in spite of handicaps.

Implied main idea: *Americans can do anything if the put their mind to it.*

2. When you hear the word "status," you are likely to think of prestige. These two words are welded together in common thinking. Sociologists, however, use status in a different way to refer to the position

that an individual occupies. That position may have a great deal of prestige, as in the case of a judge or an astronaut, or it may carry very little prestige, as in the case of a gas station attendant or a hamburger flipper at a fast-food restaurant. The status may also be looked down on, as in the case of a street corner man, an ex-convict, or a bag lady.

Implied main idea: _____

_____

_____

_____

3. Many products are repeatedly purchased. People are in the habit of buying a particular product. They give little thought or time to the routine purchase; they fully realize the product's benefits. These are called low-involvement goods because they involve a routine buying decision. People's attitudes and beliefs toward the product are already formed and are usually very positive. Cigarettes, cold drinks, beer, and many grocery items are often purchased through **routine decision making.**

Implied main idea: _____

_____

_____

_____

4. For a substance to be smelled, it must be capable of becoming a gas so than the gaseous particles can enter the nostrils. Also, the substance must be water soluble so that it can dissolve in the nasal mucus to make contact with olfactory receptors. Finally, the substance must be lipid soluble to pass through the plasma membranes of olfactory hairs and initiate an impulse.

Implied main idea: _____

_____

_____

_____

5. There as been so much written about the dangers of cigarette smoking that it is hard to believe that anyone would smoke, knowing the risks it brings and the energy drain it causes. Cigarette smoke is composed of over 4,000 chemicals, including 43 that are known to cause cancer. These chemicals include cyanide, formaldehyde, acetone, ammonia, carbon monoxide, and, of course, addictive nicotine. Advertisers spend billions of dollars a year to convince you that smoking will make you more attractive, sexier, cooler, and calmer, and will solve all your problems in life. We are a drug-using society, and the payoff is excitement and pleasure and a quick fix for problems. The fact is, however, that nicotine is a depressant and saps your energy. Recent studies also show that smoking even causes wrinkles. The risks are well documented, and close to 500,000 people die every year from smoking-related illness. Nonsmokers who are married to smokers have a 30 percent greater risk of developing lung cancer than those who are married to nonsmokers.

124 Chapter 4 Understanding Main Ideas

Implied main idea: _____

_____

_____

_____

EXERCISE 4.9

Directions: The following paragraphs have both stated ideas and implied main ideas. Decide whether the paragraph has a stated or implied main idea. If the main idea is stated, copy it on the lines provided. If the main idea is implied, write one in your own words.

1. First impressions are important. Whether you realize it or not, the image you present—your attitude and your overall delivery—is affected by your clothing. The clothes you wear during an interview are an important part of how you present yourself; you should be comfortable, but professional. You need to look like you belong in the position for which you are being interviewed. So, dress the part. If you feel great about the way you look, you will convey that image. Taking time to present an attractive, professional image will only add to your self-esteem and self-confidence.

Main idea: *Know how to dress for an interview. First impressions are important.*

2. Employment ads are a quick way to look for a variety of jobs. Although most jobs are not advertised, ads do point to general industries and specific companies where employment activity is taking place. If there were several ads for mortgage closers, you might consider sending your resumé to all the mortgage companies in your area. These ads can give you ideas about where else to look. Often there will be a classified ad announcing a Job Fair. It will state the date, time, location, and sometimes even the companies that will be represented. Read the classifieds every day. Follow the directions in the ads—phone call, a letter, and so on. Small local newspapers and professional journals carry classified ads. Some employers advertise through your local cable television network and on radio stations.

Main idea: *Ways to look for ads for jobs. Employment ads are a quick way to look for a variety of jobs.*

3. Before a person can purchase insurance on a person or thing, the law requires that he have an insurable interest in the person or thing being insured. A person cannot insure against harm to personal or real property she does not own or otherwise have legal right to use. Likewise, a person cannot insure the life of

2. What is the topic of this excerpt? _____

3. What is the main idea of paragraph 3? _____

4. What is the main idea of paragraph 5? _____

5. Is the main idea in paragraph 6 the first sentence or the second sentence?_____

6. Is the main idea in paragraph 1 stated or unstated? _____

Related Study Skills #4: Concept Mapping

A very useful way to get a better picture of the main ideas in a selection is **concept mapping**. This is a type of free-form outlining that you may use as you read to take notes. It is also a wonderful way to make sense of your notes—and your reading. When you make such a map, you force yourself to look at the main ideas and see the relationships among them.

Here is a section on gender differences from a sociology textbook. Read it and then carefully examine the map in Exercise 4.10 begun by a student. Notice how the main idea is divided and how the details fit into the whole picture to make a concise visual representation of the ideas.

Fill in details to complete the map.

Textbook Chapter Excerpt 4.3

MANHOOD IN THE MAKING

The basic presupposition of the sociological perspective on gender in that differences between the sexes are due entirely, or almost entirely, to socialization. Some analysts consider the possibility that biology may account for some differences in men's and women's behavior, possibly even for attitudinal differences, but if it does, they assume that its influence is minor. Without in any way intending to try to resolve this issue, the following materials illustrate how vastly different masculinity is conceived in diverse cultures.

Anthropologist David Gilmore wanted to find out if there were universal elements to the idea of masculinity. He surveyed anthropological data on cultures in southern Spain, the United States, Canada, Britain, Mexico, Sicily, Micronesia, Melanesia, equatorial

Africa, aboriginal South America, South Asia, East Asia, the Middle East, New Guinea, and ancient Greece. He found four basic elements associated with masculinity: (1) not being like females (to be called feminine is an insult), (2) matching or outdoing other males (which takes such forms as fighting, drinking, and gaining wealth), (3) personal accomplishment (especially sexual prowess, but also being able to withstand adversity and pain), and (4) "bigness" (of sexual organ, body, wealth, or possessions). He also found a consistent theme running through these elements—unlike femininity, masculinity does not come naturally, but must be attained. Masculinity is validated by reputation.

If Gilmore's sample of cultures had ended with these groups, we might conclude that regardless of how the specifics of the world's various expressions of masculinity may differ, they reflect a universal inherited predisposition, some inborn, underlying structure. Gilmore's sample, however, included two cultures where ideas of manliness differ sharply.

The first exception is Tahiti in the South Pacific. Tahitian males and females are similar to one another in both characteristics and roles. Both men and women are expected to be passive, yielding, and to ignore slights. Neither competitively strives for material possessions. Their blurred sex roles are manifested in the following ways: There is no expression of gender in their language, not even pronouns; children's names are not sex-specific; labor is not divided on the basis of gender.

The Semai of Central Malaysia are the second exception. The Semai, a racially mixed group of Malays, Chinese, and other people who have passed through their forest enclaves, also lack the differentiation between the sexes that most societies esteem. Their core value is not to make anyone feel bad, which means not denying or frustrating anyone. To do so could anger the spirits, which might take vengeance on the entire village. Consequently, the Semai have no contests or sporting competitions that might make a losing person feel bad. No one can give orders to another, for that might make the other feel bad. For the same reason, they can't resist someone's sexual advances. The Semai say that adultery, whether a man's or woman's, is "just a loan." Nor are they to nag another person for sex, for that, too, would be aggressive. Not concerned about family lines, they love and treat all children well, regardless of paternity. Children may not be disciplined, for that might make them feel bad, and if a child says that he or she does not feel like doing something, that is the end of the matter. If the Semai, either men or women, encounter danger, they run away and hide without shame. Women become headmen, but less often than men, and men can become midwives, but rarely do. The one gender distinction that the Semai appear to make is that the men do the hunting.

Although Gilmore's survey of cultures failed to find a universal, he did confirm a significant sociological principle—that in each human group manhood (or in the exceptional cases of the Tahitians and the Semai, personhood) is a culturally imposed ideal to which men must conform whether or not they find it personally congenial. That we can also apply to cultural ideals of femininity.

EXERCISE 4.10

Concept Map for "Manhood in the Making"

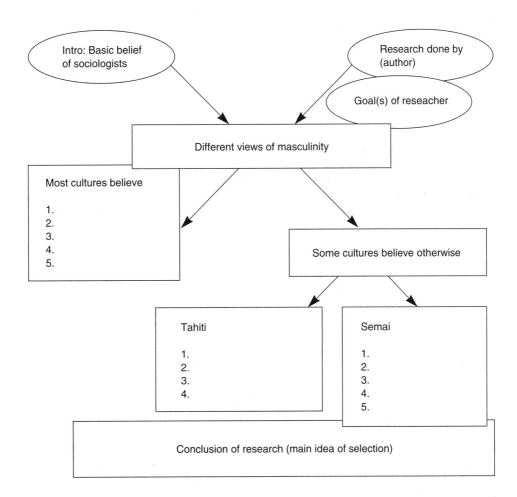

Making the Connection

Reflection Entry #4

Directions: After taking a few moments to reflect on the information in this chapter, write an essay summarizing what you have learned about understanding main ideas and how you will apply that knowledge to your textbook assignments.

_____

_____

_____

CHAPTER FIVE

Identifying Major and Minor Details

As we go through a typical day, we observe countless details—a broken traffic light, a missing button on a friend's jacket, a movie stub in a library book, the blissful look on a baby' face. Sometimes we deliberately look for the details surrounding us. Sometimes they simply pop into our eyes. Psychologists say that if we tried to note each and every detail and make sense of it, we'd have some major problems—too much stimulation.

Fortunately, all details are not of the same importance. Some we note and can quickly forget. Others have significance to our lives and work and need to be heeded. One secret of successful living may be the ability to distinguish what's important and what isn't. Most of us learn as we mature to make important distinctions. We begin to realize that the broken traffic light may be of great significance to us, but the movie ticket stub can be forgotten. In some lines of work—science and criminal detection, to name two—making distinctions is more important: the ticket stub *may* actually have significance in establishing, say, an alibi; the baby's expression reveals much to a nurse or pediatrician.

Details and their relative importance play a major role in reading college textbooks. Authors support their main idea with examples and details. They also present related information, the details of which may or may not be of major importance.

Successful readers need to learn early which details are crucial to the development of ideas and which are relatively minor. An author, for example, may support a main paragraph idea with two details of major importance, but may also present several related details that are not truly important to grasping the main idea.

Details can be facts, reasons, examples, or statistics. Their function is to explain or back up the main idea of a paragraph. All details in a paragraph support the main idea; however, they do not all have the same importance. Major details support the main idea directly. Minor details support the main idea by backing up the major details.

Before you read this chapter, take the survey on major and minor details. This survey will help you determine your strengths and weaknesses for understanding their differences.

Major and Minor Details Survey

	Never	Sometimes	Always
1. I look for major details to support the main idea.	___	___	___
2. I look for minor details to support the main idea.	___	___	___
3. I look for signal words that introduce major details.	___	___	___
4. I check to see if a detail supports or proves the main idea.	___	___	___
5. I check to see is a detail relates to other details in a significant way.	___	___	___
6. I check to see if a detail provides examples of the main idea.	___	___	___
7. I check to see if a detail defines what has been stated.	___	___	___
8. I check to see if a detail adds to or changes the main idea.	___	___	___
9. I check to see if a detail provides interest.	___	___	___
10. I check to see if a detail helps me to understand the main idea.	___	___	___

Plan of the Chapter

Chapter 5 is designed to help you better distinguish between major and minor details in paragraphs of your textbooks. You will find explanations to help you identify major details, plus several exercises based on college textbooks.

Chapter 5 also presents comments from college students about their experiences, as well as a section on Careful Reading. The chapter concludes with a Textbook Excerpt and space for your Reflection Entry.

This is a brief but important chapter. It gives you more help in identifying main idea sentences and shows you how they relate to the major and minor details of the paragraph.

Major Details

Major details are often introduced by signal words or phrases. Some examples:

First; Second; Third	Another key issue . . .
One major reason . . .	Finally
An important point . . .	Of great importance . . .
One factor . . .	In addition . . .

The downside is that not all major details are introduced by signal words or phrases. Remember to ask yourself if the detail in question supports the main idea (major detail) or another detail (minor detail).

EXERCISE 5.3

Directions: Use your textbooks to locate five paragraphs or passages to which you can apply your knowledge of identifying major and minor details. Copy the paragraphs or passages below and identify the main idea and major and minor details for each paragraph.

Paragraph 1 _____

_____

Main idea: _____

Major detail 1: _____

Minor details: _____
_____
_____
_____

Major detail 2: _____
_____
_____
_____

Minor details: _____
_____
_____
_____

Major detail 3: _____
_____
_____
_____

Minor details: _____
_____
_____
_____

Major detail 4: _____
_____
_____
_____

Minor details: _____
_____
_____
_____

Paragraph 2 _____

_____
_____
_____
_____
_____
_____
_____
_____
_____
_____
_____
_____
_____

Main idea: _____
_____
_____

Major detail 1: _____
_____
_____

Minor details: _____
_____
_____

Major detail 2: _____
_____
_____
_____

Chapter 5 Identifying Major and Minor Details

Minor details: _____
_____
_____
_____

Major detail 3: _____
_____
_____

Minor details: _____
_____
_____

Major detail 4: _____
_____
_____

Minor details: _____
_____
_____
_____

Paragraph 3 _____
_____
_____
_____
_____
_____
_____

_____
_____
_____
_____
_____
_____
_____
_____
_____
_____

Main idea: _____
_____
_____

Major detail 1: _____
_____
_____

Minor details: _____
_____
_____

Major detail 2: _____
_____
_____

Minor details: _____
_____
_____
_____

Major detail 3: _____
_____
_____
_____

Minor details: _____
_____
_____
_____

Major detail 4: _____
_____
_____
_____

Minor details: _____
_____
_____
_____

Paragraph 4 _____
_____
_____
_____
_____
_____
_____
_____
_____
_____

Main idea: _____

Major detail 1: _____

Minor details: _____

Major detail 2: _____

Minor details: _____

Major detail 3: _____

Minor details: _____

Major detail 4: _____

_____

_____

_____

Minor details: _____

_____

_____

_____

_____

Paragraph 5 _____

_____

_____

_____

_____

_____

_____

_____

_____

_____

_____

_____

_____

_____

Main idea: _____

_____

_____

Major detail 1: _____

_____

Minor details: _____

_____

_____

Major detail 2: _____

_____

_____

Minor details: _____

_____

_____

_____

Major detail 3: _____

_____

_____

Minor details: _____

_____

_____

Major detail 4: _____

_____

_____

Minor details: _____

_____

_____

_____

VIGNETTE 1

One of the most important things I discovered last year was that I could distinguish better major and minor details *after a second reading*. The first time I read a paragraph, all the details blended together in my mind, but if I read it a second time, I had a general idea of what the author was driving at and I could see the differences between the main points and the minor details. Now, when I know the assignment is really crucial to the course, I reread it and major and minor details are distinguished in my mind.

Wally R.

VIGNETTE 2

I see the difference between major and minor details better when I know the main idea of the paragraph. I love writers who put the main idea first, right at the top of the paragraph. When I know it, I can read along at a comfortable rate of speed, paying less attention to minor details because I know they are minor. They don't support the main idea and, sometimes, they have very little to do with the main idea.

Art A.

Careful Reading

Wally and Art point us in the direction of careful reading. Many less successful college readers read everything—newspapers, TV Guides, stories, and textbooks—with the same degree of care. Successful readers read some material with care, some with great care, and some casually. Checking the newspaper for the weather requires care: you are looking for a specific piece of information and don't want to miss it. But that isn't the same as reading a textbook chapter for a major test; that you read with the greatest care, trying not to miss anything. In textbook reading you need to make sure that major and minor details don't all run together in your mind.

Wally and Art also point out two specific ways of handling a textbook reading assignment. Wally notes that a first reading isn't enough: all the details blend together because you don't know that the paragraph or assignment is about. A first reading allows you to say to yourself that this is about, for example, the settlement of penal colonies in Australia, and that the main idea is that 9 out of 10 people in the colonies were convicted of crimes in England and transported. Knowing this, you can pay less attention to specific details about sentences for individual crimes. Art's idea about main ideas is clearly related: when you know the main idea, you can begin to see which details are major and which minor.

To demonstrate how these ideas of Wally's and Art's (rereading and noting the main idea) help you become a careful reader who distinguishes major from minor details, read the following paragraph from a history textbook. First read it casually, as you might read a newspaper article. Then try to identify its main idea and reread it, this time as a careful reader.

In the early 1800s the separate colonies on the Australian mainland—New South Wales, Victoria, West Australia, and South Australia—were separated by huge tracks of unexplored country, desolate and dangerous. Most communication was by sea. But already the country had become attractive to settlers from the outside world. Despite the early settlements of convicts, many people were flocking to the coastal settlements, not only from England but from the European nations and Asia. British soldiers in India often committed offenses in the hope that they would be transported to Australia. Although gold had yet to be discovered there, ships were regularly bringing the individuals and families who would develop the great coastal cities of Sydney and Melbourne.

One reading of that paragraph tells you a great deal, but if you reread it, thinking about the main idea and trying to distinguish major and minor details, you not only learn more but also probably remember more.

What is the main idea? It is that the country had become attractive to settlers. It's in the third sentence. Now, what details support this idea? Clearly, the next three sentences (that is, the remainder of the paragraph) gives you examples: settlers are coming from England, Europe, and Asia; soldiers are deliberately trying to get transported there; and ships are regularly unloading passengers. The information in the first two sentences (that there are four colonies, that they are separated, that the country is unexplored and dangerous, and that communication is by sea) does not support the main idea. This is interesting information and raises the question of why people were flocking in but none of it supports the main idea that Australia was attractive to settlers.

Being aware of the main idea—either by identifying it in the third sentence or by a quick first reading—helps you see the major details much more sharply.

Another way to help distinguish major from minor details is to ask yourself, What details do I need to truly understand the main idea? You can better answer this question by turning the main idea sentence into a question beginning with WHO, WHAT, WHERE, WHEN, WHY, or HOW.

For example, a paragraph in a marketing textbook begins: "A new product idea will move through the early stages of its life cycle when it has certain characteristics." This is clearly the main idea sentence. You can read to find the details needed to understand the main idea sentence; that is, read to find the characteristics. Or you can simply turn the sentence into the question: What are the characteristics of a new product idea moving through the early stages of its life cycle? The answers you get are the major details.

Later in the same textbook, a paragraph begins with the main idea sentence: "Many wholesalers are modernizing their warehouses and physical handling facilities." To find the major details (rather than the minor ones:), ask: HOW are many wholesalers modernizing? When you do that you discover that they are (1) using bar codes that can be read with hand-held scanners, (2) using computerized order-picking systems, (3) having delivery vehicles travel in computer-selected sequences, and so on. Distinguishing major from minor details becomes a snap!

EXERCISE 5.4

Here is a selection modified slightly from a chapter in the textbook, *Marketing: Creating Value for Consumers,* by C.A. Churchill and J.P. Peter (Irwin, 1995). The section has three paragraphs. Read each separately and answer the same three questions about each. You'll find that working logically and sequentially through each paragraph helps you better see main ideas and distinguish between major and minor details.

The three questions are:

1. *What seems to be the main idea sentence?* Remember that all paragraphs do not always have clear-cut main idea sentences, but you should try to find them and record them here.
2. *What details seem to support the main idea?* Remember that a paragraph may not include well-defined major details to support the main idea, but you need to look for them and record them here.
3. *What details supply additional information without necessarily supporting the main idea?* These are minor details. The authors believe that you should have this information, but it could be eliminated.

Principles of Motivation

Paragraph 1

To motivate employees, the marketing manager must recognize that different people are motivated by different things at different times. One employee may want to earn a lot of money, whereas another is more interested in professional growth. According to various theories of motivation, some of the incentives that may motivate employees are money, security, interesting work, relationships with co-workers, esteem, the opportunity to realize one's potential, and opportunities to be creative or to be promoted. Countless books have been written to explain human motivation.

1. Main idea:

   _____
   _____
   _____
   _____

2. Major detail(s):

   _____
   _____
   _____
   _____

3. Minor detail(s):

   _____
   _____

Paragraph 2

The manager's behavior also can motivate employees. Employees are more likely to be motivated when they can see that their boss is fair and follows the same rules they are expected to adhere to. Furthermore, the manager can motivate by treating employees with respect and by communicating what is expected of them. Successful managers learn to set good examples.

1. Main idea:

2. Major detail(s):

3. Minor detail(s):

Paragraph 3

Not only must rewards be attractive to employees, but employees must believe they can achieve them. For example, if the marketing department bases a bonus on its goal of total customer satisfaction, employees must believe that they have the power to do the things customers want. Even if the manager is confident that employees can achieve a reward, motivation will not work unless employees themselves share this belief. At the same time, however, one of the ways a manager can inspire people to do excellent work is to have high expectations (a self-fulfilling prophecy). In summary, the manager's job as motivator is to provide rewards for objectives that are challenging but achievable.

1. Main idea:

2. Major detail(s):

_____

_____

_____

_____

3. Minor detail(s):

_____

_____

_____

_____

Textbook Excerpt 5.1

Directions: After reading the following excerpt taken from a college textbook, answer the questions in the space provided.

CATEGORIES OF UNEMPLOYMENT

1. There are four types of unemployment: frictional, structural, cyclical, and seasonal. Each type has a different effect on the economy. **Frictional unemployment** refers to those people who have quit work because they did not like the job, the boss, or the working conditions, and who have not yet found a new job. It also refers to those people who are entering the labor force for the first time (for example, new graduates) or are returning to the labor force.

2. There will always be some frictional unemployment, because it take some time to find a new job or a first job. Frictional unemployment has little negative effect on the economy. Recently, about 80,000 of the unemployed were seeking their first job; another 1.87 million had been in the labor force, had left it for some reason, and had not found a new job yet; and a million more left their previous jobs for one reason or another. As you can see, a large number of the unemployed are getting their first job or are simply between jobs.

3. There is a second important group called the structurally unemployed. **Structural unemployment** refers to that unemployment caused by the restructuring of firms or by a mismatch between the skills (or location) of job seekers and the requirements (or location) of available jobs, for example, coal miners in an area where the mines have been closed. You have learned that a major cause of this type of unemployment is the decline of the manufacturing sector. Another cause is the replacement of workers by robots and other technology. Structural unemployment calls for industry retraining programs to move workers into growth industries. The difference between previous structural layoffs and the layoffs of the 1900s is this. Previous layoffs were usually temporary and involved blue-collar workers. The 1990s layoffs are largely permanent and involve white-collar workers.

4. A third kind of unemployment is **cyclical unemployment**. It occurs because of a recession or a similar downturn in the business cycle. This type of unemployment lasts until the economy recovers and businesses begin rehiring. The 1990s' unemployment figures reflect both structural and cyclical layoffs.

5. The fourth type of unemployment is **seasonal unemployment**. It occurs where the demand for labor varies over the year, as with harvesting of crops. Less than 5 percent of the unemployed fall into the latter two categories. That seems like a relatively low amount, and historically it is very low.

Source: William G. Nickels, James M. McHugh, and Susan McHugh, *Understanding Business,* 3rd ed. (Burr Ridge, Ill.: Richard D. Irwin, 1993). Copyright © 1993 by William G. Nickels. All rights reserved. Reprinted by permission.

1. Using your knowledge of context clues, defining the following words:

   a. frictional unemployment (paragraph 1) _____

   _____

   b. structural unemployment (paragraph 3) _____

   _____

   c. cyclical unemployment (paragraph 4) _____

   _____

   d. seasonal unemployment (paragraph 5) _____

   _____

2. What is the topic of this excerpt? _____

   _____

3. Write a main idea that would cover all five paragraphs: _____

   _____

   _____

   _____

idea:

One way to distinguish major from minor details is to play editor—editor of a magazine such as *Readers' Digest*. Your job is to condense articles from other magazines so that people may read them more quickly. You must cut out words. Your job is to decide which words may be cut without losing the main ideas of the original article.

The secret, of course, is to cut the minor details. You must keep the maid ideas and as many of the major details as possible. You need some major details because they often support the main ideas.

Go back to the paragraph on Australia in the early 1800s. What can you cut without losing the main ideas? You can eliminate the first sentence or say, "Despite the fact that it was dangerous, unexplored, and difficult to communicate, Australia was attractive to settlers."

Try this approach the next time you have a difficult textbook paragraph. Play editor and cut the unessential details. You end up with the main ideas and basic supporting major details. And you are more apt to remember the content of the paragraph.

4. What is the major detail of paragraph 1? _____

   What are the minor details that support it? _____

5. What is the major detail of paragraph 3? _____

   What are the minor details that support it? _____

6. What is the major detail of paragraph 4? _____

   What are the minor details that support it? _____

7. What is the major detail of paragraph 5? _____

   What are the minor details that support it? _____

Related Study Skills #5: Note Taking

As you have seen in this chapter, textbook reading assignments are full of many important major and minor details. To keep track of all these details that you need to take notes. Note taking not only helps you to focus your attention on your reading assignments; it also helps you to distinguish between what is important and what is not important. One very effective technique for taking notes is "blocking." Block notes can be taken by following six easy steps. An example of blocking follows.

1. Make two columns about two inches wide and one column about four inches wide on your note pages.
2. As you read your assignment, write the topic of the paragraph or paragraphs in the second column.
3. Write down ideas, fact, examples, and other important information in the third column.
4. Reread the assignment checking the topics and ideas, facts, examples, and other information, adding anything you may have missed. Change any topic if there is a need.
5. Check your lecture notes if your instructor has previously lectured about this material, to see if there is anything that can be added to the third column.
6. Create questions for the first column. They will help you to review and study your notes. Use the question words who, what, when, how, why, and what happened when making up your questions.

Example

Question	Topic	Ideas, Facts, Information, Examples
What are the 4 types of bones?	Types of bones	Long bones: greater length than width
		Short bones: cube-shaped, almost equal in length and width
		Flat bones: thin comprised of two parallel plates of compact bone
		Irregular bones: complex shapes
What are long bones?	Characteristics of long bones	Main cylindrical central portion called shaft
		Extremities (ends)
What are some examples of long bones?	Types of long bones	Thighs Legs Toes Arms Forearms Fingers

156 Chapter 5 Identifying Major and Minor Details

Directions: After reading the selection "Types of Bones," use the next block to finish taking notes using the block technique.

TYPES OF BONES

The bones of the body may be classified into four principal types on the basis of shape: long, short, flat, and irregular. **Long bones** have a greater length that width and consist of (1) a main, cylindrical, central portion called a shaft and (2) extremities (ends). They are slightly curved for strength. Long bones consist mostly of compact bone tissue (dense bone with few spaces), but also contain considerable amounts of spongy bone tissue (bone with large spaces). The details of compact and spongy bone are discussed shortly. Long bones include bones of the thighs, legs, toes, arms, forearms, and fingers.

Short bones are somewhat cube-shaped and nearly equal in length and width. They are spongy except at the surface where there is a thing layer of compact bone. Short bones include the wrist and ankle.

Flat bones are generally thin and are composed of two more or less parallel plates of compact bone enclosing a layer of spongy bone. Flat bones afford considerable protection and provide extensive areas for muscle attachment. Flat bones include the cranial bones, sternum (breastbone), ribs, and scapulae (shoulder blades).

Irregular bones have complex shapes and cannot be grouped into any of the three categories just described. They also vary in the amount of spongy and compact bone present. Such bones include the vertebrae (backbone) and certain facial bones.

Source: Gerald J. Tortora, Introduction to the Human Body, (New York: Harper Collins, 1994). Copyright © 1994. Reprinted by permission of Harper Collins College Publishers.

Question	Topic	Idea, Facts, Information, Examples

Chapter 5 Identifying Major and Minor Details   **157**

EXERCISE 5.6

Directions: Using one of your textbook assignments, take notes in block form in the block below.

Question	Topic	Idea, Facts, Information, Examples

Making the Connection

Reflection Entry # 5

Directions: After taking a few moments to reflect on the information in this chapter, write an essay summarizing what you have learned about identifying major and minor details and how you will apply that knowledge to your textbook reading assignments.

_____

_____

_____

CHAPTER SIX

Patterns of Organization

Authors organize their thoughts and ideas. They do not randomly present their material to readers; they follow a specific plan of organization. Using a specific plan allows authors to write so that readers find it easier to comprehend what has been written.

In this chapter, you will learn about five basic patterns that authors use. Identifying and understanding these patterns will help you to easily and quickly understand how authors organize textbook material. Understanding these patterns will also help you to organize your own academic writing.

Before you read this chapter, take the patterns of organization survey. This will help you determine your strengths and weaknesses for identifying which pattern an author is using.

Patterns of Organization Survey

	Never	Sometimes	Always
1. I watch for the author's plan when I read.	✓		
2. I look for signal words when I read.		✓	
3. I look for familiar patterns when I read.	✓		
4. I look for signal phrases when I read.	✓		
5. I can recognize if more than one pattern is used in a paragraph.	✓		
6. I use patterns of organization when I write.		✓	
7. I use signal words to help readers follow my plan.		✓	
8. I outline the reading material to see the author's plan.	✓		
9. I can recognize each of the six patterns of organization.		✓	
10. I can tell the difference between a primary pattern and a secondary pattern of organization.	✓		

Plan of the Chapter

To make sense, most speakers and writers organize their information and ideas according to some plan or pattern familiar to their listeners and readers. We all seem to realize that people will have trouble understanding us when our ideas are presented in a disorganized, out-of-order, or jumbled way. When we speak and write, we usually try to follow one of the well-known patterns of organization.

This chapter describes the five most common patterns of organization, as well as the signal words and phrases associated with each pattern. The chapter helps you understand answers to the following questions:

1. What are organizational plans or patterns?
2. Why do textbook writers and others use them?
3. Which patterns are most widely used?
4. What are the basic signal words and phrases?
5. In what ways does knowing patterns help readers?

VIGNETTE 1

Last year I took an extra science course that included a lab. Each meeting I had to write about a lab report but, unfortunately, the lab assistant wasn't exactly helpful. All she said was "Leave your lab reports on the desk on Thursdays." I had trouble. Lots. Each time I set out to write the report and each time got more and more confused. Then, one day, I realized that the lab reports *followed a plan*! This plan was like a cooking recipe: "First you do this, and next you do that, and finally you do something else." Except, in this case, I put everything into the past tense. The recipe tells you what to do; the lab report tells what you did. Once I figured out the plan, the course went along fine.

David J.

VIGNETTE 2

I belong to a club. I'm not going to tell you what kind of a club but it's the kind where every week a member has to give a short talk before the group. I really want to belong to this group but I hate public speaking and really thought I'd quit rather than get up before 30 or 40 people each month or so. My problem was solved by listening. The first two speakers of the year were fair but not very good. Then the third speaker used a plan that I think is perfect. He started right away by saying, "I have five things to tell you about . . ." I had the good sense to realize that this is the ideal organizational pattern for a shy public speaker like me. Everyone has five (or three) things to say about something. By using the pattern, I clue in my listeners to know what to expect, and, very important if I want them to like me, when I am ending. I can't get lost because I can write the five points out on a tiny card, and, best of all, it sounds authoritative. When I say "I've got five things to tell you," I sound as if I know what I'm talking about and am in command.

Ed Smith

EXERCISE 6.1

The first exercise in this chapter is based on the two vignettes. David said that he found it useful to follow a simple "first, then, next" pattern. This is known as the widely used *sequence pattern*, in which the writer tells what was done first, second, next, and so on. It is the basic pattern not only of recipes and lab reports but of history textbooks, stories, movies, and most television dramas. Ed Smith discovered that he could best organize his talks to the group by singling out three or five (or any number of) items and focusing on them. The exact sequence was less important than the clarity gained by focusing on a relatively small number of items. This pattern is called *enumeration* and is described in the next section of the chapter.

Exercise 6.1 is simple. It has two parts, each involving a search and some writing.

Part I
Locate in a newspaper, book, magazine, or some other source an example of the sequence pattern. Cut it out or duplicate it and attach it here. Then write out a short paragraph of your own in which you use the sequence pattern. You can tell how to do something, an event that you witnessed, or even a humorous story. Whatever you write must follow the sequence pattern or items being listed in some order.

Part II
Locate, again in a newspaper, magazine, or similar source, an example of the enumeration pattern. Again, cut it out or duplicate it to attach here and then write your own example of enumeration at work. You can zero in on anything in your life that seems interesting to others: "I am going to tell you three things about karate," or "Let me share five observations about stand-up comedians."

Exercise 6.1, Part 1

Attach example.

_____

_____

_____

_____

_____

_____

_____

_____

_____

Chapter 6 Patterns of Organization

Write your own example.

_____
_____
_____
_____
_____
_____
_____
_____

Exercise 6.1, Part 2

Attach example.

_____
_____
_____
_____
_____
_____
_____
_____

Write your own example.

_____
_____
_____

Five Patterns of Organization

The following is a list of the five basic patterns of organization that textbook authors follow.

1. **Enumeration.** When simply listing things, an author will use this pattern of organization. For example, an author may want to list parts, types or kinds, people, books, and so on.

2. **Sequence.** Sequence is used when an author wants to relate events or steps that take place in a <u>specific order</u>. These may be anything from historical events to a chemistry experiment.

3. **Cause and Effect.** This pattern requires the author to state a cause or causes and then discuss its effect or effects.

4. **Comparison and Contrast.** When authors use this pattern, they are showing how one thing is similar and different to another. An author may use an object, idea, concept, person, and so on when comparing and contrasting.

5. **Definition and Example.** Authors often use specialized and technical terms in their writing. To help you understand these terms they organize the material so that a definition and an example or examples immediately follow the new term.

The following paragraphs demonstrate each of the patterns of organization.

EXAMPLE OF ENUMERATION PATTERN

For symbolic interactionists, symbols are vital for social life. First, symbols lie at the root of self-concept; we symbolize our own selves, that is, we perceive ourselves in certain ways—such as young, appealing, and personable—and act accordingly. Second, without symbols our social relations would be limited to the animal level, for we would have no mechanism for perceiving others in terms of relationships (aunts, uncles, employers, teachers, and so on). Strange as it may seem, only because we have symbols can we have aunts and uncles, for it is these symbols that define for us what such relationships entail. Third, without symbols we could not build bridges and highways. Without symbols, there would be no books, movies, or musical instruments. We would have no schools or hospitals, no government, no religion. In short, as symbolic interactionists point out, symbols make social life possible.

EXAMPLE OF SEQUENCE PATTERN

Desensitization usually involves three steps. First, the client and the therapist *construct a hierarchy*. This is a list of fear-provoking situations involving the phobia and ranging from the least disturbing situation to the most disturbing one. Second, the client is taught *exercises that produce total relaxation* (described in this chapter's Application section). Once the client is relaxed, he or she proceeds to the third step by trying to *perform the least disturbing item* on the list. For fear of heights (acrophobia), this might be: "(1) Stand on the chair." The first item is repeated until no anxiety is felt. Any change from complete relaxation is a signal to clients that they must repeat the relaxation process before continuing. Slowly, clients move up the hierarchy: "(2) Climb to the top of a small stepladder"; "(3) Look down a flight of stairs"; and so on, until the last item is performed without fear: "(20) Fly in an airplane."

EXAMPLE OF CAUSE AND EFFECT PATTERN

Marijuana's typical psychological effects are a sense of euphoria or well-being, relaxation, altered time sense and perceptual distortions (Carr & Meyers). Being stoned on marijuana impairs short-term memory and slows learning—effects that can be a serious problem for frequent users (Nahas, 1979). All considered, marijuana intoxication is relatively subtle by comparison to a drug such as alcohol (Kelley et al., 1990). Despite this, it is now well established that driving a car or operating machinery while high on marijuana can be extremely hazardous. As a matter of fact, driving under the influence of any intoxicating drug is dangerous.

EXAMPLE OF COMPARISON AND CONTRAST PATTERN

Differences in expressing emotions are also evident within the same culture. For example, college professors probably show their pleasure at having done well, such as having given a good lecture, with a simple smile. In contrast, football players show their pleasure at having done well, such as scoring a touchdown, by jumping up and down, throwing the ball to the ground, shouting, lifting one another into the air, clapping one another on the shoulders, or patting one another's rear. But there is something much deeper going on here, for the difference is not limited to display. Because their socialization differs, these individuals actually experience different emotions. The college professor feels satisfaction, contentment, or pride at a job well done. In contrast, the football player feels an intense triumph that borders on pure ecstasy.

EXAMPLE OF DEFINITION AND EXAMPLE PATTERN

People who are very pleased with their particular social status may want others to recognize that they occupy that status. To gain recognition, they use status symbols, signs that identify a status. For example, people wear wedding rings to announce their marital status; uniforms, guns, and badges to proclaim that they are police officers (and to not so subtly let you know that their status gives them authority over you); and "backward" collars to declare that they are Lutheran ministers or Roman Catholic or Episcopalian priests.

Two Important Points about Patterns of Organization

Authors May Use More than One Pattern

There may be times when authors will organize material around a primary and a secondary pattern. For example, an author may choose to discuss the causes and effects of a specific war through enumerating them, or he or she may compare and contrast one presidential administration to another by listing the similarities and differences.

c. _____

4. Comparison and Contrast

a. _____

b. _____

c. _____

5. Definition and Example

a. _____

b. _____

c. _____

EXERCISE 6.5

Directions: Read the following sentences taken from various textbook chapters and decide which pattern the material will follow; enumeration, sequence, cause and effect, comparison and contrast, or definition and example. Then write down the word or words in the sentence that helped you decide.

1. Perhaps a contrast between hospices and hospitals will make the distinction clearer.

Pattern that would follow: *comparison and contrast*

Word or words: *perhaps a contrast*

2. Although the postindustrial economy has brought a greater availability of goods, it has not resulted in social equality.

Pattern that would follow: *cause and effect* ~~comparison and contrast~~

Word or words: *although, postindustrial economy resulted in*

3. The **corporation**, a legal entity treated in law as an individual, is the joint ownership of a business enterprise, whose liabilities and obligations are separate from those of its owners.

Pattern that would follow: *definition and example*

Word or words: ~~corporation~~

4. Marriages are more likely to fail in the lower social classes, and the children of the poor are thus more likely to grow up in broken homes.

Pattern that would follow: *cause and effect*

Word or words: *thus more*

5. Other social classes are not crime free, of course, but for the more privileged classes a different illegitimate opportunity structure makes other forms of crime functional.

Pattern that would follow: *comparison and contrast*

Pattern that would follow: _____

Word or words: _____

5. Textbook sentence: _____

Pattern that would follow: _____

Word or words: _____

6. Textbook sentence: _____

Pattern that would follow: _____

Word or words: _____

7. Textbook sentence: _____

Pattern that would follow: _____

Word or words: _____

174 Chapter 6 Patterns of Organization

8. Textbook sentence: _____
_____
_____
_____

Pattern that would follow: _____
_____

Word or words: none _____
_____

9. Textbook sentence: _____
_____
_____
_____

Pattern that would follow: _____
_____

Word or words: _____
_____

10. Textbook sentence: _____
_____
_____
_____

Pattern that would follow: _____
_____

Word or words: _____
_____

EXERCISE 6.7

Directions: Identify the signal words and the pattern of organization in the following paragraphs. **Note:** All paragraphs may not contain signal words.

1. Test **standardization** refers to two things. First, it means that standard procedures are used in giving the test to all people. That is, the instructions, answer forms, amount of time to work, and so forth, are

2. Sequence

3. Cause and Effect

4. Comparison and Contrast

5. Definition and Example

idea:

Patterns of organization are all around us—not just in college textbooks. One way to make sure that you are aware of the common patterns is to watch for them in unlikely places.

Start observing and collecting. Look at recipes, appliance instructions, pamphlets, newspapers, advertisements, catalogues, how-to-do-it books, manuals, magazines—everywhere. Such searching makes you supersensitive to the basic patterns of organization that all writers use.

EXERCISE 6.9

Directions: Using your knowledge of patterns of organization and signal words and phrases, write a paragraph that clearly demonstrates the following patterns: enumeration, sequence, cause and effect, comparison and contrast, and definition and example. Write your paragraphs on the lines below.

1. **Enumeration**

2. Sequence

3. Cause and Effect

4. Comparison and Contrast

5. Definition and Example

Something to Think About

Where Do Patterns Come From?

Patterns of organization are to be found in all writing, and always have been. Today writers enumerate, compare and contrast, sequence, and use the other basic plans. They did in past times, too—at the time of the American Revolution, during Shakespeare's time, during the Middle Ages. Many have wondered where the patterns came from. Did someone actually invent them? Are they built into our minds? Are they genetic? Part of our biological inheritance?

There are two theories to account for patterns of organization. Many believe they were developed by the ancient Greeks. Early Greek philosophers were concerned about rhetoric, the ways people organized words and sentences to persuade and convince. Some pre-Socratic Greek philosophers recommended organizing words and sentences in certain ways, using time order or placing cause before effect. As time went on, these early patterns were refined and polished and became part of our inheritance from classical civilizations. The patterns were further refined and developed in the Middle Ages and, particularly, in the 18th and 19th centuries. What we have in our books today, according to this theory, is directly descended from ancient times.

Recently, another theory has been advanced. According to some modern psychologists, there are only certain ways we can organize our ideas and information for presentation. We can enumerate, compare and contrast, sequence, and so on. Our minds allow only certain patterns. Other psychologists carry this point a step further and say that these patterns have been built into our genetic make-up. Through centuries of use, they say, our minds have chosen these basic patterns, and our thinking is now, to some extent, shaped by the patterns. These psychologists tend to believe that the common patterns of organization may be constricting because they force our thinking into molds and, sometimes, we fail to think in creative, original ways. Sometimes, they say, we miss solutions to problems because our thinking is shaped in nonproductive ways.

One thing is certain, however. Whether the patterns are a useful gift from the past or a set of thinking detriments, *we need to know them*. We make better sense of writing when we see the patterns authors use, and we can think more effectively ourselves when we are aware of the ways our minds are working.

Chapter Excerpt 6.1

Directions: After reading this excerpt, taken from a college textbook, answer the questions that follow.

LISTENING AND WHY WE FAIL TO LISTEN

What do we really want when we communicate with someone else? We might need a question answered; perhaps we need to affirm that a job is being done correctly; or maybe we just need to be heard. All of us have a very strong need to have other people hear us, understand us, and process the information we give them. This need is so strong that when listening is purposely withheld, our self-esteem suffers.

This tremendous need to be listened to is crucial to human relations. We should realize that other people have this need as much as we have. You'll be amazed at the results you can get when you tune into other people and their needs. The need to be a good listener to others is often ignored by people who consider themselves good communicators. In fact, nearly everyone is a poor listener. In a much quoted article in *Harvard Business Review*, Ralph Nichols and Leonard Stevens wrote, "Immediately after the average person has listened to someone talk, he remembers only half of what he heard—no matter how carefully he thought he was listening . . . Two months after listening to a talk, the average listener will remember only about 25 percent of what was said." Other recent studies have reached similar conclusions. What makes us miss so much of what we hear?

Selective Listening. Let's start with some of the more legitimate reasons for poor listening. In our society we are bombarded with messages. Because we couldn't possibly give our full attention to all these messages, we practice **selective listening**. If we are in a personal environment with even more demands on our attention, the problem is even greater. For example, picture a home with young children chattering and trying to get attention. Parents often become selective listeners just to retain their sanity. Thus, **information overload** is one cause of poor listening skills. Many other reasons for poor listening skills, though, come from habits we have established through our lives. For example, when a subject seems difficult or above our level of ability, we often fail to listen—when, if we had listened, we would have seen how clear and understandable the subject was. The opposite often happens, too. We might reject a speaker because the message seems too basic, beneath our level of knowledge. In either case, the message is lost.

When we are in a group listening to a single speaker, we can easily allow our minds to wander. If we are attending a business meeting or conference, the success of the meeting can be destroyed by this habit. One reason for this tendency is that we have a capacity for listening at a speed that far exceeds the speed of the fastest speaker. We could listen and comprehend up to 500 words per minute; the average public speaker travels through a message at about 125 words per minute. How we spend that extra time and energy often determines our effectiveness as listeners.

Tuning Out. Sometimes we simply refuse to listen to our co-workers, often out of **prejudice**. Some people won't listen to members of races they consider inferior; some men won't listen to women. Prejudice can be more subtle than these examples, though. What about a person who looks unintelligent to the listener, or whose appearance is in some way unattractive? Prejudice can also overlap with jealousy. What about a speaker who seems just a little too perfect? We need to watch our listening habits and rule out these types of prejudice. The process of doing business can be hampered by prejudice.

Red flag words and expressions can bring an immediate emotional response from a listener. We all have words that send our minds off in another direction when we hear them. Often a word triggers a reaction because of strong beliefs we have on a subject. A word such as *Communist*, for example, might cause emotions that keep some people from hearing anything else for quite a while. A word such as *sex* can get similar results, although the emotions might be more positive.

Clearly, there are many reasons why we do not hear what our co-workers are really saying. Listening expert Anthony Allesandra believes there is one major cause underlying most of our poor listening habits. From childhood we have been taught that talking requires energy, attention, and organization, but that listening is a passive, compliant position. From kindergarten onward, we are taught to be assertive, to express ourselves effectively. But until recently, little has been done to teach us **active listening**, as Dr. Allesandra calls it.

Source: Lowell Lamberton and Leslie Minor, *Human Relations* (Burr Ridge, Ill.: Richard D. Irwin, 1995). Copyright © 1995 by Richard D. Irwin. All rights reserved. Reprinted by permission.

1. From the way it is used in the sentence, you know that *compliant* probably means:

    _____ unwilling

    _____ willing

    _____ unable

2. From the way it is used here, you know that *assertive* probably means:

    _____ forthright

    _____ bossy

    _____ energetic

3. What is the main idea of the first paragraph?

    _____ We listen to get answers.

    _____ Everyone has a strong need to be heard and understood.

    _____ We need to check to see if we're doing our jobs right.

4. What is the main idea of the second paragraph?

    _____ Two months after listening to a talk, people remember only 25 percent of what was said.

    _____ Speakers sometimes forget that they need to be good listeners as well.

    _____ The need to be listened to is crucial to human relations.

5. What is the main idea of the excerpt?

   _____ Too many listeners tend to be prejudiced.

   _____ Too many listeners are passive rather than active.

   _____ Speakers tend to speak slower than listeners can listen.

6. Why do listeners fail to get most of the message?

   _____ They listen selectively.

   _____ They are waiting themselves to talk.

   _____ Speakers talk too rapidly.

7. According to the excerpt, what is an example of prejudice interfering with successful listening?

   _____ Some children won't listen to adults.

   _____ Some people can only listen to 125 words per minute.

   _____ Some men won't listen to women.

8. Which of the following is a "red flag word"?

   _____ Communist

   _____ Prejudice

   _____ Reaction

9. Why do some listeners have to listen selectively?

   _____ prejudice

   _____ information overload

   _____ assertiveness

10. Which pattern of organization serves as the basis for this chapter excerpt?

    _____ sequence

    _____ cause and effect

    _____ enumeration

Related Study Skills #6: Preparing Visuals

Often you can better understand by preparing simple *visuals*. By drawing the plan of organization on a piece of paper, you make the main parts and their relationships stand out. Here are several such visuals:

Chapter 6 Patterns of Organization

Enumeration

There are three key features of this process:

First	Second	Third

Cause and Effect

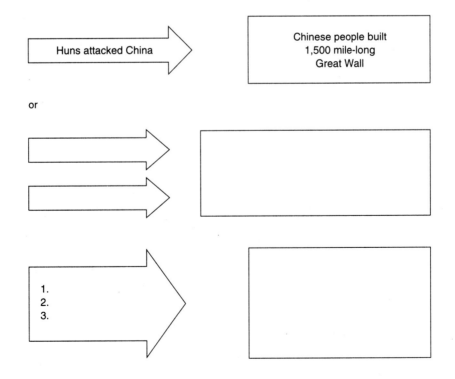

Comparison and Contrast

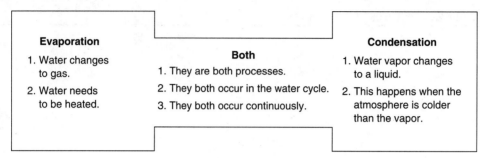

Time Sequence

```
        1800  1810  1820  1830  1840  1850  1860  1870  1880  1890  1900
─────────┼─────┼─────┼─────┼─────┼─────┼─────┼─────┼─────┼─────┼─────┼─────
                           Sources of immigration
         ⋮                       ⋮     ⋮                 ⋮           ⋮
   Scotland and England      Germany Ireland           Italy   Eastern Europe
```

EXERCISE 6.10

Select one of the paragraphs from this chapter and prepare your own visual.

Making the Connection

Reflection Entry #6

Directions: After taking a few moments to reflect on the information in this chapter, write an essay summarizing what you have learned about patterns of organization and how you will apply that knowledge to your textbook reading assignments.

# CHAPTER SEVEN

Fact and Opinion

Successful college readers are *critical* readers. They not only understand and remember what they read, but they also sense the truth and accuracy of what they read. They have learned to detect distortions, lies, and attempts to sway their judgments. They have learned to be on the watch for bias, emotional language, illogical arguments, and propaganda.

In a free society writers and publishers are generally free to print whatever they wish. Politicians are free to argue any position; advertisers are free to slant information to make their products attractive; rabble-rousers and unscrupulous fanatics are free to use their skills to convince and persuade. It becomes very important that readers in a free society sharpen and use their critical reading skills. We all need to read critically.

This chapter introduces you to the most basic critical reading skill: distinguishing factual statements from opinion statements. In everything you read—from newspapers to college textbooks—writers have made statements that are accurate and contribute to their message. However, they also introduce their own opinions. Their opinions are important to readers. Unfortunately, opinions and facts are often so intertwined that readers are misled; they accept writers' opinions as solid evidence and then misinterpret what they read.

This chapter gives you practice in discerning fact from opinion and starts you on the way to becoming a critical reader. It also introduces you to several other key critical reading skills and provides practice in distinguishing fact from opinion, plus other basic skills.

Before you read this chapter, take the fact and opinion survey. This will help you determine your strengths and weaknesses for distinguishing fact from opinion.

Fact and Opinion Survey

	Never	Sometimes	Always
1. I determine if a statement can be proven true or false through written record.	✓		
2. I determine if a statement can be proven true or false through observation.	✓		
3. I determine if a statement can be proven true or false through the testimony of others.	✓		

4. I examine statements for value words. ✓ _____ _____
5. I examine statements for judgment words. ✓ _____ _____
6. I examine statements for words or phrases of beliefs. ✓ _____ _____
7. I examine statements for references to the future. ✓ _____ _____
8. I prove facts to be true or false. ✓ _____ _____
9. I look for both facts and opinions in the same statement. ✓ _____ _____
10. I look for opinions disguised as facts. ✓ _____ _____

Plan of the Chapter

This chapter introduces you to *critical reading*. It does this in two ways. First, it focuses on the basic critical reading skill, distinguishing fact from opinion, and gives you a clear-cut explanation of how factual statements differ from opinion statements, plus a variety of interesting exercises to sharpen this key skill. Next, it gives you an overview of several other important critical reading skills so that you will see how these can be used together to make yourself an effective critical reader. As in the other chapters of this book, you will find stories from other college students, as well as a Fact and Opinion Survey, a Chapter Excerpt, and a Reflection Entry. By the end of this chapter, you will be better able to cope with misleading advertisements, slanted news stories, and various types of propaganda.

VIGNETTE 1

My brother is a sucker for those ads in the back of magazines—you know, "Lose Weight While Eating All You Want" and "Make Money at Home Addressing Envelopes." Last year, he thought he was getting too paunchy around the belly and decided to lose weight. He wrote to some company advertising in a magazine and sent them $40 for pills. He took the pills for two weeks and ate all he wanted. At the end of the two weeks, he weighed fifteen pounds more.

When our class came to the chapter on critical reading, I thought about my poor brother. If anyone ever needed some instruction in how to tell facts from opinion, he did.

Deidre McC.

VIGNETTE 2

My family is very concerned about health insurance. We've had problems, not so much with health, as with employment. My mother had no plan at work and, before my sister and I started our jobs two years ago, none of us had any real insurance.

When the politicians started to talk about this in Washington, we followed the newspaper stories with great interest. Some people said one thing; some said something else. To tell the truth, we couldn't really make sense of the stories in the paper. There were contradictions and arguments going in all directions.

Our reading class this semester had a unit on critical reading, and, for the first time, I began to realize that we all could read the newspaper but we were not reading critically. Facts and opinions were mixed in together. Some stories were biased one way; some, another. The language was emotional and people used words just to get us excited one way or another. I decided that the most important classes I had during the first two semesters of college were those in which I began to read critically.

Elizabeth W.

EXERCISE 7.1

Critical Reading: Where? When? What? Why? How?

From what you've learned so far, the WHY? is clear: we all need to read critically because writers frequently try to persuade readers, by means both fair and foul. They mix up facts with opinions and employ a variety of propagandistic tricks to lead readers to their positions. The HOW? of critical reading is what this chapter is about; you'll be shown how to use some critical reading skills to protect yourself.

This exercise focuses on the WHERE? WHEN? and WHAT? Here is a list of print materials. Think about each and place a check beside the item if it requires critical reading on your part.

✓   1. Newspaper editorials

_____ 2. Help wanted notices

✓   3. Letters to the editor

_____ 4. Death notices

_____ 5. Names and addresses in the telephone directory

_____ 6. Cigarette ads

✓   7. Nutrition facts on a soup can label

_____ 8. Dealer stickers on new car windows

_____ 9. Dictionaries

✓   10. How-to-assemble directions for a bicycle

_____ 11. Cosmetic advertisements

_____ 12. Blurb on dust jacket of mystery novel

Distinguishing Fact from Opinion

What you read in your textbooks is made up of facts, opinions, or both. It is important for you to be able to tell the difference between them so that you can effectively evaluate what you are reading. Oftentimes authors will express their opinions on a topic cleverly mixed in with the facts. This leads unskilled readers to believe that the opinions are facts. This chapter will teach you to distinguish the facts from the opinions.

Facts

A fact is a statement that can be proven true or false by using an objective form of measurement.

Three Ways to Prove a Statement True or False

1. Written records
   a. Surveys
   b. Files
   c. Reference works
   d. Official documents
   e. Forms of measurement
   f. Statistics
2. Your own observations
3. Testimony of individuals

Examples

Fact: On April 14, 1865, Abraham Lincoln was assassinated by John Wilkes Booth in a theater.

This statement can be proven true through historical records.

Fact: Mark Twain was born Samuel Clemens in Hannibal, Missouri, in 1835.

This statement can be proven true through a biographical dictionary.

Fact: The Northern star is the brightest star in the sky.

This statement can be proven through observations.

Fact: Madam Curie discovered a vaccine for polio.

This statement can be proven to be false through an encyclopedia.

Opinions

An opinion is a statement that cannot be proven to be true or false through an objective form of measurement. The reason for this is that opinions often contain subjective feelings, judgments, or beliefs. It is easy to spot an opinion because it contains value words.

Examples of Value Words

best   worst   pretty   ugly   smart   dumb   bad   good

Examples

Opinion: Richard Nixon was the **worst** president this country ever had.

Opinion: Women should have the right to have an abortion.

Opinion: There will be a third world war.

Each of the statements above reflects a belief, judgment, or value that cannot be proven true or false by an objective form of measurement.

A final note about opinions: Anything that happens in the future is an opinion. The reason for this is that since it has not happened, it cannot be proven.

Example

Opinion: Eventually, due to the lack of space on the earth, people will have to live in communities in outer space and under the ocean.

Facts and Opinions

A statement can contain both a fact and an opinion.

Example

Fact and Opinion: The **best** boxer of all time, "Boston Strong Boy" John L. Sullivan, became heavyweight champion in 1882.

In this statement, it can be proven that Sullivan was indeed a heavyweight champion in 1882, but it cannot be proven that he was the best boxer of all time.

EXERCISE 7.2

Directions: Determine if the following statements are facts, opinions, or both. Write F, O, or F & O on the lines provided.

1. __O__ Many Americans felt that the United States should never have been involved in the Vietnam war.
2. __O__ The Boston Tea Party was inevitable.
3. __F__ The hand is comprised of 42 bones.
4. __F__ B. F. Skinner was a behaviorist.
5. __F__ Omnivores are animals that are at times carnivores and at other times herbivores.
6. __F__ All college students could improve their test scores by using mnemonic devices.
7. __F+O__ The Declaration of Independence is the most important document in American history.
8. __F+O__ *Leaves of Grass*, written by Walt Whitman, should be read by all English majors.
9. __F__ A sole proprietorship is the simplest form of business ownership.
10. __F+O__ The line: "I think, therefore I am." is attributed to the great philosophical thinker Socrates.

EXERCISE 7.3

Directions: Determine if the following statements are facts, opinions, or both. Write F, O, or F & O on the lines provided.

1. **F+O** *Where the Wild Things Are*, written by Maurice Sendak, is the best-loved children's book.
2. **O** The works of Mozart will continue to bring joy to many people.
3. **O** John Kenneth Galbraith is a brilliant economist.
4. **F** According to Maslow, very few people achieve self-actualization.
5. **F** Chukchee women of 20 years of age marry baby husbands of 2 to 3 years of age.
6. **O** The American educational system is a failure.
7. **O** Women should receive the same pay as men for the same job.
8. **F+O** John F. Kennedy made more contributions to the betterment of society than any other American president.
9. **O** The best Canterbury Tale is *The Miller's Tale*.
10. **F** Man is at the bottom of the food chain.

EXERCISE 7.4

Directions: Using your textbooks, find 10 statements of fact and 10 statements of opinion. Write them on the lines provided. Be able to prove your choices.

Facts

1. _____

2. _____

3. _____

4.
5.
6.
7.
8.
9.
10.

Opinions

1.
2.
3.
4.
5.
6.
7.

8. _____

9. _____

10. _____

---

idea

Much good writing demonstrates how facts actually support opinions! A writer has carefully reflected upon a topic and come to an opinion that's clearly worth sharing with readers. The writer then uses the opinion statement as the main idea sentence for the paragraph and supports it with two, three, or more factual statements. For example, an automotive writer for a newspaper test-drives a new automobile and likes it very much. She wants to share her opinion with readers of the newspaper, but, knowing many are critical readers, she backs up the opinion with facts. Here's how her story might look:

The new XXL is a dream car—easily the best presented at the city's gala auto show this week. If holds a driver and five passengers. Its fuel economy, EPA, mpg, is 28/37. Braking from 60 mph on dry pavement is 102 ft. and on wet pavement, 120 ft. Its net horsepower is 180.

So that you can better see how facts may support an opinion, try writing such a paragraph:

Your opinion:
    Supporting fact 1
    Supporting fact 2
    Supporting fact 3

202 Chapter 7 Fact and Opinion

EXERCISE 7.5

Directions: Read the following paragraphs carefully to determine which sentences are facts and which are opinions. Write F, O, or F & O on the lines provided.

1 Have you ever seen those yellow Post-it note pads people use to stick messages up on a wall? 2 That product was developed by Art Fry, a 3M employee. 3 He needed to mark the pages of a hymnal in a way that wouldn't damage the book or fall out. 4 He came up with the idea of the sticky paper. 5 The 3M labs soon produced a sample, but the distributors thought the product was silly, and market surveys were negative. 6 Nonetheless, 3M kept sending samples to secretaries of top executives. 7 Eventually, after 12 years, the orders began pouring in, and Post-its became a $12 million winner. 8 The company continues to update the product and now offers Post-it notes made of recycled paper. 9 Post-it notes have gone international as well. 10 The pads sent to Japan are long and narrow to accommodate vertical writing.

1. _____   2. _____   3. _____   4. _____   5. _____
6. _____   7. _____   8. _____   9. _____   10. _____

1 **Organizational culture** may be defined as widely shared values within an organization that provide coherence and cooperation to achieve common goals. 2 Usually the culture of an organization is reflected in stories, traditions, and myths. 3 Anyone who has been to Disneyland or Disney World cannot fail to be impressed by the obvious values instilled by Walt Disney that permeate the organization. 4 One may have heard about or read about the focus on cleanliness, helpfulness, and friendliness, but such stories cannot prepare you for the near-perfect implementation of those values at the parks. 5 The workers seem to have absorbed the ideals into their very being so that they work joyfully and give total attention to the customer.

1. _____   2. _____   3. _____   4. _____   5. _____

Learning from the Wal-Mart Experience 1 Sam Walton developed not just a business but a true American success story. 2 He believed that success in business was dependent on several key factors, many of which he included in his three basic tenets listed above. 3 You can prepare for a business career by getting involved in campus activities and learning to (1) get along with people by practicing listening skills, (2) be a more concise and clear writer so that you can write memos and reports that are short and readable, and (3) be a public speaker by becoming an officer in a campus club and giving talks. 4 Today, corporate recruiters complain that business graduates lack creativity, people skills, aptitude for teamwork, and the ability to speak and write clearly and concisely. 5 Remember, the best way to lead is by example, and the Wal-Mart management team is a model for employees and for managers in all types of firms as well.

1. _____   2. _____   3. _____   4. _____   5. _____

1 Anyone who watches cowboy movies on television is familiar with the fast-talking salesman who sold snake oil and other all-purpose medicines off the back of a horse-drawn wagon. 2 During the 1800s, sanitary conditions in food plants were deplorable. 3 There was special concern about the sale of contaminated meat. 4 There were many questionable business practices associated with the sale of food and drugs in that period. 5 Nevertheless, it took 10 years of debate in Congress to get final passage of the Pure Food and Drug Act in 1906.

1. _____   2. _____   3. _____   4. _____   5. _____

1 Recently, the Food and Drug Administration ruled that a few food manufacturers used misleading labels. 2 Manufacturers of vegetable oils such as Mazola and HeartBeat had to take the phrase *no cholesterol* from their packages, although that statement was literally true. 3 The FDA felt that consumers would think that the product contained no fat, and that is not the case. 4 The FDA does not want food manufacturers to say anything on labels about cholesterol or polyunsaturated fat. 5 Some people feel that the FDA is going too far in restricting information on packages, but that is nonetheless the trend. 6 For example, the FDA went after Citrus Hill for calling its orange juice "Fresh Choice" when it was made from concentrate. 7 The company said right on the label that the juice was made from concentrate, but the FDA judged that the message was not clear enough. 8 The word *fresh* had to be eliminated.

1. _____ 2. _____ 3. _____ 4. _____ 5. _____
6. _____ 7. _____ 8. _____

1 It is easy to criticize business for its moral and ethical shortcomings, but we must be careful in our criticism to note that society as a whole is not too socially minded, either. 2 A recent book, *The Day America Told the Truth*, revealed that most Americans have few moral absolutes: Many decide situationally whether it's all right to steal, lie, or drink and drive. 3 This information comes from a national survey. 4 Two-thirds of the population reported never giving any time to the community. 5 Nearly one-third said they never contributed to a charity. 6 Both managers and workers cited low managerial ethics as a major cause of our competitive woes. 7 But employees report that they often violate safety standards and goof off as much as seven hours a week.

8 It is always healthy when discussing moral and ethical issues to remind everyone that ethical behavior begins with you and me. 9 We cannot expect "society" to become more moral and ethical unless we as individuals commit to becoming more moral and ethical ourselves. 10 It was estimated that consumer fraud in the auto insurance industry cost us all $17.5 billion in 1990 alone.

11 We all look forward to the day when American business and consumers will not only be the economic leaders of the world, but will be the moral and ethical leaders as well.

1. _____ 2. _____ 3. _____ 4. _____ 5. _____
6. _____ 7. _____ 8. _____ 9. _____ 10. _____
11. _____

EXERCISE 7.6

Directions: Using your textbooks, choose five paragraphs from present or upcoming reading assignments and copy them down in the space provided. Then, determine which statements are facts, opinions, or both fact and opinion. Write your answers on the lines below each paragraph.

1. _____

_____

_____

_____

| 1. ____ | 2. ____ | 3. ____ | 4. ____ | 5. ____ |
| 6. ____ | 7. ____ | 8. ____ | 9. ____ | 10. ____ |

2. _____

| 1. ____ | 2. ____ | 3. ____ | 4. ____ | 5. ____ |
| 6. ____ | 7. ____ | 8. ____ | 9. ____ | 10. ____ |

3. _____

1. _____ 2. _____ 3. _____ 4. _____ 5. _____
6. _____ 7. _____ 8. _____ 9. _____ 10. _____

4. _____
_____
_____
_____
_____
_____
_____
_____
_____
_____

1. _____ 2. _____ 3. _____ 4. _____ 5. _____
6. _____ 7. _____ 8. _____ 9. _____ 10. _____

5. _____
_____
_____
_____
_____
_____
_____
_____
_____
_____

1. _____ 2. _____ 3. _____ 4. _____ 5. _____
6. _____ 7. _____ 8. _____ 9. _____ 10. _____

EXERCISE 7.7

We expect to find facts and opinions mixed together in advertisements, political commentaries, and newspaper editorials. We do not expect confusion of fact and opinion in the telephone directory, dictionaries, or a tax form from the Internal Revenue Service. We certainly do not expect facts to be confused with opinions in college textbooks! However, the authors of college textbooks do have opinions and are expected to present them. Usually, opinions are presented in such a way that students will not interpret them as facts; nevertheless, critical readers need to be alert.

Here are statements chosen from a popular college textbook on marketing. Indicate whether each is a factual statement or an opinion by circling "F" or "O." If it is an opinion, tell what factual evidence is needed to support it.

1. There have been efforts to measure consumer satisfaction in the United States and elsewhere.

   F/O

   Factual evidence needed if O:

2. However, measuring consumer satisfaction is difficult.

   F/O

   Factual evidence needed if O:

3. This is because consumers' levels of aspiration or expectation influence their satisfaction.

   F/O

   Factual evidence needed if O:

4. Less prosperous consumers expect more out of an economy as they see the higher living standards of others.

   F/O

   Factual evidence needed if O:

5. Products considered satisfactory one day may not be considered satisfactory the next.

   F/O

   Factual evidence needed if O:

6. Once, most people were satisfied with a 19-inch black-and-white TV.

   F/O

   Factual evidence needed if O:

7. Once you've watched a newer, large-screen, color TV, the old one is never the same again.

   F/O

   Factual evidence needed if O:

8. Consumer satisfaction is a highly individual matter.

   F/O

   Factual evidence needed if O:

9. Consumer satisfaction is hard to define.

   F/O

   Factual evidence needed if O:

10. These statements appear on page 419 of the textbook.

    F/O

    Factual evidence needed if O:

EXERCISE 7.8

Directions: After reading the following selection, decide whether the statements taken from it are facts, opinions, or both. Write an F on the line if you think it is a fact, an O if you think it is an opinion, or an F & O if you think it is both.

WHEN CULTURES CLASH—PROBLEMS IN DEFINING DEVIANCE

In November 1989, sixteen-year-old Tina Isa, who lived with her parents in an apartment on the south side of St. Louis, was stabbed six times by her father, Zein, a Palestinian-born grocer who brought his family to the United States in 1985. Her mother, Maria, held Tina down as Zein ended his daughter's life.

In an eerie twist, the entire murder was captured on tape. For two years, the Isa household had been bugged by the FBI, which was monitoring Mr. Zein for possible illegal activities on behalf of the Palestinian Liberation Organization. While the surveillance unit was not staffed the night the murder occurred, Tina's screams and her parent's shouts in Arabic telling her to "die quickly" were clearly recorded—and ultimately replayed to a horrified jury.

Tina, the youngest of the Zein's seven children and the only daughter remaining at home, had clashed constantly with her parents and siblings. They strongly disapproved of her playing soccer and tennis on high school teams and of being on the cheerleading squad. Her job at a fast-food restaurant infuriated them, and when Tina went to her junior prom, her family followed her and forcibly brought her home.

Tina's mother is Roman Catholic; the rest of the Isa family is Muslim. None had assimilated into American culture like Tina. During their parents' murder trial, her sisters blamed Tina for her own murder, claiming that she had long brought shame to the family and that the parents had just done their duty. At their trial, Tina's parents showed no remorse. Sentenced to die by lethal injection, Maria Isa told the judge, "My daughter was very disrespectful and rebellious. We should not have to pay with our lives for something she did."

After Zein and Maria Isa were sentenced to death, Nocolas Gavrielides, who was born and raised in Jerusalem and is now an anthropology professor at the State University of New York, testified that the way Tina lived had offended her father's sense of honor. The parents were especially concerned that Tina would not remain a virgin and thus be unable to marry a relative of one of their sons-in-law. "Everyone growing up in the Middle East knows that being killed is a possible consequence of dishonoring the family," said Professor Gavrielides.

But others disagree, including Victor Le Vine, professor of Jewish and Near Eastern Studies at Washington University in St. Louis. "This is certainly aberrant behavior," he said. "Palestinians and other Arab refugees in the United States would regard it with horror."

In April 1985 the residents of Fresno, California, were confronted with a less shocking, but in some ways similar incident. Having decided that it was time to marry, a young Hmong refugee named Kong Moua went to a local college campus along with a group of friends and forced the girl he had selected as his mate to his house. He then had sex with her.

In the Hmong culture, Kong Moua had performed *zij poj niam*, marriage by capture. While this method of obtaining a marriage partner is not the only, or even the most frequent, way of marrying among traditional Hmong, neither is it a rare occurrence. Universal to Hmong courtship is the idea that men appear strong, women resistant and virtuous.

The apparent sincerity of Kong Moua presented a dilemma to the judge who heard his case. Under the United States legal system, Kong Moua had committed two crimes: kidnap and rape. Given Moua's cultural background, however, the judge felt uncomfortable simply applying American law. In an attempt to balance matters, he allowed Moua to plead to a lesser charge of false imprisonment, thus giving the court the leeway "to get into all these cultural issues and try to tailor a sentence that will fulfill both our needs and the Hmong needs." Moua was ordered to pay $1,000 to the girl's family and serve a ninety-day jail term.

What is the proper reaction when cultures clash? When the norms of the culture in which people were raised violate the norms of their host society, what should the proper reaction be? It is obvious that the United States cannot allow murder and rape just because of where a person was raised. But should the full force of the law be applied in such cases? If not, how can we justify two types of application?

Source: Based on Treen, Bell, and McGuire 1992; *New York Times*, October 28, 1991; and Sherman 1988. From James M. Henslin, *Sociology: A Down-To-Earth Approach* (New York: Allyn and Bacon, 1993). Copyright ©1993 by Allyn and Bacon. Reprinted by permission.

_____ 1. Tina's mother is Roman Catholic; the rest of the Isa family is Muslim.

_____ 2. During her parents' murder trial, her sisters blamed Tina for her own murder, claiming that she had brought shame to the family and that the parents had just done their duty.

_____ 3. Her mother, Maria, held Tina down as Zein ended his daughter's life.

_____ 4. Sentenced to die by lethal injection, Maria Isa told the judge, "My daughter was very disrespectful and rebellious."

_____ 5. "We should not have to pay with our lives for something she did."

_____ 6. "Everyone growing up in the Middle East knows that being killed is a possible consequence of dishonoring the family," said Professor Gavrielides.

_____ 7. "Palestinians and other Arab refugees in the United States would regard it with horror."

_____ 8. Universal to Hmong courtship is the idea that men appear strong, women resistant and virtuous.

_____ 9. Kong Moua had committed two crimes: kidnap and rape.

_____ 10. It is obvious that the United States cannot allow murder and rape just because of where a person was raised.

Critical Reading

Once you have learned to distinguish fact from opinion you are on your way to becoming a true critical reader. Three other critical reading skills you need to learn are

- Recognizing emotive language.
- Recognizing bias.
- Evaluating sources of information.

You already know a good deal about these three skills because in your daily reading through the years you have had many occasions to use them, consciously or not. Make sure now that you are aware of each and ready to spot examples in your reading.

Emotive Language

Many words that we use every day are straightforward; they carry little or no emotional overtones. Words such as *reading, teacher,* or *student* are not, for most readers, emotionally charged. Of course, if a person has had great trouble learning to read, hated (or esteemed) a particular teacher, or been an especially good or poor student, these words may trigger some emotional response. Many other words, such as *bombing, abortion*, or *love,* trigger some kind of emotional response in most readers.

Such *emotive* words work positively and negatively. Words such as *mother, baby*, or *freedom* generally carry positive responses for most readers, and words such as *murder, rape*, or *hate* tend to carry negative emotional overtones.

Most writers know all this. Poets, for example, choose words that carry exactly the kinds of emotional overtones that are needed to express and/or arouse certain emotions. Writers of novels or love letters use emotive language, sometimes with great skill. However, advertisers and propagandists know all about emotive language, too. Cigarette advertisers and political commentators understand the value of arousing certain emotions in readers and carefully craft their writing to achieve the effects they want.

One set of examples may make this clear. Your friend may be overweight. *Overweight* is a fairly neutral word to describe his condition. However, because he is your friend, you may refer to him as *chubby* or *plump*. Others, less friendly, may call him *fat* or *gross*. An underweight friend may be referred to positively as *slim* or *slender,* or negatively, as *skinny* or *scrawny*. Poets and advertisers, both, are able to use words like these in ways to make readers respond positively or negatively to the subjects they write about.

EXERCISE 7.9

Directions: Try out your skill in detecting emotive language by sorting out these words and phrases. Some are clearly favorable; some are unfavorable; some are neutral. Label each F, U, or N.

1. go-getter salesman _____

energetic salesman _____

high-pressure salesman _____

2. outmoded _____

old _____

time-tested _____

3. old _____

venerable _____

antiquated _____

4. gathering _____

crowd _____

mob _____

5. strong man _____

dictator _____

absolute ruler _____

Biased Language

Writers sometimes use emotive words to bias readers. They deliberately select words that have positive or negative emotional overtones in order to make readers feel one way or another about their subjects and ideas. Here are two examples:

Sean walked into the garage and took the bike.

Sean sneaked into the garage and stole the bike.

The City Hall official courageously maintained his innocence.

The City Hall flunky refused to admit his guilt.

These are simple examples and easy for most readers to detect. Most college readers will realize that *walk* is a neutral word but *sneaked* carries emotional overtones. Most will see the difference between "courageously maintained" and "refused to admit." However, some biased language is so carefully crafted that readers require a good deal of care. Newspaper editorials, political commentary, and most printed advertisements are written by highly skilled professionals who have learned to use language to bias readers. Here are two examples from a popular weekly news magazine.

When Democrats ran the House, smoking tended to be frowned upon in the Health and Environment subcommittee office; now congressional aides gleefully flick their ashes into a glass ashtray placed atop the previous chairman's picture.

One senator who once tried to ban smoking now must make his way to his office past aides lighting up with impunity in the hallways.

The writer seems to be reporting her observations, but, unless readers are *critical* readers, they may not pick up the bias underlying the article. Based on key words and phrases (such as "gleefully flick" or "with impunity"), uncritical readers are apt to make inferences about Republicans that may not be accurate.

Try out your skill in detecting bias by "neutralizing" a newspaper or magazine advertisement. You know that the material has been deliberately slanted in favor of the product. It contains words emotionally charged in favor of the product and also includes more opinions than facts. As a quick check on your critical reading ability, rewrite the advertisement deleting all opinions and substituting neutral words for all positive or negative emotive words.

Evaluating Sources

Another key critical reading skill is evaluating sources. Uncritical readers seem to believe almost anything; critical readers want to know the sources of the information in the material. For example, an uncritical reader will be satisfied with "A prominent historian says . . ." A critical reader wants to know who the historian is. Phrases such as "statistics prove" or "science demonstrates" are not enough for critical readers who insist upon knowing exactly where the information comes from and the date of the original source.

Some sources of information are certainly better than others. Critical readers always keep such questions as the following in their minds as they read:

1. What are the writer's qualifications?
2. Has he or she wide experience in the field?
3. Why is the writer writing this?
4. Is there any reason to think the writer is biased?
5. Are opinions supported by facts?
6. Are there emotive words and phrases?
7. Could the writer have a hidden reason for writing?
8. Where can I find other points of view?

Check your own skill in evaluating sources by selecting a page from a popular magazine and reading it to discover whether the author bothers to report sources of information. Careful authors mention sources—books, people interviewed, other articles—in their paragraphs, in footnotes, or in a section at the end (sometimes called "References"). When no sources are noted, you should be wary. When sources are mentioned, you need to evaluate them by asking yourself questions such as those given above.

Chapter Excerpt 7.1

Directions: After reading this excerpt, taken from a college textbook, answer the questions that follow.

SOME BASIC TRUTHS ABOUT COMMUNICATION

Analysis of the communication process brings out three underlying truths that will help us understand its complexity.

Meanings Sent Are Not Always Received. The first underlying truth is that the meanings transmitted are not necessarily the meanings received. No two minds have identical filters. No two minds have identical storehouses of words, gestures, facial expressions, or any other symbol forms. And no two minds attach exactly the same meanings to all the symbols they have in common. Because of these differences in minds, errors in communication are bound to occur.

Meaning Is in the Mind. A second underlying truth is that meaning is in the mind—not in the words or other symbols used. How accurately one conveys meaning in symbols depends on how skillful one is in choosing symbols and how skillful the person receiving the symbols is in interpreting the meaning intended. Thus, you should look beyond the symbols used. You should consider the communication abilities of those with whom you want to communicate. When they receive your messages, they do not look at the symbols alone. They also look for the meanings they think you intended.

The Symbols of Communication Are Imperfect. The third underlying truth is that the symbols used in communication are imperfect. One reason for this is that the symbols we use, especially words, are at best crude substitutes for the real thing. For example, the word *man* can refer to billions of human beings of whom no two are alike. The word *dog* stands for any one of countless animals that vary sharply in size, shape, color, and every other visible aspect. The word *house* can refer equally well to structures ranging from shanties to palatial mansions. The verb *run* conveys only the most general part of an action; it ignores countless variations in speed, grace, and style. These illustrations are not the exception; they are the rule. Words simply cannot account for the infinite variations of reality.

Communication is also imperfect because communications vary in their ability to convey thoughts. Some find it very difficult to select symbols that express their simplest thoughts. Variations in ability to communicate obviously lead to variations in the precision with which thoughts are expressed.

Communications across cultures is especially imperfect, for often there are no equivalent words in other cultures. For example, usually there is no precise translation for our jargon in other cultures. Words like *condo, computer virus,* and *yuppie* are not likely to have equivalents in every other culture. Similarly, other cultures have specialized words unique and necessary to them that we do not have. For instance, the Eskimos have many words for *snow,* each describing a unique type. Obviously, such distinctions are vital to their existence. We can get along very well with one word.

Although the foregoing comments bring to light difficulties, complexities, and limitations of communications, on the whole we human beings do a fairly good job of communicating. Still, miscommunication often occurs. And people who attach precise meanings to every word, who believe that meanings intended are meanings received, and who are not able to select symbols well are likely to experience more than their share.

Source: Raymond V. Lasiker, John D. Petit, Jr., and Marie E. Flatley, *Basic Business Communication*, 6th ed. (Burr Ridge, Ill.: Richard D. Irwin, 1993). Copyright © 1993 by Richard D. Irwin. All rights reserved. Reprinted by permission.

1. Using context clues, define **infinite** in paragraph 3 _____

2. Define **variations** from paragraph 4 _____

3. Define **distinctions** from paragraph 6 _____

4. What is the main idea of this excerpt? _____

5. What is the main idea of paragraph 5? _____

Chapter 7 Fact and Opinion **213**

6. What are the major and minor details in paragraph 5?

   1. Major detail _____

      a. Minor detail _____

      b Minor detail _____

      c. Minor detail _____

   2. Major detail _____

      a. Minor detail _____

      b. Minor detail _____

7. What three signal words are used in this excerpt to indicate the pattern of organization?

   a. _____

   b. _____

   c. _____

8. What is the pattern of organization in this excerpt? _____

   _____

9. Indicate whether the following statement is a fact, opinion, or both.

   Paragraph 2 _____ You should consider the communication abilities of those with whom you want to communicate.

10. Indicate whether the following statement is a fact, opinion, or both.

    Paragraph 5 _____ Similarly, other cultures have specialized words unique and necessary to them that we do not have.

Related Study Skills #7: Reviewing

Regularly, you have to demonstrate—on tests!—that you understand and remember what you read in your college textbooks. You not only need to read the assigned chapters but you need to review them for midterm and final examinations.

   To help you review more effectively, here are some suggestions for successful review.

   1. Select what is important. Go through your notes before exams and star the points that you think are basic to the course. Compare your starred items with those of other students. Do you agree? If not, why not? It may be wise to check with your instructor.

2. Review by predicting test questions. One way to do this is to turn sentences in your notes and in the book into questions. Main idea sentences often appear on exams as questions.

3. Reorganize your material. You can sharpen your mind by rearranging your notes in a different manner. For example, if your history notes are arranged in time sequence, try reorganizing them under idea headings, by cause and effect, or by key terms. By shaking your mind up, you make the material stand out.

4. Change your point of view. If you have approached the material from the memorizing angle, now try looking at it from the point of view of application. Note all the ways a person might use the ideas and information. You provide yourself with another way to remember.

5. Establish personal relationships. Go through your notes and write down a personal association with names, dates, terms, ideas, and so on. Be fanciful; don't be afraid to be off-beat or bizarre. You'll find that you may be able to remember data that would otherwise have escaped you.

6. Overlearn. Many students stop when they feel they have mastery, but this is not always sensible. Most successful students note that it's best to overlearn: review, review, review.

Remember, too, that an excellent way to learn difficult material is to teach it to someone else. If you are still not sure of an important concept, try explaining it to another student or a friend. If no one is available, pretend: imagine that you are the instructor and explain the concept to a class. You can make a simple 10-item test to administer to your imaginary class, take it yourself, and check the answers. You'll find that many difficult ideas are understood and remembered by "teaching."

Making the Connection

Reflection Entry #7

Directions: After taking a few moments to reflect on the information in this chapter, write an essay summarizing what you have learned about facts and opinions and how you will apply that knowledge to your textbook reading assignments.

_____

_____

_____

_____

_____

CHAPTER EIGHT

Inferences

Of all our thought processes, inferencing seems to be the most important. It is the first we learn and the basis for most others. No one teaches us how to make an inference—infants can do it—but we make inferences all day long, about all aspects of our lives.

What is an inference? As you will learn in this chapter, it is a guess about the unknown based upon the known. You see a friend rush by at 10:03 A.M. so you *infer* that she's late for a 10 o'clock class. You see a motorist stopped by the side of the road tightening the lug nuts on a wheel, so you infer he has had a flat tire. You see another friend holding a test paper and smiling, so you infer he did well on an examination. In each instance, you are making guesses about what you don't really know based upon certain observations that seem true.

Why study inferences if everybody is constantly making them? Some answers are implied in the examples. The first friend my have forgotten a dentist appointment and may be rushing not to class but to her dentist's office. The motorist may not have had a flat tire but felt a wheel wobble and decided to stop and make sure it was secure. The other friend may have actually done poorly on the test but learned that he had won the lottery! In other words, our guesses may not always be accurate.

Another reason to study inferences is that we make them based on knowledge. You have to have knowledge of college class schedules, car problems, and typical student responses to examinations to make the inferences about lateness, flat tires, and test success. Accurate inferences are based upon the past experiences of inference makers. You need to study the process in order to better distinguish between situations in which you can make valid inferences and those in which you cannot.

What does inferencing have to do with reading college textbooks? The authors of college textbooks make inferences on every page, in every paragraph, in every sentence. To be a successful reader you need to be aware of inferences and cautious about accepting them. Sometimes the inferences found in your books make sense; sometimes they may be inaccurate.

A value in learning about inferences is that you become a better *thinker*. You carry your knowledge of inference making into other aspects of your life and tend to think more sharply and more carefully. This chapter helps you become a better reader and a more effective thinker.

Before you read this chapter, take the inference survey, which will help you determine your strengths and weaknesses for making inferenes.

Inference Survey

	Never	Sometimes	Always
1. I watch for clues that will help me make a logical inference.	_____	_____	_____
2. I carefully consider the facts before I make an inference.	_____	_____	_____
3. I make sure that I understand the literal meaning before I try to make an inference.	_____	_____	_____
4. I look for details that will help me make a logical inference.	_____	_____	_____
5. I can support the inferences I make.	_____	_____	_____
6. I recognize that not all inferences are logical.	_____	_____	_____
7. I recognize that there can be more than one logical or correct inference.	_____	_____	_____
8. I use my own experience and background when making an inference.	_____	_____	_____
9. I read between the lines when I read textbook assignments.	_____	_____	_____
10. When I read, I am aware that an inference is not directly stated.	_____	_____	_____

Plan of the Chapter

This chapter has two goals. The first is to make you more aware of your own inference-making process so that you can make better inferences and also recognize the inferences of others. The second is to sharpen your ability to detect inferences in reading, especially your textbook reading. The achievement of these goals—even their partial achievement—will make you a better thinker. Most sloppy thinking, as you'll see, is the result of careless inferencing; people make inferences and act upon them, forgetting that they may be wildly out of line.

The chapter includes a personal Survey, some study tips, several exercises, and an end-of-chapter excerpt from an actual textbook. Remember, as you read this chapter that, although you have been an inference maker since infancy, you can refine and sharpen this important thinking skill and, in the process, make yourself not only a better thinker but a more successful reader.

Inferences in Daily Life

Before examining inferences in textbook reading, let's look at ways in which we all make inferences in our daily lives. From early childhood on, we have been making inferences. There is actually some research that shows infants making valid inferences. One famous study examined the eye movements of babies only a few months old and found that they looked at mother entering the room, at the bottle in their hand, and, then, opened their mouths. Researchers say that these infants took the evidence (mother and bottle) and made the inference that it was time to eat!

People around us constantly voice their inferences—sometimes silly ones. A neighbor bought a Mercedes-Benz; therefore, the neighbor must have a great deal of money. Another staggered to his door; therefore, he must have been drinking. A friend flunked an exam; she hadn't studied. Another regularly loses weight and regains it; he has no will power. As we know, these inferences may or may not be reasonable, but we all guide our thinking and behaviors by the inferences we make each day.

Some of us make inferences as an intrinsic part of our work. Doctors diagnose by making inferences; automotive mechanics figure out what's wrong with engines by inferencing. One good example of the professional inference maker is the detective. The legendary detective from the Arthur Conan Doyle stories, Sherlock Holmes, provides countless instances of clever inference making. He would note three or four features of a person and note occupations, hobbies, personality traits, or education. A style of shoe, pronunciation of a word, or reference to the past, and Holmes was off!

Inferences are related to facts and opinions (see Chapter 7). An observation (whether true or false) that may be verified is considered a *fact*. An expression of one's feelings about the observation is an *opinion*. A guess about the facts in an *inference*. For example, a stranger entered our classroom, looked out the window, and make three statements: (1) "There are black clouds in the sky," (2) "This part of the country has awful weather," and (3) "It will rain soon." His first statement if factual: we can look out the window and confirm or deny his observation that there are black clouds in the sky. His second statement is his opinion; we may not share it and, in fact, may like the weather in our area. The third statement is clearly an inference. It is his guess, in this case, a prediction, that it will rain, and remember, his inference is only as good as his experience of weather in this part of the country (if he recently flew in from another continent his "guess" probably will not prove accurate).

EXERCISE 8.1

Directions: Here are five sets of statements. Read each and label it F (for Fact), O (for Opinion), or I (for Inference).

1. I always received and A in mathematics. _____

   I will receive an A in College Algebra. _____

   I received As through high school in math. _____

   I am a superb math student. _____

2. Liz refused to go to the dance with me. _____

   Jan said she was busy when I asked her to go. _____

   I'll never get a date for the dance. _____

   I am not popular with women. _____

3. Senator Kane voted against tax reform. _____

   He sends his children to private schools. _____

   He will never be elected president. _____

   He isn't a good American. _____

4. I am in superb physical condition. _____

   I have never been in a hospital in my life. _____

   When I was a kid, I did have the measles. _____

   I don't need health insurance. _____

5. It was over 90 degrees yesterday. _____

   It rained all day today. _____

   The weather will be terrible tomorrow. _____

   This state has awful weather. _____

VIGNETTE 1

One of the most interesting things I learned in last semester's reading class was that little kids made inferences! I had been misled. I remember years ago learning, probably in high school, that inferencing was a "higher-level" reading skill. I assumed all this time that it was something you studied in college. Now I've been watching my own kids. And they make inferences all the time. After dinner, they watch TV but know that at seven they are supposed to do homework for an hour. Once, I'd have to speak to them. Remind them in no uncertain terms. Now I give them "The Look."

One way to enhance your ability as a inference maker and inference spotter is to remember that inferences are often predictions. When a person says, "It will rain soon," she has made an inference. It is a prediction in this case, but it is clearly a guess based upon factual evidence of some kind. When an author writes that "economic indicators suggest diminishing financial gains," he, too, although less obviously, is making in inference, a prediction based upon some evidence. When a textbook author writes: "Intermediaries, or middlemen, are sources of unnecessary costs," and then specifies such costs for some manufactured item, you may infer that the elimination of middlemen will lower costs for consumers. If the author says, "Buying directly from a factory outlet will save consumers money," he makes another inference, in this case a clear-cut prediction. You know from your study about inferences that such predictions, like all inferences, are only as good as the inference maker's knowledge of the field and remain educated guesses.

They turn the TV off and get out the books. They make an inference that I'm not going to speak. That's a silly example, maybe, but I have been aware of the thousands of times each day that children do make inferences about school, family schedules, personal relations, friends, and everything else.

Maureen O'D.

VIGNETTE 2

The most important thing I've learned in college so far is that predictions are inferences. That may sound like an overstatement of some kind but it's true. Always I took predictions at their word. You know, they were statements about the future and should be heeded. Predictions I heard on the radio or TV. Predictions I read in the papers or magazines. Now, I am, to say the least, profoundly skeptical! A prediction, I now realize, is someone talking (or writing). That person has taken observations and made a guess or inference about what's going to happen, and that person may or may not be correct. Actually, it's been good for me to know that no one really can tell what's going to happen. They're guessing just as I am.

Magnus M.

Understanding Inferences

When a reader makes an inference, he or she is making an educated guess or prediction about something that in unknown based on the facts that are given. This is a very useful skill since authors do not always directly say what they want you to know about a particular point or idea. It is up to you to be able to correctly guess what the points or ideas are that an author is trying to get across.

So why to authors not directly state what they want you to know? There are a few reasons why they do not. The first reason is that they do not always have enough space to give you all the information that is important to their reason for writing. Therefore, they expect you to be able to make inferences about what is missing. Another reason that authors do not state everything is that doing so might distract you from the more important points and thus break your concentration. Third, authors tend to leave out information that they feel you may already know.

For these reasons, as well as others, you need to learn about and enhance your knowledge of making inferences.

Making an Inference

Here are several guidelines to help you with inferencing:

1. Pay attention to the literal meaning.
2. Be mindful of details.
3. Be aware of all the facts.
4. Look for clues that are provided by the author.
5. Make sure that you can support your inference.

Example

A stranger came int our chemistry lab, looked at the professor, and said, "You are partly responsible for the smog and air pollution in our city." He looked at our class and said, "Be responsible, think of the environment." Then he quickly left the lab.

The most logical information based on the facts given is:

a. The stranger is an unbalanced person.

b. The stranger is concerned about the environment.

c. The stranger enjoys interrupting classes.

We have no evidence that the stranger likes to interrupt classes, nor do we have any evidence about the stranger's mental soundness. Therefore, based on the facts that are given, we can only infer that the stranger is concerned with the environment.

EXERCISE 8.2

Directions: Read each of the following statements and then circle the most logical inference based on the facts given. Explain your answers on the lines that follow.

1. The student flunked his psychology test.

    a. The test was too hard.

    b. He did not have enough time to finish it.

    (c.) He probably did not study for it.

    d. The instructor graded it unfairly.

    _____
    _____
    _____
    _____

2. Betty always studies in the library.

    a. It's too noisy to study at home.

    b. She meets her friends there.

    c. She likes being around people.

    (d.) She enjoys studying there.

    _____
    _____

3. Inside the dorm room there were pizza boxes, soda cans, and ice cartons.

   (a.) The occupants like pizza, soda, and ice cream.

   b. The occupants had just eaten.

   c. The occupants are slobs.

   d. The occupants had a party.

4. Four professors in academic gowns and caps were walking toward the campus.

   a. They were going to graduation ceremonies.

   (b.) The professors were going to an academic event.

   c. There is a new dress code for faculty.

   d. Their students wanted to see them in academic robes.

5. The student did not get back to her dorm until 3:00 AM.

   a. Her friend's car broke down.

   b. She was on an awesome date.

   c. She didn't know what time it was.

   (d.) Something made her get back late.

6. Harry's dorm room walls are covered with posters of motorcycles.

   a. Harry is a biker.

   (b.) Harry like posters of motorcycles.

   c. Harry owns a motorcycle.

   d. Harry works part-time selling motorcycles.

7. Mike ordered a soda while his friends ordered beer.

   (a.) Mike felt like having soda.

   b. Mike has a drinking problem.

   c. Mike does not drink.

   d. Mike is underage.

8. Kara takes three college courses.

   a. Kara is not smart enough to take four.

   b. She does not have enough money to take four.

   (c.) She probably is a part-time student.

   d. Kara could not decide on a fourth course.

9. The student was wearing a blue and white sweater.

   a. They are the school colors.

   b. It was wear-blue-and-white day.

   c. The sweater was a present.

   (d.) The student likes those colors.

10. Amy always wears sneakers to class.

    a. Amy has problems with her feet.

    b. The classroom floors are always slippery.

    (c.) Amy feels comfortable in sneakers.

    d. Shoes make too much noise.

EXERCISE 8.3

Directions: Complete the following statements. Make sure that the completed statements are logical and based on experience and the facts given.

1. We can infer from the negative response to the professor's lecture that the class _was boring_

2. We can infer from the lack of students that this particular class _is boring_

3. We can infer from the speaker's stuttering, fast pace, and constant fidgeting that _he was nervous._

4. We can infer from the smile on the professor's face that the class test papers were _very good._

5. We can infer from the sirens and massive traffic jam that _there was a wreck._

6. We can infer from the pile of library books, textbooks, and notebooks on the desk that the student was _doing a term paper._

7. We can infer from the girl's sandals, shorts, halter top, and glass of lemonade in the hand that _it was hot._

8. We can infer from all the cars, loud music, and complaining neighbors that _there was a party._

Chapter 8 Inferences 227

9. We can infer from the student's puzzled expression and inability to answer the question that _____ the student didn't know the answer.

10. We can infer from the woman's Mercedes-Benz, mink coat, and lavish jewelry that she is _____ rich.

EXERCISE 8.4

Directions: Remember, there can be more than one logical inference made based on the information given. Go back over the previous exercise and make another inference for each set of facts given.

1.

2.

3.

4.

228 Chapter 8 Inferences

5. _____
_____
_____
_____

6. _____
_____
_____
_____

7. _____
_____
_____
_____

8. _____
_____
_____
_____

9. _____
_____
_____
_____

10. _____
_____
_____
_____

Inferences in Reading

Because so much of your time as a college student is spent reading, you need to become sensitive to the inferences authors use in books. When inferences are in print—especially in a college textbook—we sometimes become less cautious, forgetting that inferences may be dangerous.

One textbook, for example, describes the famous Hawthorne Studies, noting that (1) productivity at the plant of Western Electric in Hawthorne, Illinois, increased when light was increased in work areas, (2) productivity increased when light was held constant or diminished, and (3) workers were regularly consulted about the changes. Researchers decided that increased productivity was not the result of changes in lighting arrangements but of the regular consulting. Evidently, they said, it is important that questioning and interviewing the workers affected attitudes more than the physical arrangements. This study has been described in many college textbooks, but students are not always aware of the distinctions between the factual information provided (as in 1, 2, and 3 above) and the inferences drawn by the researchers.

To get the most from your textbook reading, you need to be aware always of the inferences, or educated guesses based on the facts.

EXERCISE 8.5

Directions: After reading the paragraphs, answer the questions that follow:

1. He appeared before the voters as a man of the people. He wore ill-fitting black suits and a stove-pipe hat—repository for letters, bills, scribbled notes, and other scraps—that exaggerated his great height. He presented a worn rumpled appearance, partly because he traveled from place to place on day coaches, accompanied by only a few advisers. When local supporters came to meet him at the station, he preferred to walk with them through the streets to the scene of the debate.

Who is being discussed in this paragraph? _____

On what facts do you base your inference? _____

2. Perhaps one of the greatest benefits of weight training is that is may help prolong independence in older adults. As we age, we often lose our ability to function independently because we have lost the basic strength to climb stairs, carry groceries, get up after a fall, or even stand up. Sometimes injury or illness leads to a period of bedrest and/or reduced activity, which precipitates a sharp decline in physical fitness. Recent studies have provided a dramatic illustration of the important contributions weight training can make to the quality of life in very old people. Men and women in their eighties and nineties who participated in a weight training program made substantial gains in muscle strength, with strength increases of 30 percent in some cases. This improvement in strength significantly increased the ability of these elders to perform daily tasks. In one case, a woman was able to walk without a cane for the first time in many years.

What is the author' opinion of weight training for the elderly? _____

On what facts do you base your inference? _____

3. Addiction means having more than a strong desire for something. The experience of addiction is a negative one that distorts reality and limits participation in life. Addiction is marked by gradual reduction in awareness, a decline in self-esteem, and decreased involvement with other people and activities. Although people initially become addicted to something because it feels good, addiction is not pleasurable once the initial "high" has passed, and addicted people usually do not feel good most of the time, which results in the vicious cycle of increased cravings and abuse.

How does the author feel about addiction? _____

On what facts do you base your inference? _____

4. He was determined to change the direction in which the nation was moving. He hoped to revitalize the economy and extend the influence of the United States abroad. His inaugural address was a call for commitment: "Ask not what your country can do for you," he said. "Ask what you can do for your country." But he was neither Woodrow Wilson nor a Franklin Roosevelt when it came to bending Congress to his will. Perhaps he was too amiable, too diffident and conciliatory in his approach. A coalition of Republicans and conservative southern Democrats resisted his plans for federal aid to education, for urban renewal, for a higher minimum wage, for medical care for the aged.

Who is being discussed in this paragraph? _____

On what facts do you base your inference? _____

5. You might try an experiment for yourself. Buy an attractive but inexpensive tie and put it in a very attractive box from an exclusive store. Then buy a similar tie from an exclusive store and put it in a box from an inexpensive discount store. Tell your friends that you can't decide which tie is better and ask them to choose. If past experience is any guide, most will choose the inexpensive tie in the more expensive box. Laboratory experiments support these suggestions. The concept that explains such behavior is that people often cannot determine the value of products by physical inspection; they therefore turn to other indicators of quality such as label, packaging, brand names, and price. A higher-priced, expensively packaged item is usually perceived as better regardless or its actual physical qualities.

What can you infer about products and consumers? _____

Chapter 8 Inferences **231**

On what facts do you base your inference? _____

_____

_____

_____

EXERCISE 8.6

Directions: Using current textbook reading assignments, find five paragraphs or passages and copy them down on the lines provided. Then for each paragraph or passage, make three inferences base on the stated facts.

1. _____

_____

_____

_____

_____

_____

_____

_____

_____

_____

_____

1st inference _____

_____

_____

2nd inference _____

_____

_____

3rd inference _____

_____

2.

1st inference

2nd inference

3rd inference

3.

1st inference

2nd inference

3rd inference

4.

1st inference _____

2nd inference _____

3rd inference _____

5. _____

1st inference _____

_____

_____

_____

2nd inference _____

_____

_____

_____

3rd inference _____

_____

_____

_____

EXERCISE 8.7

To show that you can identify inferences in textbooks, read the following paragraph from a popular textbook on marketing (*Marketing: Creating Value for Consumers*, by G. A. Churchill, Jr. and J. P. Peter, Irwin, 1995). It is a well-organized paragraph with much valuable information. However, it contains at least one inference.

BUYER PERCEPTIONS

To position a product, marketers need to know how consumers or organizational buyers in its target market perceive products in that category. After sales growth of its cream soda slowed, A&W Brands conducted research to learn why. The results showed that consumers didn't know what flavor cream soda was. They tended to think of it being related to root beer.

Based on what they have learned about their target markets' perceptions, marketers determine whether they must make changes to satisfy their target markets. They may identify a need for a new type of product or for modifications to an existing product. They may learn that members of the target market don't know (or don't believe) that the organization's product actually meets the need it was positioned to meet. In that case, the problem is not with the product, but with other elements of the marketing mix.

In the case of A&W, the company saw the need for several changes to the marketing mix for its cream soda. A&W added vanilla to strengthen its taste, began running ads that stress the product's "cold, sparkling, vanilla taste," and redesigned the packaging to better differentiate the cream soda from A&W root beer. In addition, the company saw these efforts to educate consumers as an opportunity to broaden its target market to attract 12- to 24-year-olds.

To use another example, the prime customers for Turtle Wax, Inc., which makes car-care products, are men aged 18 to 35, followed by women in the same age group. Research shows that people in this age group are strongly concerned about the environment. Thus, if the company decides to position itself on the basis of being the environmentally responsible alternative, these consumers should be receptive to Turtle Wax's 20-year history of selling only biodegradable products packaged in recyclable containers.

Source: Peter Churchill, Jr., *Marketing: Creating Value for Customers* (Burr Ridge, Ill.: Richard D. Irwin, 1995). Copyright © 1995 by Richard D. Irwin. All rights reserved. Reprinted by permission.

What is the inference? _____

_____

_____

EXERCISE 8.8

Directions: After reading the following selection, complete the exercise by placing a check beside each statement that could be a possible inference.

THE ILLEGAL TRAVEL GUIDE

Manuel was a drinking buddy of Jose's, a man I had met on an earlier trip to Mexico. At forty-five, Manuel can best be described as friendly, outgoing, and enterprising.

Manuel lived in the United States for seven years and speaks fluent English. Preferring his home town in Colima, Mexico, where he can pal around with his childhood friends, Manuel always seemed to have money and free time.

When Manuel invited me to go on a business trip with him, I quickly accepted. I never could figure out how Manuel made his living and how he was able to afford a car—a luxury that none of his friends had. As we traveled from one remote village to another,

> You seldom hear people actually say that they *infer* something. It may be that the word has too formal a ring to it. However, people often signal their inferences by using one of the many synonyms for the word. They tell you that they "reckon" or "surmise." They'll say, "My guess is so-and-so" or "I assume such-and-such." The language seems to have many synonyms for infer, an indication of the importance of this mental process.
>
> One dictionary gives several options for speakers who, for some reason, want to avoid *infer: guess, reckon, surmise, assume, presume, speculate,* and *construe.* It also gives as synonyms for *inference* such words as *theory, hypothesis,* and *conjecture.* (It also notes that *imply* is quite different! The speaker or writer *implies* something, often deliberately. Here's an example: Although the instructor said there'd be no test right away, he pointed out that college regulations mandated an examination before midterm. He is *implying* that there will, indeed, be an exam. An inference, on the other hand, is an activity performed by listeners and readers. The students in class who hear him say this make the inference that there will be an exam!)
>
> To sharpen your understanding of inferences, keep a checklist of instances you note in which writers (or speakers) actually signal their inference making by saying something like "My assumption is that there will be an exam."

Manuel would gather a crowd and sell used clothing that he had heaped in the back of his older-model Ford station wagon.

While chickens ran in and out of the dirt-floored, thatched-roof hut, Manuel spoke in whispers to a slender man of about twenty-three. The sense of poverty was overwhelming. Juan, as his name turned out to be, had a partial grade school education. He also had a wife, four hungry children under the age of five—and two pigs, his main food supply. Although eager to work, he had no job—and no prospects of getting one, for there was simply no work available.

As we were drinking a Coke, the national beverage of the poor of Mexico, Manuel explained to me that he was not only selling clothing—he was also lining up migrants to the United States. For $200 he would take a man to the border and introduce him to a "wolf," who, for another $200 would surreptitiously make a night crossing into the promised land.

When I saw the hope in Juan's face, I knew nothing would stop him. He was borrowing every cent he could from every relative to get the $400 together. He would make the trip although he risked losing everything if apprehended—for wealth beckoned on the other side. He personally knew people who had been there and spoke in glowing terms of its opportunities.

Looking up from the children playing on the dirt floor with the chickens pecking about them, I saw a man who loved his family and was willing to suffer their enforced absence, as well as the uncertainties of a foreign culture whose language he did not know, in order to make the desperate try for a better life.

Juan handed me something from his billfold, and I looked at it curiously. I felt tears as I saw the tenderness with which he handled this piece of paper—his passport to opportunity—a social security card made out in his name, sent by a friend who had already made the trip and who was waiting for Juan.

It was then that I knew that the thousands of Manuels scurrying about the face of Mexico and the millions of Juans they were transporting could never be stopped—for the United States held their only dream of a better life.

Source: James M. Henslin, *Sociology: A Down-To-Earth Approach* (New York: Allyn and Bacon, 1993). Copyright © 1993 by Allyn and Bacon. Reprinted by permission.

_____ 1. Manuel and Jose are good friends.

_____ 2. Manuel went to school in the United States.

_____ 3. Manuel liked living in the United States.

_____ 4. Manuel is a very important man in his country.

_____ 5. Juan is very poor.

_____ 6. Juan's relatives are rich.

_____ 7. Juan will make a lot of money in the United States.

_____ 8. Juan will learn to speak English.

_____ 9. Juan could get caught.

_____ 10. Poor Mexicans prefer Coca-Cola to beer.

EXERCISE 8.9

Directions: After reading the following selection, complete the exercise by placing a check beside each statement that could be a possible inference. Make sure you can support your choices.

RACISM ON COLLEGE CAMPUSES

African-American students were upset, and white students didn't understand why. The economics professor had said, "Not many blacks take my class. It's too tough for them." When he was accused of racism, he denied that he had a racial bone in his body, saying that he had worked hard for thirty-two years to integrate students from different racial backgrounds. "What I said is the truth," he added. When African-American students went to the administration, the professor apologized.

At the fraternity party, the men did a vaudeville skit in which they painted their faces and hands black and sang "Mammy." "It's just good fun," the fraternity president said to his critics. The college administration ruled that blackface skits are within the students' right of free speech. Another fraternity held a slave auction to raise money for the poor. Females were "sold" to the highest bidder. The slaves had to walk their "masters" to class, carry their books, and stand in the lunch line for them. Each had SLAVE written on her forehead. When African-American students complained, the response was, "Don't make a big deal out of nothing. This is our annual fund-raising event for the poor. You're too sensitive."

The heat was on the university administration. A professor had written in his weekly column in the student newspaper that Puerto Rican students "traveled in packs" and spoke English only when they wanted to. When criticized, he replied that he had only written the truth, that it was time for minorities to be integrated into student life instead of remaining aloof.

When minority students went to the administration to demand that they "change the college environment," one of the trustees replied, "You should settle down and concentrate on your studies. I think that's the main reason your group isn't doing as well as the whites." The trustee later had to apologize.

The swastika scrawled on a wall, the burning of a cross in front of a predominantly African-American student dormitory, the use of racial slurs such as "nigger" and "kike," the mock hanging of a minority student—everyone knows that all these are blatant racism. But what about the specific events described above? One side, consisting of both minorities and whites, says that they are all racist. The other side defends them as nonracist. Both sides have adherents who say such events must be protected in the name of free speech.

What do you think? Are such incidents racist, and if so are they nevertheless defensible on the grounds of free speech? Should they be banned and the participants disciplined, or tolerated to preserve free speech? Are some minorities too sensitive? Are whites too insensitive? What should be done? Support your position by applying ideas from this chapter.

Source: James M. Henslin, *Sociology: A Down-To-Earth Approach* (New York: Allyn and Bacon, 1993). Copyright © 1993 by Allyn and Bacon. Reprinted by permission.

_____ 1. White students do not understand the background of African-Americans.

_____ 2. The economics professor has a problem with black students.

_____ 3. The fraternity president likes to imitate African-Americans.

_____ 4. The college administration believes in the right of free speech.

_____ 5. Female students like to portray slaves.

_____ 6. Minorities are outcasts on this campus.

_____ 7. The minority students do not concentrate on their studies.

_____ 8. One of the trustees is a racist.

_____ 9. The college environment on this campus is in need of change.

_____ 10. The minority and majority on this campus are indifferent to each other's feelings.

Textbook Chapter Excerpt 8.1: Final Review

Directions: After reading this excerpt, taken from a college textbook, answer the questions that follow.

WHY PEOPLE TAKE THE ENTREPRENEURIAL CHALLENGE

Today, more than 12 million Americans work for themselves. That's over twice the number recorded in 1970. Why have we experienced such and explosion of entrepreneurs in the past two decades? There are many reasons why people are willing to take the risks of starting a business. These reasons generally include the following:

Opportunity. Many immigrants do not have the necessary skills for working in today's complex organization. They *do* have the initiative and drive to work the long hours demanded by entrepreneurship. To them, the opportunity to share in the American dream is a tremendous lure. They are willing to sacrifice to see that their children have a chance for a good life. The same is true of many corporate managers who leave the security of the corporate life and try running businesses of their own.

Profit. Profit is only one reason to become an entrepreneur, but an important one. The second richest person in America is William Henry Gates III, the entrepreneur who founded Microsoft Corporation. Mr. Gates owns a Ferrari, a Porsche, and a Lexus. The richest person in America was Sam Walton, the entrepreneur who started Wal-Mart, though he was not listed as the richest person because he divided his riches among the rest of the family. The profit potential of entrepreneurship is fantastic. Tom Monaghan opened his first pizza store in Ypsilanti, Michigan, near the campus of Eastern Michigan University. He took a hunch that dormitory food probably had the same appeal as food he had eaten in an army mess hall. Later he ruled over Dominio's Pizza, the largest pizza delivery company in the world, and had a personal net worth of over $600 million.

Independence. Many entrepreneurs simply do not enjoy working for someone else. Many lawyers, for example, do not like the stress and demands of big law firms. Some have found more enjoyment and self-satisfaction in starting their own business.

Challenge. *Venture* magazine has concluded that entrepreneurs are excitement junkies who flourish on taking risks, but others disagree. Nancy Flexman and Thomas Scanlan wrote a book called *Running Your Own Business*. They contend that entrepreneurs take moderate, calculated risks; they are not just gambling. In general, though, entrepreneurs seek *achievement* more than *power.*

Source: William G. Nickels, James M. McHugh, and Susan McHugh, *Understanding Business*, 3rd. (Burr Ridge, Ill.: Richard D. Irwin, 1993). Copyright © 1993 by William G. Nickels. All rights reserved. Reprinted by permission.

1. entrepreneur means:
    a. Salesman for a business.
    b. Owner and operator of a business.
    c. Corporate lawyer.
2. The main idea of paragraph 5 is:
    a. Entrepreneurs like the challenge.
    b. Entrepreneurs do not gamble.
    c. Entrepreneurs want power.
3. One reason that people become entrepreneurs is:
    a. Happiness.
    b. Excitement.

c. Money.
4. According to this selection, Sam Walton was not listed as the richest man in America because:
   a. He did not have all his money in this country.
   b. He did not own as much as William Henry Gates III.
   c. He divided up his money among family.
5. The pattern of organization for this selection is:
   a. Cause and effect.
   b. Enumeration.
   c. Compare and contrast.
6. More people are becoming entrepreneurs. This is:
   a. Fact
   b. Opinion.
7. We can infer that being an entrepreneur is:
   a. Fun.
   b. Rewarding.
   c. Too difficult.
8. We can conclude that being an entrepreneur is:
   a. Very demanding.
   b. Takes a lot of money.
   c. For immigrants only.
9. Which of the following is the main point?
   a. There are many opportunities available.
   b. It is a definite challenge.
   c. It lets you be independent.
   d. There are many reasons for becoming an entrepreneur.
10. Summarize this selection in your own words.

_____

_____

_____

_____

_____

_____

_____

Related Study Skills #8: Memory Tricks

Memory tricks are aids that help you to remember information for later use. Why should you learn about these tricks? As a student, you are concerned about remembering information that might show up on quizzes and exams. Knowing some memory tricks and how to use them just might help you remember key information for your next quiz or exam. Memory tricks are also very useful for learning and remembering material that is not organized in a meaningful way. Two examples that come to mind are information found in textbooks and your class notes. Sometimes you read material or take notes on lectures that contain facts or ideas that do not seem to be organized in a meaningful way but still must be committed to memory. Knowing a few tricks can help you to get those facts and ideas into your memory so you can recall them when you need them.

Memory tricks (mnemonic devices, as they are also called) include nonsense words and phrases, words, phrases, sentences, rhymes, and anagrams (words or phrases formed by changing the order of the letters of another word of phrase). One of the most popular examples of a memory trick that uses one word to help you remember five words is based on the Great Lakes. Remembering the word HOMES should trigger the five names of the Great Lakes: Huron, Ontario, Michigan, Erie, and Superior. Another popular example uses a rhyme for remembering the number of days in the months of the year. Remember how it went? "Thirty days hath September, April, June, and November," and so on. A final example uses a phrase. Some mathematics students have trouble remembering the reciprocal of pi (0.318310). Rather than trying to remember seven numbers that have no organization, students recall the phrase "*Can* (3) *I* (1) *remember* (8) *the* (3) *reciprocal* (10)?" because the number of the letters in each word comes out to be the reciprocal of pi.

EXERCISE 8.10

Directions: Organize each of following groups of information by using the memory tricks described above.

1. Forms of business ownership (sole proprietorships, partnerships, corporations).

___

___

___

2. Types of bones (long bones, short bones, flat bones, irregular bones).

___

___

___

242 Chapter 8 Inferences

3. Kubler-Ross's stages of dying (denial, anger, negotiation, depression, acceptable).

_____
_____
_____

4. Maslow's hierarchy of needs (physiological needs, safety and security, love and belonging, esteem and self-esteem, self-actualization).

_____
_____
_____

5. Kohlberg's stages of moral development (punishment orientation, pleasure-seeking orientation, good boy/girl orientation, authority orientation, social-contract orientation, morality of individual principles).

_____
_____
_____

EXERCISE 8.11

Directions: Use your own class notes and textbooks to find information you need to memorize. Write what you need to memorize and which memory aid you are going to use to memorize it.

1. Information _____
_____
_____

Memory aid _____
_____
_____

2. Information _____
_____
_____

Memory aid _____
_____

3. Information _____

Memory aid _____

4. Information _____

Memory aid _____

5. Information _____

Memory aid _____

Making the Connection

Reflection Entry #8

Directions: After taking a few moments to reflect on the information in this chapter, write an essay summarizing what you have learned about inferences and how you will apply that knowledge to your textbook reading assignments.

CHAPTER NINE

Understanding Arguments

The reading we do each day ranges from the easy to the difficult. Newspapers, stories, and novels, for example, tend to be relatively easy to read: the writer's purpose and goal are apparent, the language is direct, the vocabulary is accessible, and most of the ideas are readily understood. Other kinds of reading material are not easy. Tax forms, legal documents, medical records, and so on, are apt to include difficult words, convoluted sentences, new information and ideas, and purposes and goals that elude readers.

On a scale of 1 to 10, textbooks probably are 5 and up. You can read most of them, but a few textbooks present difficulties. They, too, include words not yet in your vocabulary, involved sentence structures, and information and ideas still beyond your ready reach. However, the most difficult reading you are required to do is a special kind of reading, found not only in textbooks but often in newspapers, magazines, and other books—*argumentation*. Argumentation often includes unfamiliar words and highly sophisticated sentence structures; it also tends to aim for goals that are not apparent. And—it must be said—sometimes writers of argumentation *deliberately* use difficult words, convoluted sentences, obscure ideas, and disguised goals. They try to cloud up issues and make your reading difficult in order to win their argument!

Chapter Nine focuses on argumentation. It is designed to help you better understand the arguments you encounter in your reading, whether in textbooks or elsewhere. Can you spot the main issue? Are you able to easily identify the arguments supporting the issue? Are you aware of the arguments that are fallacious or irrelevant? Do you use all your critical reading skills when reading an argument? This chapter will sharpen the key skills you need when confronting a simple or sophisticated argument.

Before you read this chapter, take the argument survey. This survey will help you determine your strenghs and weaknesses for understanding arguments.

Argument Survey

	Never	Sometimes	Always
1. I identify the point of an argument.	___	___	___
2. I identify facts or ideas that support the point.	___	___	___

3. I identify the issue. _____ _____ _____
4. I determine the position, action, or idea the author is _____ _____ _____
   trying to get me to accept.
5. I evaluate the evidence the author provides. _____ _____ _____
6. I watch for the author's conclusions. _____ _____ _____
7. I look for words and phrases that signal a conclusion. _____ _____ _____
8. I can distinguish between a sound argument and an _____ _____ _____
   unsound argument.
9. I check to see if the evidence is relevant. _____ _____ _____
10. I check to see if the evidence is sufficient. _____ _____ _____

Plan of the Chapter

Chapter Nine examines argumentation as found in textbooks and other printed materials. Because argumentation is one of the most difficult types of reading, the chapter begins with simple examples from daily life (including the language of radio talk show callers!) Examples from books and articles are given as well as several exercises. The second part of the chapter focuses on faulty argumentation. It looks closely at several unfair tricks that speakers and writers frequently use to distort their arguments and persuade you to accept their point of view. Chapter Nine also includes tips for improving your understanding of arguments, vignettes in which students tell of their experiences, and more exercises and opportunities to sharpen your reading skills in this important area.

VIGNETTE 1

I'm glad we studied argumentation last year because my goal is law school and I know that I need to be sharp at detecting good and bad arguments. The best thing I learned was that it was important to *outline* arguments. Our instructor used to make an outline on the board. She'd write the main issue across the top of the chalkboard and then make two blocks on either side by drawing a line down the middle of the board. On the left side, she'd write the "pro" points that we'd give her—all the ideas that supported the issue. On the right side, she'd put all our "cons." The class would then have to make a decision based upon the number of points on each side and the quality of each point. (We learned that there may be fewer "pros" but each seemed to carry more weight.) I think this is a plan I can use later in law school, but I also know that it is a useful procedure in everyday thinking.

Simon T.

VIGNETTE 2

The best thing I learned from the course was the fallacies. I'd never heard of them before. They really do have a value in daily living. For example, I learned that people deliberately use tricks. "Post hoc" is when they say something caused something because it came before it. I had never thought about that but people all around me say, "Well, every time I wash my car it rains," or "We have only had wars after Democrats were elected president." I also was really impressed by what is called "Argumentum ad hominum." This is when someone criticizes an idea because of the person who says it. You know, someone says, "What does she know about kids; she's never had any," or "I wouldn't believe that because he never finished high school." One of the most important things I got out of the course was that you really have to put your thinking cap on when people argue.

Winston W.

Understanding Arguments

Arguments consist of two parts: a point or issue, and supporting points. Sometimes the supporting points are sound, valid, and logical, but there are also instances when they are not. You need to recognize when a point is being made and if that point is logically and soundly supported.

This chapter will help you understand how to write a solid argument and how to recognize and analyze an argument as a reader.

Guidelines for Reading an Argument

1. Identify the point or issue.
2. Decide what the writer is trying to convince you to accept.
3. Highlight any evidence that supports the author's point or issue.
4. Look for the author's conclusions.
5. Be aware of which side of the point or issue the author is promoting.
6. Outline the argument by writing down the points or issues and their supporting material.

Example

Here are three positions that one can take on the issue of legalizing street drugs:

All street drugs should be legalized.

Some street drugs should be legalized.

No street drugs should be legalized.

Each one needs to be supported with evidence that would prove that the position taken is the right one.

EXERCISE 9.1

Directions: After reading each of the following issues, think of three alternative positions and write them on the lines below.

1. Gay rights.

   a. _____

b. _____

c. _____

2. English as a world language.

   a. _____

   b. _____

   c. _____

3. Hunger in third world nations.

   a. _____

   b. _____

   c. _____

4. Nuclear testing.

   a. _____

   b. _____

   c. _____

5. Prayer in public schools.

   a. _____

   b. _____

c. _____

_____

EXERCISE 9.2

Directions: Choose one position from each of the five issues, then support it with three facts or other pieces of evidence.

Position 1 _____

_____

1st support _____

_____

2nd support _____

_____

3rd support _____

_____

Position 2 _____

_____

1st support _____

_____

2nd support _____

_____

3rd support _____

_____

Position 3 _____

_____

1st support _____

_____

2nd support _____

_____

3rd support _____
_____

Position 4 _____
_____

1st support _____
_____

2nd support _____
_____

3rd support _____
_____

Position 5 _____
_____

1st support _____
_____

2nd support _____
_____

3rd support _____
_____

The next exercises will help you to pick out the point or issues from the supporting material.

Example

a. Exercise increases one's ability to concentrate.
b. Exercise cuts the risk of heart attack.
c. Exercise is essential for a healthy mind and body.
d. Exercise can reduce depression.
e. Exercise can reduce fatty tissue.

The correct answer is c. The other statements clearly support healthy bodies and minds.

EXERCISE 9.3

Directions: Identify the point or issue by circling the correct letter.

1. a. A new bicycle trail will be a great asset to our neighborhood.
   b. Children who ride their bicycles in the street will be safer on the trail.
   c. The bicycle trail will provide a place for many different types of activities besides cycling.

2. a. Mike works hard every day.
   b. He often puts in extra hours when no one else will.
   c. Everyone on the job respects Mike.
   d. Mike will be a good boss.

3. a. I'd better put in extra study time.
   b. My chemistry class is a lot of work.
   c. My social life will have to be put on hold.

4. a. Children need to express themselves freely.
   b. Creative play is very important for children.
   c. Children need to be encouraged to use their imaginations.

5. a. Through divorce many children have two sets of parents.
   b. There should be a test for people who want to be parents.
   c. Parental involvement is at an all-time low.
   d. Child abuse is at an all-time high.

EXERCISE 9.4

Directions: Identify the supporting points by circling the correct letters. There will be three supporting points for each.

1. Professor McHenry is a very good teacher.
   a. He is always available for extra tutoring.
   b. He is the highest paid faculty member on campus.
   c. He is always prepared for class.
   d. His classes are lively and interesting.
   e. He has been teaching for 20 years.
   f. He always explains everything in great detail.

2. Good study habits are essential to college success.
   a. Students should have a consistent study time for each course.
   b. Students should study in an area that is conducive to study.
   c. Studying before and after classes is important.
   d. Some students achieve high grades with minimal effort.
   e. Choosing the right courses makes all the difference.
   f. Not having a tutor for difficult courses can be costly.
3. Jan is the best candidate for class president.
   a. She is captain of the debating team.
   b. She is involved in college activities.
   c. She was class president her senior year in high school.
   d. She is an active member in student government.
   e. She is concerned about student policies and rights.
   f. She has excellent leadership skills.
4. Smoking should be banned in public places.
   a. Second-hand smoke causes serious problems.
   b. Nonsmokers suffer the effects of second-hand smoke.
   c. My friend smokes three packages of cigarettes a day.
   d. Smoking pollutes the indoor air quality.
   e. People don't necessarily die from smoking.
   f. People smoke at home and at work.
5. Marijuana should be legalized.
   a. Doctors prescribe it for certain illnesses.
   b. It is less harmful than alcohol, which is legal.
   c. It has had no bad effects on anyone I know.
   d. It's not as bad as the nicotine in cigarettes.
   e. It's a good recreational drug.
   f. If it's used in moderation, studies have shown that there are no long-term effects.

EXERCISE 9.5

Directions: Think of five points that are of concern to you. Write each one beside the word Point. Then, write six supporting points—three that logically support the point and three that do *not* logically support it. When you are done, place a check beside the supporting points that logically support the point.

1. Point _____

   a. _____ Supporting point _____

   b. _____ Supporting point _____

   c. _____ Supporting point _____

   d. _____ Supporting point _____

   e. _____ Supporting point _____

   f. _____ Supporting point _____

2. Point _____

   a. _____ Supporting point _____

   b. _____ Supporting point _____

   c. _____ Supporting point _____

   d. _____ Supporting point _____

   e. _____ Supporting point _____

   f. _____ Supporting point _____

3. Point _____

a. _____ Supporting point _____
_____

b. _____ Supporting point _____
_____

c. _____ Supporting point _____
_____

d. _____ Supporting point _____
_____

e. _____ Supporting point _____
_____

f. _____ Supporting point _____
_____

4. Point _____

a. _____ Supporting point _____
_____

b. _____ Supporting point _____
_____

c. _____ Supporting point _____
_____

d. _____ Supporting point _____
_____

e. _____ Supporting point _____
_____

f. _____ Supporting point _____
_____

5. Point _____

a. _____ Supporting point _____
_____

b. _____ Supporting point _____

c. _____ Supporting point _____

d. _____ Supporting point _____

e. _____ Supporting point _____

f. _____ Supporting point _____

EXERCISE 9.6

Directions: Read this excerpt from an education book, and then answer the questions that follow it.

TO INVENT—OR NOT!

In recent years some teachers of young children have encouraged "invented spelling." They say it is an effective way to ease a child's progress into both reading and writing.

Invented spelling is simple and clearly not a new creation. When preschoolers or first graders acquire a basic knowledge of the letters of the alphabet and begin to associate them with the sounds of the language, they try—naturally—to spell some common words. Because they still lack a thorough understanding of sound-letter correspondences (something that takes at least a few years to acquire), they make mistakes: *baby* may become BABE or, even, BE; *Daddy* may appear as DADE or DDE. They are "inventing" their own spelling.

There have been two responses to invented spelling. Many teachers say that they are delighted when a child first invents a spelling, because then teachers know that the child has made the important discovery that letters and sounds are related. These teachers say that children should be encouraged to invent their personal spellings: this is a "natural" and significant first step on the road to reading and writing. They note that correction at this stage of development tends to discourage later growth and lower self-esteem. Many children, teachers say, will try less eagerly after correction and, in some cases, turn completely away from learning.

Advocates of invented spelling also note that this is a temporary stage in a child's development. As children read more and more in kindergarten and first grade, they see correct forms and, without direct admonitions, tend to spell words the way they have seen them in print. For example, after seeing *baby* in several books and stories, children self-correct and write their BABEE correctly. Advocates cite research studies that find children's invented spelling disappears as children move into second and third grade. They emphasize, in any case, that teachers do not suggest invented spelling continue into later life.

Critics insist, on the other hand, that words have correct spellings and that it is the school's responsibility to teach them. They say that the encouragement of invented spelling in early schooling creates a negative attitude toward spelling: students come to believe that one may spell a word any way that comes easily. They call attention to national testing results that indicate Americans spell less well than in previous generations. Such critics of invented spelling, many of whom are teachers themselves, see invented spelling as another signal of the decline in educational standards. "American schools," writes one prominent educator, "must maintain the highest standards if we are to compete economically with other nations of the world."

1. What is invented spelling? _____
_____
_____
_____

2. What are some arguments in favor of it? _____
_____
_____
_____

3. What are some arguments against it? _____
_____
_____
_____

4. After reading the excerpt, what is your position on invented spelling? Why? _____
_____
_____
_____

EXERCISE 9.7

Directions: Read this article and answer the questions that follow it.

LET'S LEGALIZE DRUGS!

In the United States—and most of the world today—some drugs are perfectly legal and others are not. Americans may purchase powerful drugs from their local pharmacies if they have a simple prescription from a physician. They can actually purchase many powerful drugs *without* a prescription in many cases because these drugs have been made "legal" by federal authorities. On the other hand, other drugs, such as heroine, cocaine, and even marijuana, may not be imported, produced, sold, or purchased, and billions of dollars are spent tracking down, arresting, prosecuting, and imprisoning sellers and importers.

The costs of prohibiting illegal drug use have skyrocketed and continue to grow each year. Among such costs are police and law enforcement, lawyers and court costs, and the building and maintenance of state and federal prisons. Costs also include medical care: the spread of AIDS and hepatitis through shared needles; infants poisoned prior to birth; and the care of "crack babies." Extrapolations from statistical data indicate that costs, both financial and social, will continue to rise in future decades.

What can be done? Has society any solution except prohibition and its related costs? Many people believe that an answer not only exists to such questions but that it is a simple one: *legalize drug use*! Many billions of dollars would be saved, money better to be spent on treatment for addicts and education. Tax money currently spent to support a vast—and ineffective—system could be spent on hospitals, drug clinics, social workers, and treatment programs; enough would be available to support educational programs in elementary and secondary schools to inform children and young adults of the dangers of addictive drugs. For those who object to complete legalization, new laws could restrict the sale of drugs to the young and sellers could be monitored through state or local licenses. In addition, drug sales could be heavily taxed, as tobacco and liquor are today, so that drug purchasers would be discouraged and additional tax revenues might be obtained for treatment and education.

Present policies of enforcing the sale and use of drugs have clearly not worked. For decades governments have attempted to eradicate drug use through law enforcement and have met with failure. Legalization would allow greater control of both sales and use and reduce the rising rates of drug-related deaths and violence. Other societies have legalized drugs and found sharp diminutions of crime, disease, and costs. There is really only one solution to America's drug problem: legalization!

1. What is the writer advocating? _____

_____

_____

_____

_____

2. Give at least three arguments offered to support this position. _____

_____

_____

_____

_____

3. What is your position on this issue? Give at least three arguments to support it. _____

_____

_____

_____

_____

idea

To better understand argumentation, try a visual representation of an actual argument. On the top space, write the position (such as "Drugs Should Be Legalized" or "Taxes Must Not Be Increased"). In the left block, list numerically all the points that support the position; in the right block, all the points against it. The "picture" you get often gives you a better understanding of the argument.

Position	
Pro	Con

False Argumentation or Unsound Arguments

Here are some kinds of false argumentation that you need to know.

1. **Post hoc ergo propter hoc.** This is when the reader assumes that because A came before B, A must have caused B.

    Example Letting your friends housesit did not cause the furnace to break down. The furnace would have broken down even if you had been home. Your friends did not cause the breakdown.

2. **Begging the question.** This happens when you assume something proven when actually it has not been proven.

    Example There are not too many seats in the classroom because there are enough students to fill them.

3. **Faulty dilemma.** The author presents two sides of an argument when, in fact, there are more than two sides.

    Example This country is a two-party system and, therefore, you can only vote Republican or Democratic.

4. **Ignoring the question.** You can see this when the author continues an argument while ignoring the main point or issue involved.

    Example "You played a poor game today." "Yeah, well, you're a rotten coach."

5. **Agrumentum ad hominum.** You will see this when the author sidesteps the argument by slandering or making accusations against an individual. It really is an argument that is addressing an individual rather than the intended issue.

    Example Don't vote for Mike for class president; his father is a crook and a liar.

EXERCISE 9.8

Directions: To see if you understand false argumentation, write your own examples of each kind below.

1. Post hoc ergo propter hoc _____
_____
_____

2. Begging the question _____
_____
_____

3. Faulty dilemma _____
_____
_____

4. Ignoring the question _____
_____
_____

5. Argumentum ad hominum _____
_____
_____

260 Chapter 9 Understanding Arguments

EXERCISE 9.9

Directions: Here are some examples of faulty argumentation. Read each and label it.

1. We had been sitting for some time in the beautiful Moscow underground train station, surrounded by gorgeous oil paintings, impressive tapestries, and superb statuary, when my friend commented to our official guide, "We've been here two hours and there have been no trains." The guide bristled and shouted, "Yes, and what about how African-Americans have been treated in your country?"

   This is an example of _____

2. The talk show caller reminded everyone, "We've got the liberals and the conservatives, and the liberals are Democrats and the conservatives are Republicans, and that's that. Make your choice."

   This is an example of _____

3. The important thing to remember about our candidate is that she's a mother. Mothers know about what's right and what's wrong, and, no matter what your political preference as to party, you should vote for her.

   This is an example of _____

4. Our new high school will be modeled after the famous Boston Latin School, the oldest in the nation. They divide classes this way and so shall we!

   This is an example of _____

5. During Hitler's rise to power, he emphasized to German voters that they had a choice: they could choose his National Socialist Party or the Communists. One was the party of Marx, he said, and the other the party of the true German patriots.

   This is an example of _____

6. The statistics are firm on this: when we got rid of our school dress code, student behavior became worse. By letting kids wear whatever they wanted, we got discipline problems galore.

   This is an example of _____

7. This man should not be a college counselor because he was once arrested for dealing in drugs. He got off in court but has no business counseling college students.

   This is an example of _____

8. Candidate Drizzle says, "Vote for me for school committee because I went to the public schools in this community and my opponent is the product of a posh private school. What does he know about the problems facing our schools?"

   This is an example of _____

9. Another talk show caller says, "We must have prayer in our schools! The country is going steadily downhill. There's crime and corruption everywhere you look. The violence is appalling."

   This is an example of _____

10. It's a well-known fact that when the tax rate dropped two years ago, the new bicycle factory opened in town. We must fight any attempts to raise taxes for schools or anything else.

This is an example of _____

EXERCISE 9.10

Directions: Radio talk shows are full of examples of faulty argumentation. Here is a transcript of one caller's argument. Read it and respond to the questions that follow it.

RADIO TALK SHOW CALLER

Let me tell you why we've got to get rid of welfare. The costs are killing us. We should be spending that money on building up our communities—new roads, highways, public buildings; we desperately need money for national defense and other important things. But instead, we're blowing it on people who shouldn't have it.

Sure, a few people need the money because they got laid off jobs or were sick, but most of those people are cheating us all. Before we had welfare, this country was great, rich, and powerful. Now we're in trouble. You got people buying Caddies and beer, that's what you got. One woman I heard of uses all her food stamps for booze. The paper had this story about a guy collecting welfare who had a job on the side and was getting like two salaries! That nut who called in before me doesn't know what he's talking about. He sounded like a liberal fag. Probably went to Harvard or some place like that. The truth is we've got to decide: we're going to be a first-class country or a bunch of do-gooders.

This is not the kind of argumentation found in textbooks. It is, however, the kind encountered in daily life, not only on talk show radio but in newspapers and, unfortunately, many social encounters.

1. What is the speaker arguing for? _____

_____

_____

_____

2. Give at least five points he offers to support his position. _____

_____

_____

_____

3. Does he offer any support against his position? What? _____

_____

_____

_____

262 Chapter 9 Understanding Arguments

4. He uses much faulty argumentation. Find examples of each.

   Post hoc ergo propter hoc: _____

   _____

   Begging the question: _____

   _____

   Faulty dilemma: _____

   _____

   Ignoring the question: _____

   _____

   Argumentum ad hominum: _____

5. Present an argument supporting welfare without using false argumentation. _____

   _____

   _____

   _____

Tricking Readers: Appeals in Arguments

Unscrupulous writers often try to trick their readers by appealing to readers' emotions, sympathies, fears, and prejudices. Sometimes, too, they appeal to authority, patriotism, or tradition. Here are some examples:

1. *The emotional appeal.* A writer opposed to the building of a new high school writes: "Some people I know in town are having real trouble making ends meet. The family next door is unable to buy birthday gifts for the kids anymore, and, I know, they haven't money to bring the children in for dental visits. Yet here we are asking them to pay money for a new high school when the old one is perfectly all right."

2. *The appeal to sympathy.* "We should elect Albert to the position," says another, "because that guy has gone through a terrible time these last months. First, he lost his job, his mother broke her hip, and then, he had all the trouble with his mortgage."

3. *The appeal to fear.* Writing a letter to the college newspaper, someone says, "There's no question about this: if we allow these "politically correct" police to monitor everything we say, we won't be able to open our mouths. You won't be able to chat with friends or say anything in class. It will be like living in Communist Russia."

4. *The appeal to prejudice.* The writer of an unsigned letter tells you, "If we don't put a stop soon to immigration, our country will be taken over by people who don't share our values. They get on welfare, use their money for drugs, and let their kids run wild. They aren't like us."

5. *The appeal to authority.* A friend says, "I know our English instructor doesn't seem to care about teaching but he has published three books, and, if he says not to put prepositions on the ends of sentences, he must be right."

6. *The patriotic appeal.* "Sure," writes a columnist, "Oliver North should not have plotted to sell arms to Iran, but he did it because he loves America."

7. *The appeal to tradition.* A college administrator sends out a memo reading, "Since our college began a half century age, students have worn caps and gowns to graduation, and we will adhere to this custom."

EXERCISE 9.11

Directions: These appeals are usually easy to spot. Most college students sense trickery when writers so clearly appeal to their good emotions. However, we all need to be constantly on guard. Check your sensitivity to various appeals in arguments by labeling each of the following appeals.

1. We should not send troops into every little world conflict. If we do, conscription may become national policy and we'll all find ourselves slogging through the mud in some broken-down country.

2. If we don't make English our national language and insist, by law, that everyone speak it, we lose the basic core that unites all Americans.

3. Unless we have sex education in our schools, distribute birth control devices, and make young people aware of the dangers of pregnancy, the population of the earth will expand and expand until our children will be unable to feed their children.

4. Our club has not allowed Jews or African-Americans since its founding a hundred and twenty years ago. We must keep to the wishes of our founders or disintegrate.

5. A recent article in the medical journal says that vitamins are unnecessary. People who eat normally don't need to buy and take pills.

EXERCISE 9.12

Directions: On the lines below, create five similar appeals. Label each to show that you understand the use of appeals in argument.

1. _____
   _____
   _____

2. _____
   _____
   _____

3. _____
   _____
   _____

4. _____
   _____
   _____

5. _____
   _____
   _____

The use of false argumentation often clues you in to an unfair presentation. When a writer (or speaker) resorts to the use of the faulty dilemma, begging the question, or one of the others, you should check the entire argument. To test for ability to spot unfair argument, go to the Letters-to-the-Editor section of a daily newspaper. Go through the letters and watch for one of the common unfair tricks. If you see one, go over the writer's argument to see whether it is valid.

Textbook Excerpt 9.1

Directions: After reading this excerpt, taken from a college textbook, answer the questions that follow.

KELLOGG: MARKETING BREAKFAST CEREAL

It all started back in the 1800s with Dr. H. Kellogg. He was a strict vegetarian and a leader in the Seventh Day Adventist community. Dr. Kellogg noticed that the typical American breakfast consisted of salt pork, biscuits, and ham gravy or pancakes, and molasses. As director of a health spa, Dr. Kellogg fed those who attended corn, wheat, and oatmeal—ground and baked. No salt and no sugar.

C. W. Post was one of his patients. He decided to go into business to market what was to become Post Grape-Nuts. Post added sugar to make his cereal tastier. Dr. Kellogg and his brother, Will K. Kellogg, countered by offering a sweetened cereal of their own. The breakfast battle was on.

The big Kellogg cereal in the 1800s was Corn Flakes. Guess what a big seller is today? You guessed it. Corn Flakes. Also popular is sugar-covered corn flakes (Frosted Flakes). All in all, Kellogg has about 36 per cent of the consumer market, down a little in the last couple of years. It is now in a head-to-head battle with General Mills' Total. Kellogg feels that its Just Right cereal is as nutritious as Total and has a better taste.

Let's see how Kellogg has attacked certain market segments. For adults, it has developed high-fiber cereals like Nutri-Grain, Bran Products, and Cracklin' Oat Bran plus the vitamin-pill-in-a-cereal Special K. For children, it's Froot Loops, Sugar Pops, Sugar Smacks, and Apple Jacks. For traditionalists, there are Corn Flakes, Rice Krispies, and Raisin Bran.

Post Raisin Bran is now part of General Foods. It, too, has targeted certain markets. There is Grape-Nuts for old-timers. Kids can feast on sugary cereals such as Smurf-Berry Crunch, Super Sugar Crisp, and Honey-Nut Crunch Raisin Bran. Joggers might go for C. W. Post Hearty Granola or just plain Bran Flakes. Altogether, General Foods has between 10 and 11 percent of the market.

The old Cheerios is still popular for General Mills. Honey-Nut Cheerios is also a good seller, along with Apple-Cinnamon Cheerios. Together, the Cheerio brands are the number one cereal in America. Anyone over 40 may remember eating graham crackers with milk. Now, General Mills makes it easy for you with Golden Grahams. Kids can sugar up on Trix and Lucky Charms. The General Mills market share is 24 percent or so.

General Mills is going after a larger share with two new products: Basic 4, an adult cereal that, together with milk, provides four basic food groups; and Triples, an all-family cereal combining corn, rice, and wheat. It's positioned to go up against Rice Krispies. General Mills already took a big bite out of Kellogg's Raisin Bran with its Big G's Raisin Nut Bran, Oatmeal Raisin Crisp, and Total Raisin.

A popular cereal in the Quaker Oats line is 100% Natural. They also make Life and Cap'n Crunch and Halfies. Market share—about 9 percent.

We can't forget Ralston Purina, with its 6 percent plus market share. They have given us Donkey Kong, Cookie Crisp, Waffelos, and Dinky Donuts. Their big seller is Chex. One of their latest cereals is Barbie, so young girls can have "breakfast with Barbie."

Nabisco's number-one seller is Shredded Wheat. It has only about a 4 percent market share.

Most of the best-sellers in the cereal industry are relatively nutritious. For a while, oat bran cereals were popular, but they faded with the reports that they were not as healthy as they were promoted to be.

How far have we come from the original intent of Dr. Kellogg to give us a healthy, nutritious, sugar-free, salt-free breakfast food? Cookie Crisps is 47 percent sugar. A one-ounce serving of Mr. T's Cereal has 230 milligrams of sodium. That's 30 more milligrams than Lay's packs into an equal amount of potato chips. Sugar Golden Crisp is 51 percent sugar, and Honey Smacks has 57 percent refined sweetener (including honey). In fact, there is little fiber in most children-oriented cereals.

The cereal industry is now doing $6.9 billion a year in sales. Some $50 million was spent on advertising just to introduce Basic 4 and Triples.

Source: William G. Nickels, James M. McHugh, and Susan McHugh, *Understanding Business*, 3rd ed. (Burr Ridge, Ill.: Richard D. Irwin, 1993). Copyright © 1993 by William G. Nickels. All rights reserved. Reprinted by permission.

1. Segments (paragraph 4) means:
   a. Divided parts
   b. Brands
   c. Targets
2. Faded (paragraph 11) means:
   a. Gradually changed
   b. Didn't sell well
   c. Lost popularity
3. The main idea of paragraph 1 is:
   a. Dr. Kellogg was a vegetarian and a member of a Seventh Day Adventist community.
   b. Dr. Kellogg fed his patients healthy breakfast foods.
   c. The typical American breakfast diet was poor.
4. According to the article, C. W. Post was:
   a. Unhealthy.
   b. Responsible for Froot Loops.
   c. One of Dr. Kellogg's patients.
5. Fact or opinion: A popular cereal in the Quaker Oats line is 100% Natural.
6. Fact or opinion: Most of the best-sellers in the cereal industry are relatively nutritious.
7. We can infer from this article that:
   a. People only eat cereal that is sweet.
   b. Breakfast food has become the opposite of Dr. Kellogg's intent.
   c. Adults don't eat sweet cereals.
8. Identify the point by circling the correct letter.
   a. Cookie Crisp is 47% sugar.
   b. Honey Smacks has 57% refined sugar.
   c. Mr. T's Cereal has 230 milligrams of sodium.
   d. Children's cereals are anything but nutritious.
   e. There is little fiber in children's cereal.
9. Circle the correct kind of false argumentation based on the following statement

   Consumers buy high-sugar cereals for kids because most of the cereals are over 50% sugar.

   a. Faulty dilemma
   b. Begging the question
   c. Post hoc ergo propter hoc

10. Using your own words, summarize this excerpt.

Related Study Skills #9: Library Research Skills

Good students know that presenting an argument requires sound and valid evidence. They make sure that their argument is sound and valid by using their library research skills to find solid and reliable evidence. One of the best resources your library has to offer is the periodicals. You can find the most current and also past journal, magazine, and newspaper articles in this section of the library. This section of the library also has several reference guides that can help you locate what you need. For example, most college libraries have the *Readers' Guide to Periodical Literature, Access,* and the *Popular Periodic Index.*

Most college libraries are on-line, which means that you can find the journal, magazine, and newspaper articles you need much faster by using the computer rather than the reference guides. The computer, with the aid of a printer, also allows you to print the information about the article you want as well as a brief description of the article.

Whether you use the reference guides or the computer, there are four important things you should keep in mind about periodicals: they are kept up-to-date; they tend to offer different views of an argument, problem, or situation; their articles tend to be longer and provide more information than those in reference books; and they tend to be easier to read and understand.

Directions: Use the periodical section in your college library to complete the exercise below. Make sure that you write down the name of the periodical, the date it was published, the title of the article, and the page numbers on which the article appeared. Write a brief summary of each article.

1. Locate an article on the Free Trade Agreement.

Periodical information _____

_____

_____

Summary _____

_____

_____

_____

_____

_____

_____

_____

2. Locate an article on family values.

Periodical information _____

_____

_____

Summary _____

_____

_____

_____

_____

_____

_____

3. Locate an article on the latest AIDS research.

Periodical information _____

Summary _____

4. Locate an article on domestic violence.

Periodical information _____

Summary _____

Making the Connection

Reflection Entry #9

Directions: After taking a few moments to reflect on the information in this chapter, write an essay summarizing what you have learned about arguments and how you will apply that knowledge to your textbook reading assignments.

_____
_____
_____
_____
_____
_____
_____
_____
_____
_____
_____
_____
_____
_____
_____
_____
_____
_____
_____
_____
_____
_____

CHAPTER TEN

Summarizing

It may seem strange, but the single most powerful reading strategy available to you is not primarily a reading activity. It is *summarizing,* something we usually do in speaking or, especially, in writing. When we condense or abridge material, we are more apt to understand and remember it.

When you read a section of a book, you may forget much of the contents within a few hours. (One research study found that people forgot as much as 90 percent of what they read casually within a day!) Even when you use the strategies suggested in this book (such as previewing and SQ3R), you may forget some of the assignment. Summarizing, however, helps you better comprehend new information and ideas and get them securely into long-term memory.

Why does summarizing work so well? Many reasons have been identified. For example, when you summarize material, you must:

1. Distinguish carefully between the main ideas and the minor details.
2. Be aware of the writer's plan of organization.
3. Be concerned with the purpose and goals of the material.

Summarizing, too, encourages you to read with greater care and attention, often forcing you to reread and double-check passages. The process of writing down the summary gives the additional benefit of involving you physically in the activity, thus increasing the opportunity to remember well.

Before you read this chapter, take the summarizing survey. This survey will help you determine your strengths and weaknesses for summarizing.

Summarizing Survey

	Never	Sometimes	Always
1. I summarize my reading assignments.	____	____	____
2. When I write a summary, I use my own words, not those of the author.	____	____	____
3. I write the ideas in my summary in the same order in which they appeared in the reading assignment.	____	____	____
4. I begin my summary with a topic sentence that states the most important point the author is making about the topic.	____	____	____
5. I support the topic sentence with major supporting details.	____	____	____

6. If needed, I support the major details with examples. ____ ____ ____
7. I end my summaries with a concluding sentence. ____ ____ ____
8. I write my summaries in my notebook for future reference. ____ ____ ____
9. I keep my summaries brief and to the point. ____ ____ ____
10. I reread my summaries, deleting irrelevant and redundant information. ____ ____ ____

Plan of the Chapter

This chapter focuses upon the ultimate reading/study skill—summarizing. After the Introduction and Survey, you'll find explanations of summarizing and suggestions on how to summarize effectively. There are exercises to help you summarize both brief and longer passages, as well as a section on informal types of summarizing. The chapter also includes two Vignettes in which students tell of their experiences with summarizing.

VIGNETTE 1

When I read the chapter on summarizing, I remembered a crazy experience. One day I got home before my husband and read a magazine article while having a cup of coffee. It was about macho men. When he came home, I joked that I'd read all about guys like him. He wanted to see the article and I showed him. He wanted to know what it said and I couldn't remember! I read it but I couldn't remember the details! I said I had to do something in the other room and took the magazine with me. Then I reread it, came out, and told him what it said. (He thought it was funny.) Afterwards, I wondered why I couldn't remember the first time I read it but could the second time, and then, after reading the chapter, I realized that when I read it the second time, I was making a *summary in my head*. That's what helped me to remember. (And, by the way, I can still remember what that article said a year later!)

Lorna M.

VIGNETTE 2

My brother went to law school with a remarkable guy. This man passed every exam perfectly throughout the program. Every exam, top score! The funny thing was that the guy wasn't from what you'd call an academic background. He didn't even graduate from high school! He'd dropped out of high school to go into the marines and got a high school equivalency certificate.

My brother said his technique for success was incredible. The guy'd read every case, and then he'd *summarize*. Every single case. He'd go home from work in the night and sit down before he went to sleep, read or reread the cases, and then write one-paragraph summaries. He'd read his summaries before exams while other people were rereading the whole cases in the law books. He said that it wasn't the reading of the summaries that helped him: it was the *writing* of the summaries. While writing them, he had to think through every angle and every point, decide what was what, and which was which. He also said that it was the physical act of writing that got the stuff into memory.

Manley H.

Summarizing

One of the best ways to know whether or not you understand what you read is to summarize the material in your own words. After reading several paragraphs or sections, you should try to put what you think the author said into your own words.

Summarizing, for some reason, seems to be very difficult for students to put into practice. It seems that many feel that it takes too much time and work. But students who consistently practice this skill actually understand the reading assignment better than those who do not. The reason is that writing out a summary forces you to think through the author's message. You become involved in the thinking process.

This chapter will offer some suggestions for summarizing and some practical applications.

Suggestions for Summarizing

1. Use the main ideas of the reading assignment. They can provide you with the foundation for your summary.

2. Be sure to write the main ideas in the order in which they appeared in the reading assignment. This will ensure that you are following the author's plan and that your summary will be logical.

3. Take care to use your own words, not the author's words. Your own words will provide you with a better basis for understanding. Using your own words also forces you to think through what the author has said. Further, it requires you to look up unfamiliar words and to put them into familiar terms.

When you are preparing to write a good summary, it helps when you recall the values of summarizing.

Remember to:

- Note the writer's main idea.
- Identify the purpose of the piece of writing.
- Distinguish between relevant and irrelevant material.
- Note the key evidence offered in support of the thesis or main idea.
- Look for the underlying structure of the piece (pattern of organization).
- Note transitional words and phrases (such as "on the other hand," "because," or "for example").
- Follow the sequence of the material.

Some good questions to ask yourself as you work grow out of the above seven points:

1. Can I put the basic, main idea into a single sentence? What is it?

2. What is the purpose behind this? Why did the writer write it?

3. What's irrelevant? What can I cut? If this were to fit onto a small card, what might I delete?

4. Does the writer support the main idea? Can I put this into a single sentence? What is it?

5. What's the plan? Comparison/contrast? Cause/effect? Sequence? Can I put the summary in the same plan?

6. What are the transitional words and phrases used? What do they tell me? ("Next" and "Finally" say it is a chronological sequence.)

7. Can I use the same plan and sequence in the summary? How? What will it look like on paper?

Summarizing is an extremely valuable and highly useful reading/learning strategy, but it is sometimes difficult. Many college students have come to rely on more specific approaches to summarizing, such as the Six-Step Approach or the 15-10-5 Approach. You may find them useful to you.

Here's how they work.

In the Six-Step Approach, you

- Cut all unnecessary or trivial material.
- Cut everything that may be important but repetitious (that is, it's been said once already!).
- Use a general term for a list of terms (for example, say "office supplies" rather than "paper, pencils, pens, paper clips, rubber bands, etc.").
- Use a general term instead of all the parts of an action or events (for example, say "got gas," instead of "he drove up to the pump, inserted the nozzle, watched the meter, gave the attendant his credit card," etc.).
- Pick the topic, or main idea, sentence.
- Make up a topic sentence if there isn't one.

In the *15-10-5 Approach*, you read the passage that must be summarized and write down the *15* most important pieces of information. Then you go back and cut—ruthlessly—to the *10* most important pieces. And then you return and cut, even more ruthlessly, to the *5* pieces of information. You have: A SUMMARY!

Example of Summarizing

The following paragraphs on mental retardation have been summarized for you. Read this excerpt, then read the summary carefully, noting how it has been written to include only the *main points* of the excerpt.

MENTAL RETARDATION

The most distinctive feature of mental retardation is inadequate intellectual functioning. Long before formal tests were developed to assess intelligence, the mentally retarded were identified by a lack of age-appropriate skills in learning and caring for themselves. Once intelligence tests were developed, numbers were assigned to indicate the degree of mental retardation. But it is not unusual to find two retarded people with the same low IQ, one of whom is married, employed, and involved in the community, and the other requiring constant supervision in an institution. These differences in social competence led psychologists to include deficits in adaptive behavior in their definition of mental retardation. **Mental Retardation** *is a condition of limited mental ability in which the individual has low IQ, usually below 70 on a traditional intelligence test, and has difficulty adapting to everyday life.* About five million Americans fit this definition of mental retardation.

There are different classifications of mental retardation. About 89 percent of the mentally retarded fall into the mild category, with IQs of 55 to 70. About 6 percent are classified as moderately retarded, with IQs of 40 to 54; these people can attain a second-grade level of skills and may be able to support themselves as adults through some type of labor. About 3.5 percent of the mentally retarded are in the severe category, with IQs of 25 to 39; these individuals learn to walk and engage in very simple tasks, but require extensive supervision. Fewer than 1 percent have IQs below 25; they fall into the profoundly mentally retarded classification and are in need of constant supervision.

Summary

About five million Americans are mentally retarded. They have IQ scores of below 70 and have trouble caring for themselves. Most of them (about 95 percent) can attain a second-grade level of skills and may be able to support themselves.

A Word about Paraphrasing

In preparing your summaries, you *paraphrase;* that is, you put the author's words into your own language. Usually, when you are summarizing sections from textbooks or articles from journals, the author's language tends to be "heavy" or "learned." Especially in textbooks, authors use technical terms, the professional language of the field (its jargon), and long, involved sentences. Sometimes it seems as if authors deliberately use language that is hard to read. As a summarizer (and successful student!), you need to "cut this language down to size," to simplify it, make it easier to read.

Actually, the process of paraphrasing is valuable in itself. When you paraphrase, you understand better. As you rephrase the textbook author's language into your own everyday language, you improve the chances that you'll understand and remember it.

Here is an example.

An author of a textbook on management writes, "The value of presentational speaking is important for three reasons: managers must provide rational explanations to colleagues, products and services are becoming more complex, and consumers increasingly demand insights into sophisticated technologies." Put into ordinary language, this may be: "Managers need to speak effectively to explain their products and services to colleagues and consumers." Boiled down further, this may become: "Managers must be good explainers." The author writes, "Strategic communicators must avoid assumptions that may be incorrect and unreliable and that result in miscommunications." Paraphrased into simpler language, this may become: "Speakers must try to give correct and reliable communications." Summarized, this may become: "Speakers should tell the truth," or something similar.

To make sure you understand the role paraphrasing plays in summarizing, take the following paragraph (also from a management textbook) and put it, first, into your own words, and then, into a shortened form. That is, first paraphrase it, and then summarize it.

Perhaps the most persuasive communication barrier results from hierarchical rank. In any interview situation, the parties involved know who holds the balance of power. Although a higher-ranking person may encourage candor, the lower-level person may fear such openness. It is only human to worry about the reactions of people in powerful positions, so candor frequently suffers.

Your paraphrase: _____

_____

_____

_____

Your summary: _____

_____

_____

_____

EXERCISE 10.1

Summarizing Paragraphs

Directions: After reading the following paragraphs, write a summary for each on the lines provided.

STRESS AND THE IMMUNE SYSTEM

The immune system serves three basic functions: to recognize foreign cells and attack them, to develop antibodies to recognize foreign invaders in the future, and to send white blood cells to the location of an injury to speed healing. Chronic stress can suppress the functioning of the immune system, so that just by being stressed for long periods of time, we can actually weaken our immune system and fall victim to an illness that we would normally fight off with ease.

Summary _____

_____

_____

_____

_____

_____

_____

DATABASES

Computers offer the most advanced method of conducting secondary research. As you know, the capacity of computers to collect and retrieve information has been expanding phenomenally. Business research has been a primary beneficiary of that expansion. Much of the information routinely recorded in printed form and accessed through directories, encyclopedias, bibliographies, indexes, and the like, is now collected and stored in computer files as well. When these files of related information, known collectively as databases, are accessed by computer, the result is research that can be more extensive, complete, and accurate than any conducted manually.

Summary _____

_____

_____

_____

_____

_____

_____

_____

ALCOHOL ABUSE

Who is likely to be an alcoholic? Alcoholics may be difficult to identify because they can be found in all occupational groups. They can be any age, members of any ethnic or racial group, male or female. Alcohol abuse alone cost the American economy almost $92 billion in 1991, according to some estimates. This was up from $70 billion in 1985. Costs are expected to rise to $124 billion by 1997. About three-fourths of the cost is due to lost productivity. This includes lost productivity due to early death by alcohol-related illness or by automobile accidents. In 1991, about 13 percent of the total cost was for treatment costs, and these are expected to rise by 74 percent by 1997.

Summary _____

_____

_____

_____

_____

_____

_____

_____

Many students don't realize it but their textbooks often include chapter summaries! Textbook authors prepare thorough and accurate summaries of chapters, and place them at the end of chapters. Successful college readers know this and read the summaries before they read the chapters. Such prereading of summaries gives a reader an excellent preview of what's to come, as well as a kind of verbal map of the territory to be explored.

No matter how well prepared the authors' summaries may be, they are never as effective as summaries you write yourself. When you write, you are forced to distinguish between main ideas and minor details, to note the organization, to identify the purpose, and so on. The summary printed in the book deprives you of certain learning opportunities. However, some students employ an extremely powerful technique: they read the chapter, write a summary, and then compare their summaries with the author's! This, of course, necessitates much rereading and going back and forth between both summaries and the chapter. Some say this is the ultimate reading/study technique!

Summarizing Longer Excerpts

Directions: After reading the following textbook excerpts, write a summary for each on the lines provided.

IMPROVING YOUR LISTENING ABILITY

Improving your listening is largely a matter of mental conditioning—of concentrating on the activity of sensing. You have to want to improve it, for listening is a willful act. If you are like most of us, you are often tempted not to listen or you find it easier not to listen. We human beings tend to avoid work; and listening may be work.

After you have decided that you want to listen better, you must make an effort to pay attention. How you do this will depend on your mental make-up, for the effort requires disciplining the mind. You must force yourself to be alert, to pay attention to the words spoken.

In addition to working on the improvement of your sensing, you should work on the accuracy of your filtering. To do this, you will need to think in terms of what words mean to the speakers who use them rather than what the dictionary says they mean or what they mean in your mind. You must try to think as the speaker thinks—judging the speaker's words by the speaker's knowledge, experiences, viewpoints, and such. Like improving your sensing, improving your filtering requires conscious effort.

Remembering what you hear also requires conscious effort. Certainly, there are limits to what the mind can retain; but authorities agree that few of us come close to them. By taking care to hear what is said and by working to make your filtering process give you more accurate meanings to the words you hear, you add strength to messages you receive. The result should be improved retention.

Source: Raymond V. Lesikar, John D. Petit, Jr., and Marie E. Flatley, *Basic Business Communications*, 6th ed. (Burr Ridge, Ill.: Richard D. Irwin, 1993). Copyright © 1993 Richard D. Irwin, Inc. All rights reserved. Reprinted by permission.

Summary _____

_____

_____

_____

WHAT ARE SENSATION AND PERCEPTION?

How do you know the color of grass, that a smell is sweet, that a sound is a sigh, and that the lights around the shore are dim? You know these things because of your senses. All outside information comes into us through our senses. Without vision, hearing, touch, taste, smell, and other *senses,* your brain would be isolated from the world: you would live in a dark silence—a tasteless, colorless, feelingless void.

Sensation is the process of detecting and encoding stimulus energy in the world. Stimuli emit physical energy—light, sound, and heat, for example. The sense organs detect this energy and then transform it into a code that can be transmitted to the brain. The first step in "sensing" the world is the work of receptor cells, which respond to certain forms of energy. The retina of the eye is sensitive to light, and special cells in the ear are sensitive to sound, for example. This physical energy is transformed into electrical impulses; the information carried by these electrical impulses travels through nerve fibers that connect the sense organs with the central nervous system. Once in the brain, information about the external world travels to the appropriate area of the cerebral cortex.

Perception is the process of organizing and interpreting sensory information to give it meaning. The retinas on our eyes record a fast-moving silver object in the sky, but they do not "see" a passenger jet; our eardrum vibrates in a particular way, but it does not "hear" a Beethoven symphony. Organizing and interpreting what we sense—that is, "seeing" and "hearing" meaningful patterns in sensory information—is perception.

In our everyday lives, the two processes of sensation and perception are virtually inseparable. When the brain receives sensory information, for example, it automatically interprets the information. Because of this, most contemporary psychologists refer to sensation and perception as a unified information processing system.

Source: John W. Santrack, *Psychology,* 4th ed. (Dubuque, Iowa: Times Mirror Higher Education Group, 1995). Copyright © Times Mirror Higher Education Group, Inc. All rights reserved. Reprinted by permission.

Summary _____

Informal Types of Summarizing

Some students are intimidated by the formalities of summary writing. They recognize the obvious values of summarizing the material in books they need to understand and remember, but they are somewhat put off by the "rules and regulations."

Here are three informal types of summarizing that anyone can use on almost any textbook material. One doesn't even require writing!

> **idea.**
>
> Several students have recommended a very sophisticated learning trick based on summary writing. As they read through the textbook, they write summaries for each chapter section. They save these summaries in their class notebooks for study before an exam. But—and this is the trick—they take a bottle of White-Out and erase every fifth word in their summaries. A couple of days before the exam, they go back to fill in the missing words. If they can fill them all in without trouble, they figure that they know that section of the book. If they have trouble, they know they need to reread and study the section. It's a simple technique but they say it works.

1. Recall the well-known 5Ws-plus-H approach traditionally used by news reporters. When sent on an assignment, they must get maximum information in minimum time. They must put this information in their articles so that readers get it all with the least reading possible. They ask, as you know, What? Where? When? Who? Why? and How? You can use this technique to make quick, informal summaries of textbook material. Read the assignment, and jot down in your notes answers to these six key questions. You have a summary. You can later, if necessary, develop it into a formal one-paragraph summary or use your notes as-is to prepare for an exam.

2. Imagine that you work for a digest magazine (such as *Reader's Digest*). Your job is to condense or abridge articles that have already appeared in other magazines so that your busy readers may read them in less time. Instead of going to other magazines, however, take chapters or sections of chapters from your textbook. Read the chapter carefully with the intention of summarizing clearly in your mind. Then write a summary. These may be kept in your class notebook to serve as the basis for review and pre-exam preparation.

3. The third informal type of summarizing appears too informal to discuss, yet it works with great effectiveness. *Tell someone*. Have you noticed how easy it is to forget film and TV stories? You see them once and forget them so effectively you may as well not have seen them at all! However, on those occasions when, for one reason or another, you actually tell a friend or family member about the movie or TV program, you find that the telling got the story into memory. When you have occasion to tell *someone else* (about a really sensational or thoroughly bad show!), your summary is not only better but easier to recall.

Most students rarely have opportunities to talk about chapters in their textbooks! It's hard to bring topics from chemistry or marketing into ordinary conversations. However, on those rare occasions when a topic does come up in conversation, you may find yourself actually *summarizing* a textbook section. The principles that govern summarizing as a learning technique apply here, just as they do in formal classroom summarizing: you must distinguish major from minor, note organization, eliminate unnecessary details, and so on.

You can try this out with another student in the class, or, even better, with a small group of students. Find a time and place and *talk the book*. Make sure that prior to the meeting you have all read the assignment; then share your informal summaries. Many students through the years have found that this is a highly effective study approach.

EXERCISE 10.2

Directions: Try out these three informal summarizing techniques here.

1. From a textbook that you are reading this week, select one section and summarize it using the 5Ws-plus-H technique.

___

2. From a textbook that you are reading, select a section and condense it for a digest-type magazine.

___

3. Organize a study group of students to make oral summaries of sections of the textbook you are all currently reading. In the space below, tell how many people were in your group, how often you met, for how long, and how effective you found this oral summary approach to reading and study.

___

EXERCISE 10.3

Directions: Select three textbook reading assignments from different courses and summarize the first section of the assignment for each.

Assignment 1

Title of Course: _____

_____

Title of Chapter: _____

_____

Title of Section: _____

_____

Summary: _____

_____

_____

_____

_____

_____

_____

Assignment 2

Title of Course: _____

_____

Title of Chapter: _____

_____

Title of Section: _____

_____

Summary: _____

_____

_____

_____

_____

_____

Assignment 3

Title of Course: _____

Title of Chapter: _____

Title of Section: _____

Summary: _____
_____
_____
_____
_____
_____

EXERCISE 10.4

Directions: Choose one of your courses and summarize the lecture notes from the last class you attended.

Title of course: _____

Title of lecture: _____

Summary: _____
_____
_____
_____
_____
_____

EXERCISE 10.5

Directions: After reading the following short selection, summarize it using the skills and techniques you have learned in this chapter.

THE BROWNING OF AMERICA

Studies of population trends in the United States indicate a future that surprises many. Currently, almost on American in four defines himself or herself as Hispanic or nonwhite. If current trends in immigration and birth persist, by the year 2000 the population of Asian Americans will increase about 22 percent, that of Hispanic Americans about 21 percent, and that of African Americans about 12 percent. During this same period, whites are expected to increase by a puny 2 percent.

By the year 2020, the number of Hispanic Americans and nonwhites will double, to nearly 115 million, but the white population will show no increase at all (see Chapter 20). The year 2056, when someone born today will be is his or her sixties, is expected to be the watershed year, for then the "average" American will trace his or her descent to Africa, Asia, the Hispanic world, the Pacific Islands, Arabia—to almost anywhere but white Europe.

In some places, the future has already arrived. In the entire state of New York, 40 percent of elementary and secondary schoolchildren belong to an ethnic minority. In California, 51 percent of schoolchildren are Hispanic American and nonwhite: 31 percent Hispanic American, 11 percent Asian American, and 9 percent African American.

A truly multicultural society will pose unique problems and opportunities. For example, in 2056, when "minorities" are expected to outnumber whites, there will be a large number of retirees but dwindling numbers of workers who pay taxes for their Social Security benefits. For race and ethnic relations, the significance is that most of the retirees will be white, and most of the workers from today's minorities.

White Americans, who have enjoyed a privileged status in the United States, are unlikely to welcome this changed balance. Political backlashes of various sorts are likely. For example, the "English First" movement is a reaction to the growing influence of Spanish-speaking Americans. Similarly, African Americans, who feel that they have waited the longest and endured the most in the fight for equal opportunity, resist gains made by Hispanic Americans. They also feel that as affirmative action has been broadened to include even white women, it has become of less value for them.

Finally, this change will mean a rethinking of American history as citizens debate the source of the nation's successes and just what its "unalterable" beliefs and other national symbols are. No longer, for example, will the meaning of the Alamo and the West be clear. Did the Alamo represent the heroic action of dedicated Americans against huge odds—or the well-deserved death of extremists bent on wresting territory from Mexico? Was the West settled by individuals determined to find economic opportunity and freedom from oppression—or a savage conquest, just another brutal expression of white imperialism?

While we cannot predict the particulars, of one thing we can be certain—that the future will be challenging as the United States undergoes this fundamental transformation in its population.

Source: Henry 1990; Whitman 1987. From James M. Henslin, *Sociology: A Down-To-Earth Approach* (New York: Allyn and Bacon, 1993). Copyright © 1993 by Allyn and Bacon. Reprinted by permission.

Your Summary _____

_____

_____

_____

EXERCISE 10.6

Directions: After reading the following short selection, summarize it using the skills and techniques you have learned in this chapter.

THE AMISH—GEMEINSCHAFT COMMUNITIES IN A GESELLSCHAFT SOCIETY

American society exhibits all the characteristics Ferdinand Tönnies identified as these of *Gesellschaft* society. Impersonal associations pervade everyday life. Local, state, and federal governments regulate many activities. Impersonal corporations hire people not based on long-term, meaningful relationships, but on their value to the bottom line. Similarly, when it comes to firing workers, the bottom line takes precedence over personal relationships. And, perhaps even more significant, millions of Americans do not even know their neighbors.

Within the United States, a handful of small communities exhibit characteristics that depart from those of the larger society. One such example is the Old Order Amish, followers of a sect that broke away from the Swiss-German Mennonite church in the late 1600s, settling in Pennsylvania around 1727. Today, more than 130,000 Old Order Amish live in the United States. The largest concentration, about 14,000, reside in Lancaster County, Pennsylvania. The Amish can also be found in about twenty other states and in Ontario, Canada, but 70 percent live in just three states: Pennsylvania, Ohio, and Indiana. The Amish, who believe that birth control is wrong, have doubled in size in just the past two decades.

To the nearly five million tourists that pass through Lancaster County each year, the quiet pastures and almost identical white farmhouses, simple barns, horse- or mule-drawn carts, and clothes calmly flapping on lines to dry convey a sense of peace and wholeness reminiscent of another era. Just sixty-five miles from Philadelphia, "Amish country" is, in many ways, a world away.

The Amish faith rests upon separation from the world, taking Christ's Sermon on the Mount literally, and obedience to the church's teachings and leaders. The rejection of worldly concerns, Donald Kraybill writes in *The Riddle of Amish Culture*, "provides the foundation of such Amish values as humility, faithfulness, thrift, tradition, communal goals, joy of work, a slow-paced life, and trust in divine providence."

The village life that Tönnies identified as fostering *Gemeinschaft* communities—and which he correctly predicted was fast being lost to industrialization—is very much alive among the Amish. The Amish make their decisions in weekly meetings, where, by consensus, the develop a set of rules, or *ordnung,* that guide their behavior. Religion and the discipline that it calls for is the glue that holds these communities together. Brotherly love and the welfare of the community are paramount values. Most Amish farm on plots of one hundred acres or less, keeping their farms small so that horses can be used instead of tractors and neighbors can pitch in with the chores. In this way, intimacy—a sense of community—is maintained.

The Amish are bound by countless other communal ties, including language (a dialect of German known as Pennsylvania Dutch), a distinctive style of plain dress that has remained unchanged for almost three hundred years, and church-sponsored schools. Nearly all Amish marry, and divorce is forbidden. The family is a vital ingredient in Amish life; all major events take place in the home, including weddings and funerals, worship services, even births. Most Amish children attend church schools only until the age of thirteen. To go to school beyond the eighth grade would expose them to "worldly concerns" and give them information considered of no value to farm life. The Amish pay local, state, and federal taxes, but they pool their resources to fund their own welfare system, and therefore do not pay Social Security taxes. They won the right to be left out of the Social Security system only after drawn-out court battles. They believe that all violence is bad, even in personal self-defense, and register as conscientious objectors during times of war.

The Amish cannot, of course, resist all change. Instead, they attempt to adapt to change in ways that will cause the least harm to their core values. Because of land shortages and encroaching urbanization, some young Amish men cannot find farms. Some have turned to farm-related businesses, cottage industries, and woodworking trades. They go to great lengths to avoid leaving the home. The Amish believe that when the husband works away from the home, all aspects of life, from the marital relationship to the care of the children, seem to change—certainly an excellent sociological insight. They also believe that if a man receives a paycheck he will think that his work is of more value than his wife's. For the Amish, intimate, or *Gemeinschaft,* society is absolutely essential to their way of life.

Source: Based on Bender 1990; Hostetler 1980; Jones 1990; Kephart 1987; Kraybill 1989; Raymond 1990; Ruth 1990; Ziegenhals 1991. From James M. Henslin, *Sociology: A Down-To-Earth Approach* (New York: Allyn and Bacon, 1993). Copyright © 1993 by Allyn and Bacon. Reprinted by permission.

Your Summary

Textbook Excerpt 10.1

Directions: After reading the following textbook excerpt, answer the questions on the lines provided.

THE SIX STAGES OF CHANGE

We process major transitions through basic recognizable steps. This author was close to a family whose mother died unexpectedly. All eight members of the family—except one—reacted openly, showing the emotions they felt in various ways. But one of the adult sons remained unemotional, not showing any feelings except the surface statements of sorrow. The other family members were quick to say, "I'm worried about Sui-Toon. He's not letting it out. When it finally comes out, he's going to have a rough time." None of them are psychologists, but they were right. Several months later, Sui-Toon broke down and spent several weeks in severe depression. The family members were acknowledging that we all need to go through certain steps in dealing with a personal loss—steps that cannot and should not be avoided.

There are six **stages of personal change** that make up the process of healthy reaction to such change. An emotionally healthy person takes each of these steps in order. Suffering through personal losses is not abnormal, nor is acknowledging your suffering a sign of weakness or inability. The truth is that failing to go through each of these steps is often detrimental. If you skip one, you will most likely have to return to it at some time.

1. **Emotional standstill.** The first reaction we usually have to the news of a sudden death, for example, is to come to an emotional standstill. "Oh no!" we say. "How did it happen? When?" In shock there is a gap between rational thinking and emotions. When ex-Beatle Paul McCartney was sought out by the British press on the day after John Lennon's murder, he told them that he was sorry, but that he just couldn't "take it all in right now." His was a typical reaction: shock had done away with other emotions for the time being.

Even when an event is expected, as in the case of a prolonged dying process, a bad marriage that both partners knew would eventually end in divorce, or an expected job loss, an element of shock exists. The reality of the event produces a different mental state, no matter how much advance notice we have.

2. **Denial and anger.** "I just don't believe it!" is a typical response to a major change event. Although many of us can accept in our minds what has happened, we continue to deny it with our emotions. Ideally, this denial period is over in a few weeks or months. The longer the period lasts, the longer it will take to move through the healing process.

At times, the denial is replaced by anger, usually containing an element of helplessness, of being a victim unable to prevent the change. Most psychologists advise expressing this anger in ways that will not harm others. This is the point where support groups can be helpful. Having other people who will listen and empathize with you and your anger is often a great help in itself.

3. **Helplessness.** We could call this step "trying but still failing." At this step the person is still suffering from the loss, but is afraid to "bottom out," because despair is a helpless condition, and most of us don't want to feel helpless. Thus, we usually make one of two mistakes. Either we try to share our emotions with too many people, or we retreat into isolation. Both extremes are negative. The first is a quick way to lose friends, and the second is self-destructive. To move through this stage effectively, we must be constantly aware of the reality of others; most friends cannot, and should not, enter into our sorrow with us. We must treat the others in our lives only to small doses of our grief.

4. **Bottoming out.** At this bottom point, for the first time since the event, you find yourself able to let go of the emotional burden that has been weighing you down. Often a person knows when this point has been reached by a peaceful feeling that comes upon awakening some morning. More often, the step itself is gradual. Bottoming out means releasing the thoughts, tensions, memories, and emotions that force you to hold onto the past. At this point, you are allowing the life-completing processes to take their course. The shock, the denial, and the anger are becoming memories.

5. **Experimenting.** Now that you have bottomed out and are on your way to recovery, your normal curiosities and desires to experiment come back to life. If the event was a divorce or death of a spouse, this is the stage where it becomes possible to spend time with the

opposite sex with romantic intentions. If it was a loss of a job, the experimentation is with tasks and opportunities you probably wouldn't have considered before. You now have emotions left over for other people and other projects; not so much of your energy is being consumed by your own recovery. For this reason, you are likely to be better company for others. (Note, though, that we are often forced into another job out of financial necessity, before we are emotionally ready to adapt. In such a case, the bottoming out and experimenting must be done in a different context.)

6. **Completion.** *Some call this step rebirth.* Although that term might sound dramatic, it is somewhat accurate. The cycle you have gone through is complete. This is not to say that you won't ever be haunted by the past, nor does it mean there won't be days when you feel you've gone right back to step one of the earlier steps. That sort of occasional *regression* is also normal. But you now have a new perspective. Far from being blocked out, the event has become a part of your active memory, a part that you can think about without pain.

Source Loweil Lamberton and Leslie Minor, *Human Relations* (Burr Ridge, Ill.: Richard D. Irwin, 1995). Copyright © 1995 by Richard D. Irwin. All rights reserved. Reprinted by permission.

Vocabulary in Context:

1. detrimental _____

_____

2. empathize _____

_____

3. regression _____

_____

4. What is the main idea of this excerpt? _____

_____

_____

_____

5. List six major details that support the main idea.

a. _____

b. _____

c. _____

d. _____

e. _____

f. _____

6. Which of the following patterns of organization did the author use? _____

   a. sequence (time order)
   b. enumeration
   c. cause and effect
   d. generalization

7. _____ Fact or opinion: There are six stages of personal change that make up the process of healthy reaction to such change.

8. _____ Yes or no: The author implies that a person who is suffering due to a loss would not lose friends if he or she "bottoms out."

9. Identify which statement makes a point and which two support it.

   a. _____ Failing to go through the stages could be detrimental.

   b. _____ Following the six stages of personal change helps people react to change in a healthy way.

   c. _____ Skipping a stage might mean having to return to it.

10. Summarize this excerpt. _____

Related Study Skills #10: Graphic Materials

The true test of understanding graphic material is being able to summarize a chart, graph, drawing, map, or table in your own words. To be able to summarize the graphic, you need to know exactly what it represents. The following guidelines will help you to get the kind of information you need to understand and summarize all types of graphics.

- **First, begin by reading the title.** The title tells you what the graphic is about and how it fits into the assignment you are reading. It is also a one-line summary of the entire graphic.
- **Second, read any introductory information.** Graphics usually have a sentence or two or a brief paragraph that will provide information that will help you in interpreting them.
- **Third, determine the purpose of the graphic.** There is a reason that the information is graphically displayed rather than given in sentences and paragraphs. If the reason is not clear, try turning the title of the graphic into a question. The answer to the question is often the purpose of the graphic.
- **Fourth, determine the type of graphic being displayed.** Different types of graphics have different purposes. A line graph has a different purpose from a pie graph and a process chart has a different purpose from an organizational chart. Identifying the type of graphic helps you to determine its purpose.
- **Fifth, make sure you read all the information that is given on the graphic.** There are a lot of clues that are provided by the information along the sides, across the top, and across the bottom. Ignoring this information may lead to an incorrect understanding of the graphic.
- **Sixth, be sure you understand what is being measured.** Is the graphic using numbers, ideas, things, places, or people? If you do not know what is being measured, then you cannot make sense out of the graphic.
- **Seventh, see if there are any codes or keys.** These are sometimes used to save space and at the same time provide important information.
- **Eighth, find the relationship between the graphic and the text.** Reading the text around the graphic will help you to better understand the relationship between the two.
- **Ninth, try to identify the main idea of the graphic.** Think back to the title, purpose, and type of graphic. Then write a main idea for the graphic in a complete sentence.
- **Finally, summarize the graphic in your own words.** By summarizing the graphic in your own words, you will be able to see how well you understood it. Summarizing is the true test of understanding.

EXERCISE 10.7

Directions: To see how well you can read and understand graphics, look at the graph on the next page, then follow the guidelines above to complete this exercise.

1. What kind of graphic is this? _____

_____

2. What is its purpose? _____

_____

_____

Figure 3–9 Government spending and revenue. Most of the government's revenue comes from you and me and other taxpayers in the form of taxes and social security payments. Corporate taxes provide a much smaller revenue source. The bulk of spending goes to individuals in the form of welfare, social security, and related programs. Defense takes a little less than 20%. The national debt gobbles up 14 percent in interest payments.

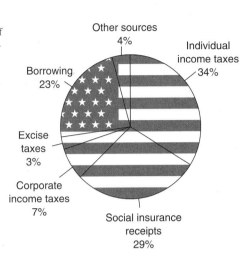

Revenue
Where it comes from . . .

- Other sources 4%
- Individual income taxes 34%
- Borrowing 23%
- Excise taxes 3%
- Corporate income taxes 7%
- Social insurance receipts 29%

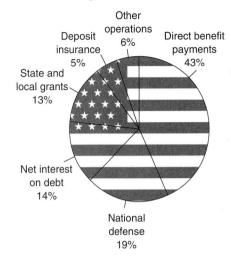

Spending
Where it goes . . .

- Other operations 6%
- Deposit insurance 5%
- Direct benefit payments 43%
- State and local grants 13%
- Net interest on debt 14%
- National defense 19%

Source: William G. Nickels, James M. McHugh, and Susan McHugh, *Understanding Business*, 3rd ed. Adapted by permission.

3. What is the title of this graphic? _____

4. How many items are in each graphic? _____

5. What is the largest source of revenue? _____

6. What is the smallest source of revenue? _____

7. Where does most of the spending go? _____

8. Where does the least amount of the spending go? _____

9. How much revenue does corporate income tax generate? _____

10. Summarize the information in this graphic in your own words.

Making the Connection

Reflection Entry #10

Directions: After taking a few moments to reflect on the information in this chapter, write an essay summarizing what you have learned about summarizing and how you will apply that knowledge to your textbook reading assignments.

_____
_____
_____
_____
_____
_____
_____
_____
_____
_____
_____
_____
_____
_____
_____
_____
_____
_____
_____
_____
_____
_____
_____

Ten Practice Tests

Directions: After reading the following practice tests, answer the questions by circling the correct answers and by writing the correct answers on the lines provided.

Practice Test 1

The Chemical Senses

In the spring of 1985 a group of chemists practically turned American society upside down simply by shifting a few carbon, hydrogen, and oxygen atoms. Or so it seemed when the Coca-Cola company changed the formula for Coke. The uproar forced the company to bring back the original flavor that summer—even after spending millions of dollars advertising the virtues of the new Coke. The chemists at the Coca-Cola company were dealing with one of the chemical senses—the gustatory (or taste) sense. The other chemical sense, the olfactory sense, involves smell. Both taste and smell differ from other senses—seeing, hearing, and the skin senses, for example—because they react to *chemicals,* whereas the other senses react to *energy.*

Taste It's not the prettiest sight you've ever seen, but try this anyway. Take a drink of milk and allow it to coat your tongue. Then go to a mirror, stick out your tongue, and look carefully at its surface. You should be able to see rounded bumps above the surface of your tongue (Matlin, 1988). Those bumps, called **papillae,** *contain your taste buds, the receptors for taste.* About 10,000 of these taste buds are located on your tongue, around your mouth, and even in your throat.

Taste buds respond to four main qualities: sweet, sour, bitter, and salty. Although all areas of the tongue can detect each of the four tastes, different regions of the tongue are more sensitive to one taste than another. The tip of the tongue is the most sensitive to sweet; the rear of the tongue is the most sensitive to bitter; just behind the area for sweet is the most sensitive area for salt; and just behind that is the most sensitive for sour.

Smell Smell is an important but mysterious sense. We take time to see a sunset or a play, to hear a symphony or a rock concert, and to feel the tension leave our muscles during a massage. But have you ever thought of taking the time to indulge

Note: All the excerpts in these practice tests are from John W. Santrock, *Psychology,* 4th ed. (Dubuque, Iowa: Times Mirror Higher Education Group, 1995) Copyright © 1995 by Times Mirror Education Group, Inc. All rights reserved. Reprinted by permission.

your sense of smell (Matlin, 1988)? Probably not, but smell can kindle pleasure or trigger discomfort—when we inhale the aroma of a fresh flower or when we encounter a skunk, for example.

We detect the scent of a fresh flower or a skunk when airborne molecules of an odor reach tiny receptor cells in the roof of our nasal cavity. The **olfactory epithelium**, *located at the top of the nasal cavity, is the sheet of receptor cells for smell.* These receptor sites are covered with millions of minute hairlike antennae that project through mucous in the nasal cavity and make contact with air on its way to the throat and lungs. Ordinarily, only a small part of the air you inhale passes the smell receptors. That is why we sometimes have to sniff deeply to get the full odor of an interesting or alarming smell—the bouquet of a fine wine or the odor of escaping gas, for example. Doing so changes the normal flow of air so that more air, with its odorous molecules, contacts the receptors.

You have just read about how taste can be classified into four main categories; sweet, sour, salty, and bitter. Are there agreed-upon main categories of odors, too? Some researchers argue that there are seven primary odors—florals, peppermint, ethereal (as in the gas, ether), musky, camphoraceous (such as mothballs), pungent, and putrid (Amoore, 1970). However, the consensus is that olfactory researchers have yet to demonstrate that different categories of smell have distinct chemical make-ups and receptor sites on the olfactory epithelium (Schiffman & Gatlin, 1930).

How good are you at recognizing smells? Without practice, most people do a rather poor job of identifying odors. But the human olfactory sense can be improved. Perfumers, as perfume testers are called, can distinguish between 100 and 200 different fragrances. If you have or have had a dog, though, you probably know that canines have a keener sense of smell than humans. One reason is that a dog's smell receptors are located along the main airflow route and a dog's smell-receptor sites are 100 times larger than yours.

1. Gustatory sense refers to:
    a. Smell
    b. Papillae
    c. Taste

2. Olfactory refers to:
    a. Hairlike antennae
    b. Smell
    c. Chemicals

3. What is the main idea of paragraph 3?

    Taste buds respond to 4 qualities

4. True or False: Taste can be classified into four main categories: sweet, cold, sour, and hot.

5. This excerpt follows which pattern of organization?
    a. Compare and contrast
    b. Cause and effect
    c. Enumeration

6. Fact or **Opinion**: Smell is an important but mysterious sense.
7. The author implies that:
   a. Identifying smells correctly takes practice.
   b. Only perfumers identify smells correctly.
   c. Animals have a keener sense of smell than humans.
8. From this excerpt, we can conclude that the smell of a freshly baked apple pie could induce a feeling of:
   a. Sadness   **b.** Pleasure   c. Discontent
9. From this excerpt, we can conclude that:
   a. Humans would be better off it they had the same keen sense of smell as dogs.
   b. More research needs to be done on the different categories of smell.
   c. The sense of taste is more important than the sense of smell.
10. Summarize this excerpt in your own words.

omit

Practice Test 2

Extrasensory Perception

Our eyes, mouth, nose, and skin provide us with sensory information about the external world. Our perceptions are based on our interpretation of this sensory information. Some people, though, claim that they can perceive the world through something other than normal sensory pathways. Literally, **extrasensory perception (ESP)** *is perception which occurs outside of the use of any known sensory process.* The majority of psychologists do not believe in ESP. However, a small number of psychologists do investigate ESP (Persinger & Kripper, in press).

Extrasensory experiences fall into three main categories. The first is **telepathy,** *which involves the transfer of thought from one person to another.* For example, this skill is supposedly possessed by people who can "read" another person's mind. If two people are playing cards and one person can tell what cards the other person picked up, telepathy is taking place. **Precognition** *involves "knowing" events before they happen.* For example, a fortune teller might claim to see into the future and tell you what will happen to you in the coming year. Or an astrologist might predict that a major earthquake will take place in Los Angeles in June of next year. **Clairvoyance** *involves the ability to perceive remote events that are not in sight.* For example, a person at a movie theater senses a burglar breaking into his house at that moment. **Psychokinesis,** closely associated with ESP, *is the mind-over-matter phenomenon of being able to move objects without touching them.* For example, a person may mentally get a chair to rise off the floor or shatter a glass merely by staring at it.

One of the most famous claims of ESP involved Uri Geller, a psychic who supposedly performed mind-boggling feats. Observers saw Geller correctly predict the number on a die rolled in a closed box 8 out of 8 times, reproduce drawings that were hidden in sealed envelopes, bend forks without touching them, and start broken watches. While he had worked as a magician, Geller claimed his supernatural powers were created by energy sent from another universe. Careful investigation of Geller's feats revealed they were nothing more than a magician's tricks. For example, in the case of the die, Geller was allowed to shake the box and open it himself, giving him an opportunity to manipulate the die (Randi, 1980).

Through their astonishing stage performance, many psychics are very convincing. They seemingly are able to levitate tables, communicate with spirits, and read an audience member's mind. Many psychics, like Uri Geller, are also magicians who have the ability to perform sleight-of-hand maneuvers and dramatic manipulations that go unnoticed by most human eyes. One magician's personal goal, though, is to expose the hoaxes of the psychics. James Randi (1980) has investigated a number of psychics' claims and publicized their failures.

Not only have magicians such as Randi investigated the psychics' claims, but scientists have also examines ESP in experimental contexts. Some ESP enthusiasts believe that the phenomenon is more likely to occur when a subject is totally relaxed and deprived of sensory input. In this kind of experiment, the subject lies down and half a ping-pong ball is placed over each eye, affixed with cotton and tape. An experimenter watches through a one-way mirror from an adjacent room, listening to a recording of the subject's statements. At an agreed-upon time, someone from another location concentrates on the message to be sent mind-to-mind.

Carl Sargent (1987) has used this procedure in a number of telepathy experiments and reported a great deal of ESP success. In one experiment, Sargent has a "sender" mentally transmit an image of one of four pictures selected from one of 27 randomly selected sets of four pictures. Immediately afterward, the experimenter and the subject examined a duplicate set of four pictures and together judged and ranked their degree of correspondence with the subject's recorded impression. Experimental psychologist Susan Blackmore (1987) was skeptical about Sargent's success in ESP experiments, so she visited his laboratory at Cambridge University in England and observed a number of his telepathy sessions. With the subject shown four pictures, the success rate expected by chance was 25 percent (1 of 4 pictures). In the experimental sessions observed by Blackmore, the subjects were correct 50 percent of the time, a hit rate far exceeding chance.

Sargent supposedly invokes a number of elaborate procedures to protect randomization, experimenter bias, unbiased selection by the subject, and so on. Blackmore was still skeptical, finding some disturbing flaws in the way Sargent's experiments were conducted. In some sessions, Sargent did the randomization of the pictures himself, putting himself where he could manipulate the ordering of the pictures. In other sessions, he came in while the subject was judging the pictures and "pushed" the subject toward the picture that had been "transmitted" by the "sender."

No one has been able to replicate the high hit rates in Sargent's experiments. Proponents of ESP, such as Sargent, claim that they have demonstrated the existence of ESP, but critics such as Blackmore demand to see or experience the same phenomena themselves. Replication is one of the hallmarks of scientific investigation, yet replication has been a major thorn in the side of the ESP researchers. ESP phenomena have not been reproducible when rigorous experimental standards are applied (Alcock, 1989; Hines, 1988; Hines & Dennison, 1989; Jensen, 1989; Nickell, 1989).

1. Replication means

    a. Randomization   b. Selection   c. Reproduction

2. What is the main idea of paragraph 5?

_____

_____

_____

_____

_____

3. According to the excerpt, extrasensory perception is
   a. Performed only by magicians
   b. Not accepted by most psychologists
   c. Used only by Uri Geller
4. The following sentence sets up which pattern of organization?
   Extrasensory experiences fall into three main categories.
   a. Enumeration/simple list   b. Compare and contrast   c. Generalization
5. Fact or Opinion: One of the most famous claims of ESP involved Uri Geller, a psychic who supposedly performed mind-boggling feats.
6. Fact or Opinion: Through their astonishing stage performance, many psychics are very convincing.
7. What can you conclude about Sargent's experiments?

_____

_____

_____

8. Based on this excerpt, we can conclude that:
   a. Magicians do not believe in psychics.
   b. Magicians and psychics use the same tricks.
   c. Magicians are similar to psychics.
9. We can infer from Sargent's experiment that
   a. He cheated.   b. He knew his subjects.   c. The experiments were fixed.
10. Summarize this excerpt in your own words.

_____

_____

_____

_____

_____

_____

_____

10. Summarize this excerpt in your own words.

Practice Test 5

Do Animals Have Language?

Many animal species do have complex and ingenious ways to signal danger and to communicate about basic needs such as food and sex. For example, in one species of firefly the female has learned to imitate the flashing signal of another species to lure the aliens into her territory. Then she eats them. But is this language in the human sense? And what about higher animals, such as apes? Is ape language similar to human language? Can we teach language to them?

Some researchers believe apes can learn language. One simian celebrity in this field is a chimp named Washoe, who was adopted when she was about 10-months-old (Gardner & Gardner, 1971). Since apes do not have the vocal apparatus to speak, the researchers tried to teach Washoe the American Sign language, which is one of the sign languages of the deaf. Washoe used sign language during everyday activities, such as meals, play, and car rides. In two years, Washoe learned 38 different signs and by the age of five she had a vocabulary of 160 signs. Washoe learned how to put signs together in novel ways, such as "you drink" and "you me tickle." A number of other efforts to teach language to chimps have had similar results (Premack, 1986).

The debate about chimpanzees' ability to use language focuses on two key issues: Can apes understand the meaning of symbols; that is, can they comprehend that one thing stands for another? And can apes learn syntax; that is, can they learn the mechanics and rules that give human language its creative productivity? The first of these issues may have been settled recently by Sue Savage-Rumbaugh and Duane Rumbaugh (1990). The researchers found strong evidence that two chimps named Sherman and Austin can understand symbols (see figure 10). For example, if Sherman or Austin are sitting in a room, and a symbol for an object is displayed on a screen, they will go into another room, find the object, and bring it back. If the object is not there, they will come back empty-handed (Cowley, 1988). Austin can play a game in which one chimp points to a symbol for food (M & Ms), and the other chimp selects the food from a tray, then they both eat it. These observations are clear evidence that chimps can understand symbols (Rumbaugh & others, 1991).

However, there still is no strong evidence that chimps can learn syntax. Perhaps other animals can. Ron Schusterman has worked with a sea lion named "Rocky," teaching him to follow commands such as "ball fetch" and "disc ball fetch." The first command means that Rocky should take a disc to a ball in his tank. The second command means that Rocky should take the ball to the disc. Although Rocky and other sea lions make some errors in decoding these complex commands, they perform much better than chance, indicating they have learned rules that link the ordering of symbols to abstract meanings. Such rules are either syntax or something close to it.

The debate over whether or not animals can use language to express thoughts is far from resolved. Researchers do agree that animals can communicate with each other and that some can be trained to manipulate language-like symbols. While such accomplishments may be remarkable, they fall far short of human language, with its infinite number of novel phrases to convey the richness and subtleties of meaning that are the foundation of human relationships.

1. What does syntax mean?

   _____

   _____

   _____

2. What is the main idea of paragraph 2?
   a. Since apes do not have the vocal apparatus to speak, the researchers tried to teach Washoe the American Sign language of the deaf.
   b. Some researchers believe apes can learn language.
   c. A number of other efforts to teach language to chimps have had similar results.

3. What two things will determine a chimp's ability to use language?

   _____

   _____

   _____

   _____

4. Washoe could communicate through _____

   _____

   _____

5. Fact or Opinion: Washoe is a very intelligent ape.

6. Fact or Opinion: Sherman and Austin's game proves that chimps understand language.

7. We can infer that apes and chimps can learn language because:
   a. All apes can use sign language
   b. A chimp named Washoe has a vocabulary of 160 signs
   c. They have vocal apparatus

8. Using the facts in this excerpt, support the following point with three supporting points.

   Animals can communicate.

   1. _____

   2. _____

   3. _____

9. Using the facts in thes excerpt, support the following point with three supporting points:

Animals can learn syntax

1. _____

2. _____

3. _____

10. Summarize this excerpt in your own words.

_____
_____
_____
_____
_____
_____
_____
_____
_____
_____
_____
_____

Practice Test 6

Culture and the Expression of Emotions

In *The Expression of the Emotions in Man and Animals,* Charles Darwin (1872) argued that the facial expressions of human beings are innate, not learned; are the same in all cultures around the world; and evolved from the emotions of animals. Darwin compared the similarity of human snarls of anger with the growls of dogs and the hisses of cats. He compared the giggling of chimpanzees when they are tickled under their arms with human laughter.

Today psychologists still believe that emotions, especially facial expressions of emotion, have strong biological ties. For example, children who are blind from birth and have never observed the smile or frown on another person's face, still smile or frown in the same way that children with normal vision do.

The universality of facial expressions and the ability of people from different cultures to accurately label the emotion that lies behind the facial expression has been extensively researched. Psychologist Paul Ekman's (1980, 1985, 1993) careful observations reveal that our many faces of emotion do not vary significantly from one culture to another. For example, Ekman and his colleague photographed people expressing emotions such as happiness, fear, surprise, disgust, and grief. They found that when they showed the photographs to other people from the United States, Chile, Japan, Brazil, and Borneo (an Indonesian island in the western Pacific Ocean), each person tended to label the same faces with the same emotions (Ekman & Friesen, 1968). In another study the focus was on the way the Fore tribe, an isolated Stone Age culture in New Guinea, matched descriptions of emotions with facial expressions (Ekman & Friesen, 1971). Before Ekman's visit, most of the Fore had never seen a Caucasian face. Ekman showed them photographs of American faces expressing emotions such as fear, happiness, anger, and surprise. Then he read stories about people in emotional situations. The Fore were able to match the descriptions of emotions with the facial expressions in the photographs. The similarity of facial expressions of emotions by persons in New Guinea and the United States is shown in figure 12.

While facial expressions of basic emotions appear to be universal across cultures, display rules for emotion are not culturally universal. **Display rules** *are sociocultural standards that determine when, where, and how emotions should be expressed.* For example, while happiness is a universally expressed emotion, when, where, and how it is displayed may vary from one culture to another. The same is true for other emotions such as fear, sadness, and anger. For example, members of the Utku culture in Alaska discourage anger by cultivating acceptance and by dissociating themselves from any display of anger (Briggs, 1970). If a trip is hampered by an unexpected snowstorm, the Utku do not become frustrated, but accept the presence of the snowstorm and build an igloo. Most of us would not act as mildly in the face of subzero weather and barriers to our travel.

In addition to facial expressions, emotions are also expressed in many other nonverbal signals of body movement, posture, and gesture. Some basic nonverbal signals appear to be universal indicators of certain emotions, just as facial expressions are. For example, when people are depressed it shows not only in their sad facial expression, but also in their slow body movement, downturned head, and slumped posture (Blanck, Buck, & Rosenthal, 1986).

Many nonverbal signals of emotion, though, vary from one culture to another. For example, male-to-male kissing is commonplace is some cultures, such as Yemen (in the Middle East), but uncommon in other cultures, such as the United States. And, the "thumb up" sign, which means either everything is OK or the desire to hitch a ride in most cultures, is an insult in Greece, similar to a raised third finger in the United States (Morris & others, 1979).

1. What is the main idea of the last paragraph?

_____

_____

_____

2. Darwin compared humans to:
   a. Objects in other cultures.
   b. Different animals.
   c. Matched descriptions.

3. Which pattern of organization does the first paragraph follow?

_____

4. Which words tipped you off?

_____

_____

5. Which pattern of organization does the entire excerpt follow?

_____

6. Which words tipped you off?

_____

_____

7. Fact or Opinion: Based on the Utku example, most of us would not act as _____ mildly in the face of subzero weather and barriers to our travel plans.

8. We can infer that the Utku people:
   a. Make the best out of bad situations.
   b. Are smarter than most cultures.
   c. Like to build igloos.

9. What can you conclude about nonverbal signals?

10. Summarize this excerpt in your own words.

Practice Test 7

What Is Language?

It is our ability to communicate in spoken and written language that sets us completely apart from all other animals. Our language allows us to describe past events in detail, and to plan for the future in carefully considered steps. Language gives us the opportunity to pass knowledge along from generation to generation and to create a rich cultural heritage.

Every culture depends on language. Human languages number in the thousands, differing so much on the surface that many of us despair of learning more than even one. Yet all human languages have some common characteristics. **Language** *is a system of symbols used to communicate with others. In humans, language is characterized by rules to organize it and infinite generativity.* **Infinite generativity** *is a person's ability to produce an endless number of meaningful sentences using a finite set of words and rules, which makes language a highly creative enterprise.* Studies on the structure and mechanics of language include phonology, morphology, syntax and semantics, each of which we now discuss in turn.

Language is made up of basic sounds or phonemes. In the English language there are approximately 36 phonemes. **Phonology** *is the study of language's sound system.* Phonological rules ensure that certain sound sequences occur (for example, *sp, ba,* or *ar*) and others do not (for example, *zx,* or *qp*). A good example of a phoneme in the English language is /k/, the sound represented by the letter k in the word ski and the letter c in the word cat. While the /k/ sound is slightly different in these two words, the variation is not distinguished and the /k/ sound is described as a single phoneme. In some languages, such as Arabic, this kind of variation represents separate phonemes.

Morphology *refers to the rules for combining morphemes, the smallest string of sounds that gives meaning to what we say and hear.* Every word in the English language is made up of one or more morphemes. Some words consist of a single morpheme (for example, *help*), while others are made up of more than one morpheme (for example, *helper,* which has two morphemes, *help + er,* with the er meaning "one who," in this case "one who helps.") However, not all morphemes are words (for example, *pre-, -tion,* and *-ing*). Just as the rules that govern phonemes ensure that certain sound sequences occur, the rules that govern morphemes ensure that certain strings of sounds occur in particular sequences. For example, we would not reorder *helper* to *erhelp*.

Syntax *involves the way words are combined to form acceptable phrases and sentences.* If I say to you, "Bob slugged Tom" and "Bob was slugged by Tom," you know who did the slugging and who was slugged in each case because we share the same syntactic understanding of sentence structure. You also understand that the sentence, "You didn't stay, did you?" is a grammatical sentence but that "You didn't stay, didn't you?" is unacceptable and ambiguous.

Semantics *refers to the meaning of words and sentences.* Every word has a set of semantic features. *Girl* and *woman,* for example, share the same semantic features as the words *female* and *human* but differ in regard to age. Words have semantic restriction on how they can be used in sentences. The sentence "The bicycle talked the boy into buying a candy bar" is syntactically correct but semantically incorrect. The sentence violates our semantic knowledge—bicycles do not talk.

1. Phoneme means:

   a. /k/ b. Language c. Basic sounds

2. What is the main idea of paragraph 2?

3. What is the purpose of having phonological rules?

4. What do the rules that govern morphemes ensure?

5. What would happen if we did not pay attention to syntax?

6. Why is it important for words to have semantic restrictions?

7. Fact or Opinion: Language gives us the opportunity to pass knowledge along from generation to generation and to create a rich cultural heritage.

8. Using the facts in this excerpt, support the following point with three supporting points:

   Language has to be governed by rules.

   1. _____
   2. _____
   3. _____

9. What can you conclude about language?

   _____
   _____
   _____
   _____

10. Summarize this excerpt in your own words.

Practice Test 8

Gender Similarities and Differences

There is a growing consensus that differences between the sexes are greatly exaggerated (Hyde, 1981; Hyde, 1991; Hyde in press. Linn & Hyde, 1991). It is not unusual to find statements such as the following: "While only 32 percent of the women were found to . . . , fully 37 percent of the men were . . ." This difference of 5 percent is probably a very small difference, and may not even be statistically significant or capable of being replicated in a separate study (Denmark & others, 1988). And when statements are made about female-male comparisons, such as "males out-perform females in math," this does not mean all females versus all males. Rather, it usually means the average math achievement scores for males at certain ages is higher than the average math achievement scores for females. The math achievement scores of females and males overlap considerably, so that while an average difference may favor males, many females have higher math achievement than many males. Further, there is a tendency to think of differences between females and males as biologically based. Remember that when differences occur they may be influenced by society and culture.

Let's now examine some of the differences between the sexes, keeping in mind that (a) the differences are averages; (b) even when differences are reported, there is considerable overlap between the sexes; and (c) the differences may be due primarily to biological factors, sociocultural factors, or both. First, we examine physical and biological differences, then turn to cognitive and social differences.

Females, on average, live longer than males (McBride, 1993). Females are also less likely than males to develop certain physical disorders. Estrogen strengthens the immune system, making females more resistant to some kinds of infection, for example, and female hormones signal the liver to produce more "good" cholesterol, which makes their blood vessels more "elastic." Testosterone triggers the production of low-density lipoprotein, which clogs blood vessels, and as a result, males have twice the risk of coronary disease as females. Higher levels of stress hormones cause faster clotting in males, but also higher blood pressure. Adult females have about twice the body fat of their male counterparts, most concentrated around breasts and hips; in males, fat is more likely to go to the abdomen. Males grow about 10 percent taller than females on average. Male hormones promote the growth of long bones; female hormones stop such growth at puberty. In short, there are many physical differences between females and males. But are there as many cognitive differences?

In a classic review of gender differences in 1974, Eleanor Maccoby and Carol Jacklin concluded that males have better math skills and better visual and spatial ability (the kind of skills an architect would need to design a building's angles and dimensions), while females have better verbal abilities. Recently, however, Maccoby (1987, 1990) revised her conclusion about several gender dimensions. Verbal differences between the sexes have virtually disappeared, she now says, though the math and spatial differences still exist.

A number of researchers believe there are more cognitive similarities than there are differences between females and males. They also believe that the differences that do exist, such as the mathematical differences, have been exaggerated. Males do outperform females in math, but only for a certain portion of the population—the gifted (Hyde, in press). Further, males do not always outperform females on all mathematical tasks; consistent differences occur only in the ability to rotate objects mentally (Linn & Petersen, 1986). And keep in mind our earlier comment about the considerable overlap between females and males. Figure 4 shows the small average difference on mathematical tasks that favors males, but also clearly reveals the substantial overlap in the mathematical abilities of females and males. Combined with the fact that females no longer have higher scores on the verbal section of the SAT, we can conclude that cognitive differences between females and males do not exist in many areas, are disappearing in other areas, and are small when they do exist.

Males are more active and aggressive than females (Maccoby, 1987; Maccoby & Jacklin, 1974). The consistent difference in aggression often appears in children's development as early as two years of age. Although males and females do not experience different emotions, they frequently differ in the emotions they feel free to express in public and how they express those emotions (Doyle & Paludi, 1991; Paludi, 1992). Females tend to be better at "reading" emotions (Malatesta, 1990). With regard to helping behavior, social psychologists Alice Eagly and Maureen Crowley (1986) argue that the female gender role fosters behavior that is nurturant and caring, while the male gender role promotes behavior that is heroic and chivalrous. They found that males were more likely to help in situations in which there was a perceived danger and in which males felt most competent to help. For example, males are more likely than females to help when a person is standing by the roadside with a flat tire, a situation involving some danger and a circumstance in which many males feel a sense of competence—automobile problems. In contrast, if the situation involves volunteering time to help a problem child, most researchers have found more helping females because there is little danger present for the helper and because females feel more competent in nurturing (Hyde, 1990). As early as elementary school, girls show more caregiving behavior (Zahn-Waxler, 1990). However, in cultures where boys and girls both care for younger siblings, boys and girls are more similar in their nurturant behavior (Whiting, 1989).

Might the way females and males are socialized as they grow up produce differences in the way they talk with each other? Sociolinguist Deborah Tannen (1990) thinks so. To read about her provocative ideas on women and men in conversation, turn to Explorations in Psychology 2.

1. What is the main idea of paragraph 4?

Tells about the differences between the males and females.

2. List some physical and biological differences between the sexes.

Females live longer. Females have twice the body fat. Males grow 10 percent taller than females on average.

3. List some cognitive differences between the sexes.

Males do outperform females in math. Males do not always outperform females on all mathematical tasks; consistent differences occur only in the ability to rotate objects mentally.

4. List some social differences between the sexes.

5. Which pattern of organization does the author follow?

Comparison and contrast

6. True or ~~False~~: Men outperform women on all mathematical tasks.

7. ~~Fact~~ or Opinion: Females feel more competent in a nurturing situation than men.

8. We can infer that men are more likely to:
   a. Hide their feelings in public.
   b. Feel free to express their feelings in public.
   c. Not know how to express their feelings in public.

9. Using facts from this excerpt, prove the following statement:

The cognitive differences between females and males do not exist in many areas, are disappearing in other areas, and are small when they do exist.

10. Summarize this excerpt in your own words.

Practice Test 9

Smoking

The year 1988 marked the seventy-fifth anniversary of the introduction of Camel cigarettes. Selected magazines surprised readers with elaborate pup-up advertisements for Camels. Camel's ad theme was "75 years and still smokin'." Coincidentally, 1988 was also the seventy-fifth anniversary of the American Cancer Society.

In 1989 the Surgeon General and his advisory committee issued a report, *Reducing the Health Consequences of Smoking: 25 Years of Progress.* It was released 25 years after the original warnings that cigarettes are responsible for major health problems, especially lung cancer. New evidence was presented to show that smoking is even more harmful than previously thought. The report indicated that, in 1985, for example, cigarette smoking accounted for more than one-fifth of all deaths in the United States—20 percent higher than previously believed. Thirty percent of all cancer deaths are attributed to smoking, as are 21 percent of all coronary heart disease deaths, and 82 percent of chronic pulmonary disease deaths.

Researchers are also increasingly finding that passive smoke (environmental smoke inhaled by nonsmokers who live or work around smokers) carries health risks (Sandler & others, 1989). Passive smoke is estimated to be the culprit in as many as 8,000 lung cancer deaths a year in the United States. Children of smokers are at special risk for respiratory and middle-ear diseases. For children under the age of five, the risk of upper respiratory tract infection is doubled if their mothers smoke.

The Surgeon General's 1989 report contains some good news, however. Fewer people smoke today and almost half of all living adults who ever smoked have quit. In particular, the prevalence of smoking among men fell from over 50 percent in 1965 to about 30 percent in 1989. As a consequence, a half-century's uninterrupted escalation in the rate of death due to lung cancer among males has ceased. And the incidence of lung cancer among White males has fallen. Although approximately 56 million Americans 15 to 84 years of age were smokers in 1985, the Surgeon General's report estimates that 91 million would have been smoking had there been no changes in smoking and health knowledge, norms, and policy over the past quarter century (Warner, 1989).

However, the bad news is that over 50 million Americans continue to smoke, most having failed at attempts to quit. Why, in the face of the damaging figure that more than one-fifth of all deaths are due to smoking, do so many people still smoke?

Smoking Is Addictive and Reinforcing Most adult smokers would like to quit, but their addiction to nicotine often turns their efforts into dismal failures. Nicotine, the active drug in cigarettes, is a stimulant that increases a smoker's energy and alertness, a pleasurable experience that is positively reinforcing. Nicotine also causes the release of acetylcholine and endorphin neurotransmitters, which have a calming and pain-reducing effect. However, smoking not only works as a positive reinforcer; it also works as a negative reinforcer by ending a smoker's painful craving for nicotine. A smoker gets relief from this painful aversive state simply by smoking another cigarette.

We are rational, cognitive beings. Can't we develop enough self-control to overcome these pleasurable, immediate, reinforcing circumstances by thinking about the delayed, long-term, damaging consequences of smoking? As indicated earlier, many adults have quit smoking because they recognize that it is "suicide in slow motion," but the immediate pleasurable effects of smoking are extremely difficult to overcome.

Preventing Smoking   Smoking usually begins during childhood and adolescence. Adolescent smoking reached it peak in the early 1980s when 29 percent of high school seniors smoked on a daily basis. In 1989 this rate remained at 29 percent (Johnston, O'Malley, & Bachman, 1990). The smoking rate is at a level that will cut short the lives of many adolescents. Despite the growing awareness that it is important to keep children from starting to smoke in the first place, there are fewer restrictions on children's access to cigarettes today than there were in 1964, and the existing restrictions are rarely reinforced (United States Department of Health and Human Services, 1989).

Traditional school health programs appear to have succeeded in educating adolescents about the long-term health consequences of smoking but have had little effect on adolescent smoking *behavior.* That is, teens who smoke know all the facts about the health risks such as lung cancer, emphysema, and "suicide in slow motion," but they go ahead and smoke just as much anyway (Miller & Slap, 1989). As a result of this gap between what teens "know" and what the "do" in regard to smoking, researchers are focusing on the factors that place teens at high risk for future smoking, especially social pressures from peers, family members, and the media (Urberg, Shyu, & Liang, 1990). The tobacco industry preys on young peoples' desire to feel grown up by including "cool" people who smoke in their advertisements—successful young women smoking Virginia Slims cigarettes and rugged, handsome men smoking Marlboros, for example, The advertisements encourage adolescents to associate cigarette smoking with a successful and, ironically, athletic/active lifestyle. Legislators are trying to introduce more stringent laws to further regulate the tobacco industry.

In recent years, American health concerns have focused not only on smoking, but on eating as well. Next, we well discuss some of the eating habits that cause people problems.

1. What is the main idea of paragraph 8?

_____

_____

_____

2. What accounted for more than one-fifth of all deaths in 1985?

3. What are the effects of passive smoke?

4. Which pattern of organization does the author follow?

5. Fact or Opinion: The smoking rate is at a level that will cut short the lives of many adolescents.

6. We can infer that young people smoke because _____

7. Using the facts in this excerpt, support the following point with three supporting points:

   Cigarette smoking is harmful.

   1. _____
   2. _____
   3. _____

8. What can you conclude about existing restrictions on children's access to cigarettes?

9. What can you conclude about cigarette advertising?

_____
_____
_____
_____

10. Summarize this excerpt in your own words.

_____
_____
_____
_____
_____
_____
_____
_____
_____
_____
_____
_____

Practice Test 10

Attraction

What attracts us to others and motivates us to spend more time with them? Does just being around someone increase the likelihood a relationship will develop? Do birds of a feather flock together; that is, are we likely to associate with those who are similar to us? How important are the attractiveness and personality characteristics of another person?

Proximity and Similarity Physical proximity does not guarantee that we will develop a positive relationship with another person. Familiarity can breed contempt, but familiarity is a condition that is necessary for a close relationship to develop. For the most part, friends and lovers have been around each other for a long time; they may have grown up together, gone to high school or college together, worked together, or gone to the same social events. Once we have been exposed to someone for a period of time, what is it that makes the relationship breed friendship and even love?

Birds of a feather do indeed flock together. One of the most powerful lessons generated by the study of close relationships is that we like to associate with people who are similar to us. Our friends, as well as our lovers, are much more like us than unlike us. We have similar attitudes, behavior, and characteristics, as well as clothes, intelligence, personality, other friends, values, life-style, physical attractiveness, and so on. In some limited cases and on some isolated characteristics, opposites may attract. An introvert may wish to be with an extrovert, or someone with little money may wish to associate with someone who has a lot of money, for example. But overall we are attracted to individuals with similar rather than opposite characteristics (Berndt & Perry, 1990). In one study, for example, the old adage "misery loves company" was supported as depressed college students preferred to meet unhappy others while nondepressed college students preferred to meet happy others (Wenzlaff & Prohaska, 1989). The fact that individuals are attracted to each other on the basis of similar characteristics and attitudes is reflected in the questions that computer-dating services ask their clients (see table 1).

Consensual validation *provides an explanation of why people are attracted to others who are similar to them. Our own attitudes and behavior are supported when someone else's attitudes and behavior are similar to ours—their attitudes and behavior validate ours.* People tend to shy away from the unknown. We may tend, instead, to prefer people whose attitudes and behavior we can predict. And similarity implies that we will enjoy doing things with the other person, which often requires a partner who likes the same things and has similar attitudes.

Physical Attraction From the long list of characteristics on which partners in close relationships can be similar, one deserves special mention: physical attractiveness. How important is physical attractiveness in determining whether we like or love someone? In one experiment, college students assumed that a computer had determined their date on the basis of similar interests, but actually the dates were randomly assigned (Walster & others, 1966). The college students' social skills, physical appearance, intelligence, and personality were measured. Then a dance was set up for the matched partners. At intermission, the partners were asked in private to indicate the most positive aspects of their date that contributed to his or her attractiveness. The overwhelming reason was looks, not other factors such as personality or intelligence. Other research has documented the importance of physical attraction in close relationships; it has been associated with the number of dates female college students have in a year, how popular someone is with peers, attention given to an infant, positive encounters with teachers, and selection of a marital partner (Simpson, Campbell, & Berscheid, 1986).

Why do we want to be associated with attractive individuals? Again, as with similarity, it is rewarding to be around physically attractive people. It provides us with consensual validation that we too are attractive. As part of the rewarding experience, our self-image is enhanced. It also is aesthetically pleasing to look at physically attractive individuals. We assume that if individuals are physically attractive they will have other desirable traits that will interest us.

But we all can't have Sharon Stone or Tom Cruise as our friend or lover. How do we deal with this in our relationships? While beautiful women and handsome men seem to have an advantage, in the end, we usually seek out someone at our own level of attractiveness. Most of us come away with a reasonably good chance of finding a "good match." Research indicates that this **matching hypothesis**—*that while we may prefer a more attractive person in the abstract, in the real world we end up choosing someone who is close to our own level of attractiveness*—holds up (Kalick & Hamilton, 1986).

Heterosexual men and women differ on the importance they place on good looks when they seek an intimate partner. Women tend to rate traits such as considerateness, honesty, dependability, kindness, and understanding as most important; men list good looks, cooking skills, and frugality first (Buss & Barnes, 1986).

Several additional points help to clarify the role of physical beauty and attraction in our close relationships. Much of the research has focused on initial or short-term encounters; attraction over the course of months and years often is not evaluated. As relationships endure, physical attraction probably assumes less importance. Rocky Dennis, as portrayed in the movie *Mask,* is a case in point (see figure 1). His peers and even his mother initially wanted to avoid Rocky, whose face was severely distorted. But over the course of his childhood and adolescent years, the avoidance turned into attraction and love as people got to know him.

Our criteria for beauty may vary from one culture to another and from one point in history to another, so although attempts are being made to quantify beauty and to arrive at the ultimate criteria for such things as a beautiful female face, beauty is relative. In the 1940s and 1950s in the United States, a Marilyn Monroe body build (a well-rounded, shapely appearance) and face was the cultural ideal for women. In the 1970s, some women aspired to look like Twiggy and other virtually anorexic females. In the 1990s, the desire for thinness has not ended, but what is culturally beautiful is no longer pleasantly plump or anorexic but, rather, a tall stature with moderate curves. The current image of attractiveness also includes body toning through physical exercise and healthy eating habits. As we will see next, though, there is more to close relationships than physical attraction.

Personality Characteristics When you think of what attracts you to someone else, certain personality characteristics probably come to mind. Wouldn't you rather be around someone who is sincere, honest, understanding, loyal, truthful, trustworthy, intelligent, and dependable than someone who is a phony, mean, obnoxious, insulting, greedy, conceited, rude, and thoughtless? In one investigation, these and other personality traits were among those we like and do not like, respectively (Anderson, 1968)(see table 2).

1. Define *matching hypothesis*.

2. What is the main idea of paragraph 3?

3. What do women look for in a mate?

4. What do men look for in a mate?

5. True or False: Looks are more important to women than men.

6. Fact or Opinion: Physical attractiveness is more important than personality.

7. We can infer that if you are attractive, you will choose _____

8. Using the facts in this excerpt, support the following point with three supporting points:

   People want to be associated with attractive individuals.

   1. _____

   2. _____

   3. _____

9. What can you conclude about attraction?

   _____

   _____

   _____

   _____

10. Summarize this excerpt in your own words.

    _____

    _____

    _____

    _____

    _____

    _____

    _____

    _____

    _____

    _____

    _____

SOURCES AND ACKNOWLEDGMENTS

The authors acknowledge the following sources for their contributions to this text:

Boone, Louise E., and David L. Kurtz. *Contemporary Business*, 1994 ed. Fort Worth: The Dryden Press, 1993

Frown, Theodore L., and H. Eugene LeMay, Jr. *Chemistry: The Central Science*, 4th ed. Englewood Cliffs, N.J.: Prentice Hall, 1988.

Churchill, Peter, Jr. *Marketing: Creativing Value for Customer*. Burr Ridge, Ill.: Richard D. Irwin, Inc., 1995.

Coon, Dennis. *Introduction to Psychology*, 6th ed. St. Paul, Minn.: West Publishing Company, 1980.

Enger, Eldon D. *Concepts in Biology*, 7th ed. Dubuque, Iowa: Times Mirror Higher Education Group, Inc., 1994.

Gagnon, Patricia J., and Karen Silva. *Travel Career Development*, 5th ed. Burr Ridge, Ill.: Richard D. Irwin, Inc., 1993.

Garrity John A. *The American Nation: A History of the United States,* 7th ed. New York: HarperCollins Publishers, Inc., 1991.

Henslin, James M. *Sociology: A Down-to-Earth Approach*. New York: Allyn and Bacon, 1993.

Lamberton, Lowell, and Leslie Minor. *Human Relations*. Burr Ridge, Ill.: Richard D. Irwin, Inc., 1995.

Lesikar, Raymond, John D. Petit, Jr., and Marie Flatley. *Basic Business Communication*, 6th ed. Burr Ridge, Ill.: Richard D. Irwin, Inc., 1993.

Lopez, Victor D. *Business Law: An Introduction*, Homewood, Ill.: Irwin Mirror Press, 1993.

Nickels, William G., James M. McHugh, and Susan McHugh. *Understanding Business*, 3rd ed. Burr Ridge, Ill.: Richard D. Irwin, Inc., 1993.

Tortora, Gerald J. *Introduction to the Human Body.* New York: HarperCollins College Publishers, 1994.

SUBJECT INDEX

A

Academic writing, 157
Access, 263
Active reading/learning, 107
Affixes, 101, 105
Alternative positions, 243
Antonyms, 76
Appeal. *See* Authority; Emotional appeal; Fear; Patriotic appeal; Prejudice; Sympathy; Tradition
Appearance, 6
Appositives, 77
Argumentation, 241, 242. *See also* False argumentation
Arguments. *See* Unsound arguments
   appeals, 258-260
   connection, 266
   example, 243
   reading guidelines, 243
   soundness, 242
   study skills, 263-265
   survey, 241-242
   understanding, 241-266
Argumentum ad hominum, 255
Assignment(s). *See* Course assignments; Fuzzy assignments; Reading; Textbooks
   defining, 6-9, 14
   notebook, 8
   reading, 14
   tracking, 9-10
Author(s), 161, 162, 193, 208
   information, 5
   plan, 158
Authority, appeal, 259

B

Beliefs, 192, 194
Bias, recognition, 205
Biased language, 207
Blocking, 153, 154
Boldface, 65
Brainstorming, 42-44, 69
Breakdowns, 22
Built-in definitions, 99

C

Careful reading, 146-148
Cause and effect pattern, 161, 162, 165, 166, 168, 176, 177-178, 181-182, 187
Cause/effect, 270
Charts, 9. *See also* Organizational chart; Process chart
Class discussions, 98
Clause markers, 76
Closed mode, 36
Clues, 217
Codes, 286
College learning, 3, 6
College textbooks, 1, 14, 23, 103, 107, 129, 150, 184, 191, 203, 208, 210, 213, 224, 225, 235, 261
College writing, 107
Comfort zone, 38
Comparison and contrast pattern, 161, 162, 165, 167, 168, 176, 178-179, 182, 188
Comparisons and contrasts, 9
Comparison/contrast, 270
Comprehension, 96. *See also* Reading
Concept mapping, 125
Concluding sentence, 268
Contents. *See* Table of Contents
Context clues, 99, 103
   checking, 96
   types, 76-83
   word definitions, 75-83
Course assignments, 8, 21
Course content, 99
Creative intelligence, 33-35
Creative person, 36-37
Creativity. *See* Perceptions; Workplace
   connection, 30-31
   definition, 31
   increasing, 35-41
Critical readers, 191, 205, 207, 208
Critical reading, 191-193, 205-208
   skills, 205, 207

D

Daily life, inferences, 214-217
Decisiveness, 38

Definition(s), 76. *See also* Built-in definitions
Definition and example pattern, 161, 162, 165, 167, 168, 176, 179, 182-183
Description, 76
Details, 129, 130, 147, 148, 217, 276. *See also* Major details; Minor details; Supporting details; Unessential details
Dictionary, 96, 99, 100. *See also* Technical dictionary
Dilemma. *See* Faulty dilemma
Drucker, Peter, 38

E

Either/or fallacy, 38
Emotional appeal, 258
Emotional overtones, 206, 207
Emotive language, 206-207
   recognition, 205
Enumeration pattern, 159, 161, 165-166, 168, 176-177, 180, 187
Episodic memory, 24
Essay, 239
Essay-type examinations, 99
Evidence, 242
Examples, 76, 129, 153
Excerpts, 14-15, 103, 112-113, 123-126, 150-152, 184-186, 208-210, 235-236, 251, 261-263, 274, 283
Exercises, 11-15, 19-20, 23-27, 29-45, 70, 110-128, 132-145, 154-156, 159-160, 164-183, 196-204, 218-240, 243-266, 272-288
   worksheet, 25

F

5 W's and H. *See* Who, what, where, when, why, and how
Fact(s), 129, 153, 191-212, 215-217. *See also* Supporting fact
   connection, 211-212
   opinion, distinguishing, 193-204
   study skills, 210-211
   survey, 191-192

Index

Factual statements, 191, 203
False argumentation, 254-258
Faulty dilemma, 255
Fear, appeal, 258
Final paragraphs, 11
Footnotes, 208
Fuzzy assignments, 7, 9

G

General statement, 119
Glossary, 5, 6, 22, 74, 99, 100. *See also* Technical terms
Grammatical clues, 77
Graph. *See* Line graph; Pie graph
Graphic
    main idea, 286
    purpose, 286
    text relationship, 286
    type, 286
Graphic materials, 285-286
Group work, 7
Groups, creative methods, 42-44
Guide questions, 6

H

Hawthorne Studies, 224
Headings, 2, 11, 65, 108
Headnotes, 6, 11

I

Idea box, 1, 7, 25, 28, 39, 84, 101, 117, 147, 151, 173, 180, 199, 216, 232, 254, 260, 274, 276
Ideas, 153, 157
Ideas into action, 39
Illustrations, 4-6, 22
Illustrative material, 2
Implied main ideas, 119-123
Index, 4, 5
    example, 18
    knowledge, 19
Index cards, 98
Inference markers, 213
Inference-making process, 214
Inferences, 213-240. *See also* Daily life; Reading
    connection, 239-240
    making, 217-218
    study skills, 237-239
    survey, 214
    understanding, 217-224
Information sources, recognition, 205
Intelligence. *See* Creative intelligence
Interest level, 6

Introduction, 2, 5
Introductory information, 286
Introductory pages, 4
Introductory paragraphs, 11
Introductory sentences, 108
Issue, 243
    identification, 241

J

Judgment words, 191
Judgments, 194

K

Keys, 286
Known, What I Want to Know, What I Have Learned (KWL), 69, 70

L

LAQ/PV. *See* Look ahead, question/predict, verify
Learning. *See* College learning keys, 73-106
Lecture notes, 153, 279
Lectures, 237
    help, 100
Libraries, 263-265
Library of Congress, 4
Library research skills, 263
Light, 225
Line graph, 286
Lists, 9, 99
Literal meaning, 217
Long-term memory, 22, 24
Look ahead, question/predict, verify (LAQ/PV), 25
Looking ahead, 14
    importance, 2-3

M

Main ideas, 22, 131-149, 269, 270. *See also* Graphic; Implied main ideas; Unstated main ideas
    connection, 127-128
    locations, 113-119
    students, remarks, 108-109
    study skills, 125
    survey, 108
    topics, comparison, 111-112
    understanding, 107-128
Main points, 270
Main-idea sentences, 107, 113, 114, 148

Major details
    connection, 155-156
    identification, 129-156
    study skills, 152-155
    survey, 130
Marginal explanations, 22
Matching game. *See* Words
Material, reorganization, 211
Meaning, 22
Memory, 19, 98. *See also* Episodic memory; Long-term memory; Semantic memory; Short-term memory
    kinds, 24
Minor details
    connection, 155-156
    identification, 129-156
    study skills, 152-155
    survey, 130
    tricks, 237
Mistakes, making, 40-41
Mnemonic devices, 24-25, 74, 98, 237
Motivation, 148-150
Multilevel marketing, 39

N

Neutralizing, 207
Note organization, 276
Notebook, 23, 74, 100, 268, 276
Notes, 27, 210, 237, 276. *See also* Lecture notes
Notetaking, 152-153

O

OK5R. *See* Overview, key idea, read, record, recite, review, and reflect
Open mode, 36
Opening statements, 170
Opinion, 191-212, 215-216. *See also* Fact(s)
    connection, 211-212
    distinguishing. *See* Fact
    statements, 191
    study skills, 210-211
    survey, 191-192
Opportunities, 37
Oral summary approach, 277
Organization, patterns, 157-190, 269
    connection, 190
    important points, 162-183
    study skills, 186-189
    survey, 158
Organizational chart, 286
Osborne, 43
Outline, 11
Overlearning, 211

Index

Overview, key idea, read, record, recite, review, and reflect (OK5R), 25
Overviews, 6

P

PQ4R. *See* Preview, question, read, reflect, recite, and review
Paragraphs, 108, 113-114, 116-119, 129, 136, 146, 172, 201. *See also* Final paragraphs; Introductory paragraphs
Paraphrasing, 271-272
Passages, 136
Patriotic appeal, 259
Patterns. *See* Cause and effect pattern; Comparison and contrast pattern; Definition and example pattern; Enumeration pattern; Organization; Primary pattern; Secondary pattern; Sequence pattern
   origin, 183-184
   usage, 162
Perceptions
   creativity, 31-33
   ordinariness, 34
Performance, 38
Personal questions, 23
Personal relationships, establishing, 211
Pie graph, 286
Plan, 270
Point, 243. *See also* Supporting points
Point of view, 21, 22
   changing, 211
Popular Periodic Index, 263
Positive reinforcement, 41
Post hoc ergo propter hoc, 254
PQRST. *See* Preview, question, read, state, and test
Practice tests, 289-322
Predictions, 27, 28, 46-47. *See also* Test questions
   accuracy, 48
Preface, 4, 5
Prefixes, 75, 84-86, 87-88, 90-91, 93-94
Prejudice, appeal, 259
Preview, question, read, reflect, recite, and review (PQ4R), 25
Preview, question, read, state, and test (PQRST), 25
Previewing, 1-20, 21-23, 267
   connection, 20
   skills summary, 2
   study skills, 16-17
Primary problem, 162
Problems, 37-38
Process chart, 286
Publication, information, 4, 5

Punctuation, 77
Purpose, 269. *See also* Reading with purpose
   setting, 27-28

Q

Questions, 23, 26, 27, 109, 123, 153. *See also* Personal questions
   begging, 254
   ignoring, 255

R

Readers' Guide to Periodical Literature, 263
Reading. *See* Assignment(s); Careful reading; Critical reading; Speed reading; Textbooks
   assignment, 7-9, 14, 22, 96, 104, 267, 269
   comprehension, 28
   ease, 6
   experience, 21
   guidelines. *See* Arguments
   inferences, 224-231
   material, outlining, 158
   rate, 10, 13
   skill, 216
   strategy, 267
Reading with purpose, 21-72
   connection, 71-72
   practices, 23-27, 29-33
   questions, 65
   review, 68
   study skills, 69-70
   survey, 22, 64
Reading/study skill, 268
Reasons, 129
Record, 15
Reference guides, 263
References, 208
Research skills. *See* Library research skills
Reviewing, 25
Reviews, 6
Right answer. *See* Second right answer
Roots, 75, 84, 86-95, 101, 105
Rules, breaking, 39-40

S

Second right answer, 38
Secondary pattern, 162
Self-esteem, 37
Self-image, 36
Self-instruction, 109

Self-perception, 37
Semantic memory, 25
Sentences, 183, 271. *See also* Concluding sentence; Introductory sentences; Main-idea sentences
   structure, 241
   writing, 98
Sequence, 270
Sequence pattern, 158-159, 161, 165, 166, 168, 176, 177, 181
Short-term memory, 99
Signal words/phrases, 130, 157, 158, 162-165, 173-176
Skimming, 4, 10-20, 25
   practices, 11-20
Sound, 95-96
Sources, evaluation, 207-208
Speed reading, 10
Spelling, 100
SPIN. *See* Survey, predict, infer, note
SQ3R. *See* Survey, question, read, recite, review
SSCD approach. *See* Vocabulary
Statement, truth/falsity, 194
Statistics, 129
Structural clues, 74, 96, 101
Structure, usage, 101
Study aids, 5
Study alert, 1, 16, 69, 104, 125, 152, 186, 263, 285
Study area, 7
Study guides, 22
Study helps, 22
Study skill, 19, 69
Subheadings, 2, 26, 65
Subjective feelings, 194
Subtitle(s), 5, 11, 26, 108
Suffixes, 75, 86-87, 90, 96
Summarizing, 25, 106, 127, 155, 190, 239, 266-288
   connection, 288
   example, 270
   informal types, 275-285
   study skills, 285-288
   suggestions, 269-270
   survey, 267-268
Summary approach. *See* Oral summary approach
Summary writing, formalities, 275
Summary/summaries, 2, 6, 11, 44-45, 76-77
Supporting fact, 199
Supporting details, 267
Supporting material, 246
Supporting points, 243, 247, 249
Survey, predict, infer, note (SPIN), 25
Survey, question, read, recite, review (SQ3R), 21-23, 25, 27, 28, 64-68, 267

Sympathy, 258
Synonyms, 76

T

Table of Contents, 4, 5
Technical dictionary, 99
Technical terms, 271
  glossary, 5
Technical vocabulary, 73
  learning techniques, 98-103
Technical words, usage, 99
Test questions, prediction, 211
Textbook reading assignment, 71, 93, 106, 109, 146, 152, 155, 190, 211, 227, 239, 266
Textbook writers, 157
Textbooks. *See* College textbooks
  assignments, 22, 96, 127
  checking, 3-5
  comparison, 6
  help, 99-100
  material, 13
  reading, 3, 214
  strategy, 2
  word, 93-94
Thinker, 213
Thinking process, 269
Time estimate, 22
Time sequence, 188

Title(s), 4, 5, 11, 21, 108, 286. *See also* Subtitle(s)
  page, 3
Topics, 119, 131, 153
  comparison. *See* Main ideas
  identification, 109-111
Tradition, appeal, 259
Transitional words/phrases, 269, 270
Typographical aids, 5, 6

U

Understanding, 269. *See* Arguments; Main ideas
Unessential details, 151
University of Texas, 7
Unsound arguments, 254-258
Unstated main ideas, 119-123

V

Value words, 194-195
Vignettes, 9-10, 26, 73-75, 108-109, 146, 157-158, 192-193, 216-217, 242-243, 268
Visuals, 186-189
Vocabulary, 2, 241. *See* Technical vocabulary
  aids, 4

Vocabulary (*continued*)
  college students, remarks, 73-75
  connection, 106
  help, 6
  remembering, 73-106
  skills survey, 73-75, 104-105
  SSCD approach, 73, 95-97
von Oech, Roger, 39, 40

W

Who, what, where, when, and how (5W's and H), 28, 147, 193, 276, 277
Word association, 98
Word definitions. *See* Context clues
Word parts, 84-86, 94-95
Words, 269. *See also* Judgment words; Technical words
  forms, 98
  groups, 105
  matching game, 98
  organization, 183
  usage, 98
  writing, 98
Workplace, creativity, 41-42
Worksheet. *See* Exercises
Writing. *See* Sentences
Writing assignments, 98